Developing Consultation Skills

*A Guide to Training,
Development, and Assessment
for Human Services
Professionals*

Richard Dean Parsons
Joel Meyers

Developing Consultation Skills

 Jossey-Bass Publishers

San Francisco • Washington • London • 1984

DEVELOPING CONSULTATION SKILLS
*A Guide to Training, Development, and Assessment
for Human Services Professionals*
by Richard Dean Parsons and Joel Meyers

Library of Congress Cataloging in Publication Data

Parsons, Richard D.
    Developing consultation skills.

    Bibliography: p. 233
    Includes index.
    1. Psychiatric consultation. 2. Mental illness—
Prevention. I. Meyers, Joel. II. Title.
RC455.2.C65P37   1984   616.89   84-5744
ISBN 0-87589-605-7 (alk. paper)

Manufactured in the United States of America

The paper in this book meets the guidelines for
permanence and durability of the Committee on
Production Guidelines for Book Longevity of the
Council on Library Resources.

JACKET DESIGN BY WILLI BAUM

FIRST EDITION

Code 8419

The Jossey-Bass
Social and Behavioral Science Series

We dedicate this book to

George Joseph Flournoy
Charles Polin
John Hanna Parsons
Reb Isser Chochlowitz

Their characteristics of intelligence, patience, and the understanding of others and their values regarding education and the pursuit of excellence have influenced us in many ways—probably more than we know.

Preface

In 1979, when our first book on consultation was published (*Mental Health Consultation in the Schools,* by Meyers, Parsons, and Martin, 1979), we noted that consultation had increasingly become the subject of professional discussion, research, training, and practice. During the few short years since, the value of mental health consultation, be it in a school, mental health, or organizational setting, has become all the more apparent. Fiscal deficits, government cutbacks, and the ever-increasing social pressures and resulting emotional needs have exacerbated the disparity between the demand for psychological services and the number of competent professionals available. Consultation offers the realistic possibility of providing effective psychological services for a large number of emotionally needy people in a variety of settings despite the scarcity of professional personnel.

This shortfall in personnel available as helpgivers has fueled a debate over the need for indirect service delivery such as that found in consultation. Consultation not only is efficient as an indirect mode of service delivery but also is a realistic and reasonable alternative to the typical deficiency or disease orientation taken by most mental health professionals. Mental health consultants use consultation as a method of reaching many people as well as a method of fostering individual and institutional growth and thus the prevention, rather than the remediation, of emotional problems. Most professionals writing about consultation have indicated its potential as an approach to primary and secondary prevention, but few have indicated any specific ways prevention can be attained. Moreover, the consultation literature is based on a deficit model focused on remediation rather than growth. This book develops a preventive conceptual framework that shapes all the consultation techniques we present.

The late 1970s and early 1980s have already seen an increasing number of professionals working as mental health consultants. These professionals—for whom the approaches delineated in this book are appropriate—include clinical psychologists, community psychiatrists, community and consulting psychologists, industrial psychologists, social workers, nurses, pastoral counselors, school psychologists, and special educators. This growth not only reflects that consultation has become "fashionable" but also depicts the real social demand for this kind of mental health assistance. As Gallessich (1982) notes, however, a discrepancy is apparent between this social need and the available professional competencies. Many texts have appeared recently that offer excellent reviews of the literature and finely developed theoretical models (for example, Gallessich, 1982; Curtis and Zins, 1981), but the professional seeking the real "how to" knowledge of skill development and application is often overwhelmed by scientific jargon and model building. The present book bridges the gap between the consultant's intellectual quest for theory and heuristics and the practical demands for skills and competence in performance. The need for a book that focuses on consultation *skills* was underscored at the National Conference on Consultation Training in August 1980 (Alpert and Meyers, 1983). One of the consistent topics of discussion at that conference was the need to delineate specific consultation skills and approaches to training. It is with this need in mind that we present this comprehensive approach to skills development, to be used by practitioners, trainers, and consultant trainees.

The uniqueness and special contribution of this book rest on three factors. First, we offer a *collaborative model* for the process of consultation that integrates the techniques described throughout this book. This comprehensive model draws support from the literatures on social psychology, consultation, and general helping relationships.

Second, the text goes beyond providing the traditional "lip service" to the importance of *preventive* mental health service delivery. Chapter One presents a conceptual framework that links prevention to consultation, and Chapters Six through Ten point to the specific assessment and intervention strategies that facilitate the goals of prevention. Although others have suggested that consultation can facilitate prevention, this book is the first to take the next logical step and indicate concretely how it can be accomplished.

The third special and unique focus of this text is its use of a *skills* approach to consultation. This skills orientation sets the book apart from most texts in this field, which have a fact-and-information focus. In addition to asking the reader to perceive, understand, and store the material presented, most of the chapters ask the reader to practice the skills. To provide such practice in skill development, learning exercises are presented.

The focus on skills and skill development creates a book that can be used flexibly in two ways. It can be used as a traditional text, read to provide information about theories, research, and particular consulting skills. This information can be obtained by reading straight through the book, approaching the learning exercises and illustrations as a part of the text. Such an approach will focus the reader's attention on what the skills of consultation are.

A second way is to use the book as part of an approach to the development of consultation skills. In this approach the exercises are carried out as the book is read—sometimes requiring that reading be stopped while the reader works with a small group of colleagues, listens to and assesses an audiotape (or videotape) of consultation, or practices the consultation

skills on the job. Some specific ideas about using this text for
self-assessment and professional development are presented in
the epilogue. *However, it is underscored from the beginning
that to use the book in this second way, the reader must audiotape at least one consultation session.* The tape will then be
used to complete many of the exercises provided in the book.

This book focuses on consultation skills as well as some
crucial conceptual issues. It is assumed that the reader has prior
background in the literature of consultation. For example, having read *Mental Health Consultation in the Schools* (Meyers,
Parsons, and Martin, 1979) is helpful. In addition to our assumption about the reader's prior information, it is important
to be certain that we have a common understanding of consultation. Accordingly, for purposes of this book, the following
definition of consultation is used (see Meyers, Parsons, and Martin, 1979): Consultation is a technique that always has the following six characteristics: (1) it is a helping or problem-solving
process; (2) it occurs between a professional helpgiver and a
helpseeker who has responsibility for the welfare of another
person; (3) it is a voluntary relationship; (4) the helpgiver and
helpseeker share in solving the problem; (5) the goal is to help
solve a current work problem of the helpseeker; and (6) the
helpseeker profits from the relationship in such a way that future problems may be handled more sensitively and skillfully.
(The helpgiver will be referred to as the *consultant,* the helpseeker as the *consultee,* and the person for whom the consultee
has responsibility as the *client*.)

Part One first presents the rationale for a preventive orientation (Chapter One) and the collaborative model of consultation (Chapter Two). Part Two presents the process skills
necessary for successful collaborative consultation: skills for
understanding the interpersonal relationship (Chapter Three),
communication skills (Chapter Four), and basic attitudes
needed to maintain the relationship (Chapter Five). Part Three
then discusses the skills necessary for implementing the different approaches to consultation: Chapter Six describes skills
used for each stage of consultation; Chapter Seven, skills for
direct service to the client; Chapter Eight, skills for indirect

service to the client; Chapter Nine, skills for service to the consultee; and Chapter Ten, skills for service to the system. Finally, Part Four focuses on evaluation skills (Chapter Eleven) and professional development (Epilogue).

No book is produced by its authors in isolation, and this work is no exception. Of course, many of the significant influences on our thinking are referenced throughout the book. Nevertheless, some people deserve particular mention, especially Roy Martin, whose ideas run through much of this work. In addition, special thanks to James Annichiarico, who taught Meyers about direct confrontation; William Erchul and Aileen Hill for their contributions to Chapter Two; Judith Pfeffer and Vicki Erlbaum for their contributions to Chapter Seven; and Dolores Carrol, Jennifer Rodriguez, and Irma Rocca de Torres for their contributions to Chapter One. Finally, our families have provided support, patience, humor, ideas, and hours of manuscript improvement. For the many times they filled in as both parents while "Daddy worked," we especially thank our wives, Karen Parsons and Barbara Meyers. And for their own special type of "understanding" and "supply of preventive mental health," we thank our children—Jonathan, Drew, and Kristian Parsons and Raina and Adena Meyers.

June 1984   Richard Dean Parsons
                                                              Aston, Pennsylvania

                                                                    Joel Meyers
                                                        Philadelphia, Pennsylvania

Contents

Exercises

The Authors

Richard Dean Parsons is associate professor of psychology at Neumann College, Aston, Pennsylvania. He is a graduate of Temple University, where he was awarded both his M.A. degree (1971) and Ph.D. degree (1976) in psychology. Parsons is a licensed psychologist and a certified school psychologist. He has given over 100 workshops for parents, educators, and human services professionals on a myriad of topics aimed at facilitating the growth and development of children through direct and consultative services. He has authored or coauthored over eighteen professional articles and texts, including *Mental Health Consultation in the Schools* (1979).

Parsons maintains a private psychotherapy practice and provides consultation services to schools and professionals in a three-county area. In addition to professional membership in the American Psychological Association, the National Association of School Psychologists, and the state and local associations, Parsons has been listed in *American Men and Women of Science* (1978) and *American Catholic Who's Who* (1980).

Joel Meyers is professor in the Department of School Psychology at Temple University, Philadelphia, where he has trained mental health consultants for over ten years. He graduated from the University of Texas at Austin, where he was awarded his Ph.D. degree (1971) in educational psychology. Meyers has served as a consultant to a variety of educational institutions in the Philadelphia area as well as other parts of the country. He is a member of the American Educational Research Association, the American Psychological Association, the National Association of School Psychologists, and the Pennsylvania Psychological Association.

Meyers has published over thirty professional articles, book chapters, and books and has made numerous professional speeches and presentations at local, state, and national meetings. Most of his research, writing, and teaching has focused on consultation. He served as director (1979-1980) of the National School Psychology Inservice Training Network, housed at the University of Minnesota, and he was codirector of the National Conference on Consultation Training held in Montreal in August 1980.

Developing Consultation Skills

A Guide to Training,
Development, and Assessment
for Human Services
Professionals

CHAPTER ONE

Goals of Primary Prevention

Over twenty years ago George Albee's work for the Joint Commission on Mental Health demonstrated convincingly that the gap between the number of mental health professionals available and the number of people needing their services was increasing. As a result of Albee's findings and other observations pointing to the inadequacy of traditional, one-to-one delivery approaches, interest in the development of innovative techniques is growing rapidly.

Albee's predictions have been borne out. Even though more mental health professionals are being trained today, the demand for services has increased at a much faster rate. The natural growth of population, and with it the growth of those identified as needing help; the increased sophistication and sensitivity of diagnostic tools, and with them the increased effectiveness of problem identification; and finally, the stress and press originating from socioeconomic conditions have all contributed to the growing demand for mental health services.

Following his extensive research on this topic, Albee

1

(1980) has concluded that a major change in approach to the delivery of mental health services is essential. Albee advocates a paradigm shift (Kuhn, 1970) in which professionals focus on primary prevention rather than remediation of mental health problems. We concur with Albee's assessment and view mental health consultation as one approach to service delivery that can promote this shift toward a preventive focus. Although a number of mental health professionals give lip service to the need for and basic value of prevention, little has been done to translate this good idea into practice.

This introductory chapter defines primary and secondary prevention and demonstrates that mental health consultation can and should be integrated into the preventive mental health movement. The preventive framework to be presented serves as one basis for conceptualizing the model of consultation presented later in this chapter.

Consultation as a Preventive Technique

It is useful to distinguish primary, secondary, and tertiary prevention. Primary prevention is based on the notion that the entire population should benefit from mental health services; the goal is to promote growth rather than to remediate or restore. Such efforts would reduce the incidence of mental health problems for all people. Primary prevention includes efforts to prevent the occurrence of a disorder in a particular population, generally by promoting the emotional well-being of those in a group or community. Its "clientele" is the population as a whole or subgroups that are at risk for developing mental health problems.

Secondary prevention focuses on problems that have begun to appear. The goal is to shorten the duration and impact of the disorder by intervening before it becomes severe. Techniques associated with early identification and treatment are emphasized.

Tertiary prevention consists in those techniques designed to reduce the consequences of severe dysfunction after it occurs.

Consultation can be used to implement primary, secondary, and tertiary prevention. Although the traditional emphasis has been on secondary and tertiary prevention, the immediate priority is to develop consultation approaches that promote the primary prevention of mental health problems.

It can be difficult to persuade organizations to allocate resources for preventive techniques, as consultation is frequently not requested until a crisis occurs. Consultation, however, offers a pragmatic approach to prevention, since it includes techniques designed to respond to such crises. By beginning with remediation and crisis intervention techniques, the consultant can increase the likelihood of acceptance for preventive approaches.

Researchers have developed a beginning data base supporting the efficacy of some primary prevention techniques (for example, Cowen, 1977; Albee, 1982). Three basic approaches to primary prevention can be distinguished: (1) analysis and modification of social environments, (2) development of competence and adaptive capacities, and (3) stress reduction.

1. There is an increasing body of research suggesting that *social environments* can have a profound effect on mental health. Barker and Gump (1964) were among the first to consider the impact of school environments; others (Broussard, 1976; Klaus and Kennell, 1976) have studied crucial environmental factors in the relationship between infant and caregivers. Kelly (1968) has repeatedly suggested the importance of adequate matching between person and environment in order to maximize adaptation and mental health.

Moos and his associates (Moos, 1973, 1974a, 1974b) have developed a series of scales to assess social environments. These scales provide concrete techniques that consultants can use. In applications of the scales, three characteristics have emerged repeatedly: relational factors, personal development factors, and system maintenance factors. Moos has begun to determine the impact of these three factors on attitudes, behavior, adaptation, health, and mental health.

2. Perhaps the most important goal of preventive approaches is the *development of competence and adaptive capacities*. This growth will, in turn, prevent future problems. To develop the technology to accomplish this goal, several questions

need to be answered: What are the core skills that provide the basis for adjustment? Can curricula and related teaching techniques be developed to help people learn these skills? When a particular skill is learned or a competence developed, will emotional adjustment improve? When skills or competencies are developed or when adjustment improves, will these changes be maintained?

These questions have been addressed by several research teams attempting to develop cognitive, interpersonal problem-solving skills (for example, Spivack and Shure, 1973; Allen and others, 1976). Children have been taught such skills as sensitivity to others, awareness of the effects of one's behavior, perception of feelings, development of alternative strategies, and awareness of means/ends relationships. Numerous other factors may be related to competence—questioning skills, planning skills, and so forth—and these approaches need not be limited to children, even though that has been the focus of most research to date. A unique feature of such programs is that an educational orientation is used in which a curriculum is developed to teach the skills to children regardless of whether they exhibit problems. (Alternatively, the skills can be taught to parents, who, in turn, teach their children.) Results suggest that skill development improves competence and emotional adjustment for a variety of children—for example, emotionally disturbed children as well as those with no apparent adjustment problems. Further, children taught these skills develop fewer social/emotional difficulties later. Chapter Eight presents in detail the factors and procedures involved in the development of competence and adaptive capacity.

3. *Stress reduction* is another effective preventive technique. There is ample evidence that environmental stress results in mental health problems. Although specific causal relations between one stressor and one particular outcome have not been found, general relations between stress and mental health have been identified. Such factors as marital status, bereavement, loss of a job, and natural disasters have been shown to result in mental health problems. Stress reduction techniques seek to reduce the impact of such factors by reducing their frequency and/or

by developing one's capacity to deal with such stress. Anticipatory guidance, psychological inoculation, and anxiety reduction are examples of stress reduction techniques (Phillips, Martin, and Meyers, 1972). Further, social support systems can be built and strengthened, since these resources often help people cope with stress more effectively (see, for example, Caplan and Killilea, 1976). The use of stress reduction in consultation is discussed in more detail in Chapter Nine.

The Consultation Model

The model presented here provides a system for delivering consultation with a focus on primary and secondary prevention. This model, initially based on Gerald Caplan's (1970) work, is derived from Meyers, Parsons, and Martin (1979). It defines four categories of consultation: (1) direct service to the client, (2) indirect service to the client, (3) service to the consultee, and (4) service to the system. These four categories are defined briefly below; more detailed discussions of them can be found in Chapters Seven through Ten.

Direct service to the client (Level I) seeks to modify the behavior, attitudes, and feelings of a particular client or clients who present a problem or problems. Data about the client are gathered directly by the consultant, using individual testing, interview, and behavior observation.

Indirect service to the client (Level II) also aims to change the behavior, attitudes, or feelings of the client(s) who has been referred by the consultee. In contrast to the first approach, however, the data are not gathered directly by the consultant. Instead, someone else, such as the consultee, gathers the necessary data.

In *service to the consultee (Level III)* the target for service is the consultee rather than the consultee's client. The goal at this level is to change the behavior, attitudes, or feelings of the consultee. This approach derives from Caplan's (1970) consultee-centered case consultation. The goals for the consultee may include the following: to increase knowledge, to develop skill(s), to promote self-confidence, and to maintain an objective view of the work situation. Although the primary goal is to change the consultee, it is assumed that the change in the consultee will result in changes for the client as well.

The goal of *service to the system (Level IV)* is to improve the organizational functioning of the system as a whole. This result should lead to improved mental health for both clients and individual consultees in the organization.

These approaches to consultation are viewed as four levels in a continuum from direct to indirect service. For example, direct service to the client (Level I) includes direct assessment of the client by the consultant. This form of consultation is labeled Level I because it is the one in which the consultant has the most direct contact with the client. In contrast, service to the system uses techniques in which the consultant is most removed from the client and is therefore labeled Level IV.

The four levels of consultation provide an integrated model based on the principle that services should be given in the most parsimonious manner that is maximally effective. This model emphasizes the approaches that include the least direct contact with the client, and it includes a decision rule to determine which category of service to provide. The consultant first determines whether the request for help is best dealt with as a situation in which an organizational factor accounts for the identified problem. If so, the consultant is to work at the systems level (Level IV); if not, the consultant should consider whether the consultee is the key factor associated with the request for service. If the consultant determines that the consultee is the significant factor, then Level III will be provided rather than either of the more direct approaches (Levels I and II). Should the client be identified as the primary target for consultation, the consultant should first consider having the consultee gather the data (Level II). The consultant will gather data directly (Level I) only when the complexity of the problem or the ineffectiveness of other approaches warrants it.

Figure 1 (adapted from Meyers, Parsons, and Martin, 1979) provides a picture of the various levels and how they are integrated in the delivery of consultation services. As should be clear both from the preceding brief presentation and from Figure

Figure 1. Stages of the Consultation Process.

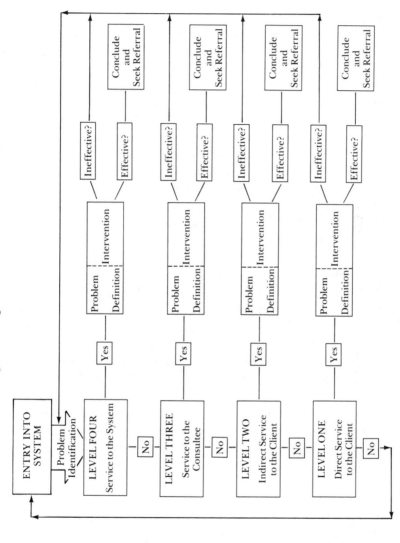

1, this model reverses the traditional framework for delivery of mental health services. Instead of assuming that the problem lies within the client and beginning with individual assessment, this approach assumes that the environment (that is, the system or consultee) has a major role to play, and therefore the preference is to begin work with these elements and work indirectly with the client. This focus on indirect service increases the consultant's potential to have an impact on many clients and to prevent development of problems in some.

The following example of consultation to a college dormitory staff illustrates how this model can work in practice. A dormitory resident, a twenty-one-year-old male senior, was referred to the consultant. Mike, as we shall call him, had a history of frequent behavioral disturbances associated with alcohol abuse. The most recent incident was discovered when a foul smell was reported to the chief dorm counselor. A search revealed that the smell was caused by a dead raccoon that had been hidden in a cabinet in the lobby—by Mike, it was learned later. The dorm counselors, furious, wanted Mike expelled. The first step in expulsion was the referral to the consultant.

The consultant's role included helping the counseling staff with problems they had in dealing with individual residents who had difficulty adjusting to college and dormitory life. Sometimes consultation services were based on individual diagnostic work-ups by the consultant (Level I consultation), and at other times the counseling staff gathered observational data as the basis for consultation (Level II consultation). Frequently, recommendations were carried out by counseling staff in the dormitory. In more serious situations, however, the resident was referred to the campus counseling center. Although the consultant's role was to do Levels I and II consultation, his long-term goal was to expand services to include service to the consultee (Level III) and service to the system (Level IV). There were organizational problems that clearly suggested the need for Level IV consultation.

The director of dormitory counselors had an authoritarian style in which policies and procedures were dictated to the staff. Although there was a monthly meeting that provided for some communication, more typically memos were used. Staff input was neither requested nor encouraged. Working under this system, the counselors felt overworked and underpaid, and they resented the nonprofessional way they were treated. The result was rigid dormitory rules that were seen as arbitrary by the students who were expected to help enforce them. Two contradictory behaviors became evident in most of the dorms. First, the counselors and student floor leaders were inconsistent in enforcing rules. Second, when a violation was not ignored, it was enforced with unusual severity and rigidity. It was clear that the atmosphere in the dorms was marked by poor communication, tension, and a general air of conflict.

In response to the referral, the consultant evaluated Mike (Level I consultation) and learned that the incident of the raccoon was related to the antagonism between residents and the counseling staff. Placing the dead raccoon in the lobby had been an act of defiance directed toward those in authority. Expulsion or even counseling for Mike was not the answer, since this situation reflected a systemic problem. The consultant used this information to renegotiate his role in this dorm by talking to the two dorm counselors. An agreement was reached to initiate organizational consultation (Level IV).

All residents of the dorm, the eight floor leaders, and the two dormitory counselors were surveyed to determine their perceptions of the dorm. Interviews with the ten staff members and with ten students followed. Then a feedback session was held with the staff and selected students to discuss the data and reach consensus about the major issues that needed to be addressed. It was agreed that the two dorm counselors were too arbitrary and rigid about the rules, that the staff enforced rules inconsistently, and that the residents and student floor leaders had no input into developing the rules. It was also agreed that the counselors were frustrated because of the director's authoritarian style.

This diagnosis resulted in the following outcomes: (1) The dorm counselors and student floor leaders agreed to hold a monthly meeting in which the residents could have input into the regulations for dormitory life. The purpose was to open communication among all members of the dormitory. (2) The staff resolved to enforce rules more consistently. (3) The consultant used these data as a basis for approaching the director of dormitory counselors to suggest a similar process of organizational consultation for the entire staff. A massive program of service to the system (Level IV) resulted, whose main outcomes were increased communication and staff input into programmatic decisions. Not only were these Level IV interventions successful, but their success increased effectiveness at other levels of consultation. For example, the consultant had recommended that Mike receive counseling and remain a dorm resident rather than being expelled (Level I). Interestingly, although this recommendation had been rejected initially, it was accepted after the organizational consultation.

Prevention and Mental Health Consultation

Mental health consultation has the potential to achieve preventive goals because of its focus on generalization, or transfer, effects. Regardless of the immediate effects on the client or consultee, the most important goal is to provide generalized effects that help similar clients in the present and the future. Through the principle of generalization, consultation can achieve preventive goals. If the *consultee's* behavior or attitudes change significantly, such change may have a positive impact on nonreferred clients and thus help to prevent development of future problems for them.

Even though consultation does have this potential, too often the frame of reference used by consultants reflects a deficit model. The model is often inherent in the process, because consultation is most typically initiated by a consultee in crisis. The crisis situation focuses attention on remediation of the problem (the crisis or deficit) and may draw attention away from the goals of promoting growth and competence.

The deficit model is clearly evident in the first two approaches in the consultation model. Both direct service to the client and indirect service to the client are initiated because of a referral regarding an individual client's problem. The typical result is for the consultee to implement techniques designed to remediate this problem. However, these client-centered approaches to consultation could be expanded to meet preventive goals directly; Chapters Seven and Eight discuss some ways this can be accomplished.

At first glance, service to the consultee seems to be more consistent with a preventive orientation because the consultee is the focus, rather than the client. Focusing on the consultee provides increased opportunity for effects that may generalize to others in the client population. Nevertheless, a deficit model is often in effect, and it reduces the potential to achieve preventive goals. In this instance the deficit is seen as inherent in the consultee rather than in the client. For example, Caplan (1970) states four reasons for consultee-centered consultation: lack of knowledge, lack of skill, lack of confidence, and lack of objectivity on the part of the consultee. Use of the word *lack* focuses the consultant's attention on the consultee's limitations, rather than considering areas of strength and areas of potential growth for the consultee. The more positive focus on growth can prevent a wider range of problems than the more restricted focus that necessarily occurs when attempting to remediate a particular deficit. For example, rather than being viewed as a corrective to lack of knowledge or lack of confidence, consultation should be initiated to increase knowledge and self-confidence or promote growth by the consultee. Chapter Nine elaborates some of the ways this preventive framework can be implemented using service to the consultee.

Service to the system is also initiated, typically, with a request to remediate a specific or general problem of the organization. Certainly prevention can result, because the attention given to the system can have multiple effects on the client population. Nevertheless, preventive goals would be served even better if these efforts were implemented on a regular basis to achieve constructive goals, rather than being limited to the resolution of crises or problems. Chapter Ten addresses these issues in more detail.

❧ CHAPTER TWO ❧

Need for Collaborative Relationships

This chapter describes the theoretical and empirical support for a collaborative model of the consultation process and delineates this collaborative model, which forms the framework for the consultation process presented in this book. One source of support for this model is the literature on helping relationships in general and consultation in particular. A second source of support is the social psychology literature.

Consultation Literature

One of the earliest and most influential writers in the field of consultation was Gerald Caplan (1964, 1970). Caplan's early description of consultation as a collaborative process was based on a differentiation of consultation from psychotherapy. In that context consultation was described as an approach that is focused on a work-related problem of the consultee, rather than a personal problem. This focus helps to maintain the professional identity of the consultee. Several professionals since

Caplan have described the collaborative nature of consultation, stressing several common principles.

Interchange Between Colleagues. One important collaborative principle is that consultation involves two professionals, the consultant and the consultee, who each have their own area of expertise. Consultation is therefore viewed as an interchange between professional colleagues. This principle helps to avoid a hierarchal relationship in which the consultant is viewed as the "expert" who is superior to the consultee.

It is not always easy to achieve this collegial relationship. One reason is that the consultee may feel inadequate and therefore tend to view the consultant as superior. Frequently consultees act on this assumption by downgrading their own skills in order to reinforce the notion that the consultant is superior. Caplan refers to such behavior as "one-downsmanship." The consultant must counteract the consultee's efforts to establish a hierarchal relationship; Caplan (1970) suggests that the consultant respond to deference with deference.

Other professionals concur with Caplan, arguing that consultation is unique because it is an interchange between colleagues who maintain a nonhierarchal relationship while working together (for example, Alpert, 1977; Altrocchi, 1972; Gutkin and Curtis, 1982; Lambert, in press; Meyers, 1981; Newman, 1967; Sarason and others, 1966). These authors present the consultant as a facilitator who helps the consultee develop unique approaches to the problem situation, and they emphasize *active involvement of the consultee* in the consultation process.

Emphasis on the Consultee's Role. One technique that helps to develop a collaborative relationship is to deemphasize the consultant's role in the development of intervention plans. The consultant can accomplish this by asking the consultee to make suggestions and by providing verbal recognition of the consultee's contributions to the intervention plans. Specific techniques for increasing such consultee contributions (brainstorming, divergent Delphi) will be discussed in Chapter Six. Throughout consultation the goal is to encourage the consultee's involvement in the process of change, thus facilitating the consultee's feeling of responsibility for implementing the recommendations resulting from consultation.

Freedom to Accept or Reject. The consultant can facilitate a collaborative relationship by communicating clearly that the consultee has the freedom to accept or reject whatever the consultant might say. Moreover, the consultee needs to understand that rejecting an idea is truly acceptable to the consultant and that no harmful repercussions will result. One way the consultant can facilitate the consultee's understanding of this freedom is to present recommendations tentatively.

Despite all that has been written about collaborative approaches to the consultation process, they can be difficult to implement. The fact that a consultant has been asked to enter a system in order to provide some expertise for a work-related problem encourages the notion that the consultant is special, different, and superior. Moreover, the consultant has knowledge, information, and insight that he or she wants the consultee to accept, and any effort to influence the consultee to accept these ideas may interfere with collaboration. To overcome this impediment, the consultant and consultee must identify the unique contribution of each to the relationship. Further, the consultant must develop a style of collaborative influence in which final control over what to do is left with the consultee.

In an incisive review of the literature, Erchul and Gallessich (1981) argue that although support for collaborative approaches is abundant, apparent violations of this principle are numerous. They found that most often it is the consultant who determines the problem, the assessment techniques, and the intervention strategies.

It is difficult to use an influence process while interacting in a collaborative manner, and there is probably no one way to establish a collaborative relationship. Each consultant must develop a unique style built on the principles of collaborative consultation. The scale shown in Exhibit 1 describes numerous ways in which the consultant can interact collaboratively. It can be used to assess the consultant's collaborative efforts and to help the consultant develop an effective collaborative style.

Exhibit 1. Consultant Observational Assessment Form.

Operational Definitions

Directions: For each category listed, rate the observed consultant interaction in terms of the degree to which you feel the description applies. Use the following Likert-type scale for each category: 5 = strongly agree, 4 = agree, 3 = no opinion, 2 = disagree, 1 = strongly disagree.

1. *Expert-facilitator*—focuses on the consultant's approach to solving the problem. "Expertness" is shown by advice giving, taking over the responsibility for problem resolution, and analyzing the problem according to the consultant's frame of reference. Facilitation is shown by attempts to elicit the consultee's observations, ideas, and previous actions. The consultee is a significant part of the problem clarification and solution.

2. *Relationship*—focuses on the way the consultant seems to view the consultee. Is the consultee viewed as a colleague or contributor to the process? Or is the consultee viewed as a recipient of the consultant's ideas and information?

3. *Empathy*—does the consultant communicate an accurate perception of the consultee's phenomenological world?

4. *Support*—does the consultant reinforce the consultee or convey agreement with the consultee over the reality of the problem?

5. *Interest* (verbal/nonverbal)—does the consultant convey interest and involvement in the relationship with the consultee?

6. *Trust*—is the consultant judgmental and critical, or does the consultant avoid evaluative statements about the consultee?

7. *Ventilation*—does the consultant allow for free expression of feelings by the consultee?

8. *Questioning*—does the questioning generally contribute to the effectiveness of the problem solving and allow the consultee to expand in depth and breadth?

9. *Summarization*—does the consultant periodically summarize the main ideas and use this process to check his or her understanding of the consultee?

10. *Problem clarification*—is the consultant able to identify and clarify the specific concerns of the consultee, or does the consultant ask questions that seem off target?

11. *Strategy generation*—does the interaction result in ideas for coping with the problem, and does the consultee contribute to these ideas?

12. *Follow-up*—is the decision for follow-up left up to the consultee, and does the consultant clearly manifest availability should such follow-up be desired?

13. *Evaluator*—is the consultant evaluative, critical, and judgmental or simply a descriptive information processor?

Source: Adapted from Curtis and Anderson (1975).

Research on Collaborative Consultation. Although the ideas behind collaborative consultation have been generated from conceptual frameworks and practical experience, there have been some beginning efforts to research the factors facilitating the development and effectiveness of collaborative consultation. For the most part, these investigations have been one-shot efforts, with few systematic series of research studies initiated by one researcher. One line of research has been conducted by Marvin Fine at the University of Kansas. This work began when Fine observed that the failure of a behavior modification program was due to the consultant's insensitivity to the unstated concerns of the teacher (Fine, Nesbitt, and Tyler, 1974). This observation was followed by a study demonstrating that the best predictor of teacher satisfaction was the teacher's perception of the consultant's facilitative characteristics (Schowengerdt, Fine, and Poggio, 1976). Facilitativeness was defined as genuineness, empathy, and respect, each a characteristic of collaborative consultation.

Curtis's work at the University of Cincinnati has provided further support for the collaborative model. Curtis and Zins (1981) found that teachers, regardless of their characteristics, preferred consultants who expressed an understanding of their difficult teaching situation. In an additional study using the Consultant Observational Assessment Form (see Exhibit 1), Curtis and Watson (1980) found that teachers' problem clarification skills improved more with consultants who were skilled in the collaborative model than with consultants who were not. This research suggests that collaborative consultation was effective. More important, the increase in problem clarification skills suggests that collaborative consultation may have generalized effects on teachers beyond the particular consultation case. Such generalized effects may be the most important single outcome of consultation (Meyers, 1981). In addition to helping the person referred by the consultee (that is, the client), consultation seeks these sorts of educative and preventive effects for improved functioning by the consultee with similar clients in the future. In this way consultation can have a broader impact than if the goal were simply to help the referred client. Curtis's research suggests that collaborative techniques have the potential to produce such generalized effects.

Other isolated studies provide support for collaborative consultation approaches. Wilcox (1977), studying group consultation, found that consultee attitude toward consultation was predicted by a "humanist factor," which included the consultant's recognizing feelings, allowing the consultee to feel free to express feelings, and welcoming different viewpoints from the consultee. Each of these elements is consistent with the collaborative model. Further research (for example, Hinkle, Silverstein, and Walton, 1977; Wenger, 1979) suggests that collaborative conditions facilitate implementation of recommendations and consultee satisfaction.

Example of Collaborative Consultation. An example of consultation in a day program for retarded adults at a community mental health center illustrates the collaborative model. The program leader, a social worker, was concerned because one of her clients was often disruptive, making daily work sessions difficult and field trips almost impossible. Consultation resulted in the recommendation that the social worker use a structured behavior modification program, which was successful in controlling the client's disruptive behavior. This recommendation was made in the context of a collaborative relationship that maintained the active involvement of the consultee. The following transcript illustrates how this influence process was implemented in a collaborative manner.

Transcript	*Analysis of Collaborative Interaction*
Consultee: Frank doesn't show any fear. I have punished him several times, but I have not been getting the results I want. He just doesn't seem to care when he loses recess privileges, if he is not permitted to go on a field trip, or even when I call	

his parents. He has no respect
for my authority!

Consultant: Why do you think
he fails to respond to authority?

Consultant wishes to challenge consultee's assumption that lack of respect is the primary problem. (1)
The challenge is posed tentatively,
using a question format, so consultee can still reject consultant's viewpoint. (2) Consultee's active involvement is encouraged by asking her to
generate the alternative ideas.

Consultee: Well—he has been
punished so much over the
years that I wonder whether
he is immune to punishment,
and maybe . . . [long pause] .

Consultant: Maybe what?

Rather than interject his point of
view during this silence, consultant
encourages consultee to keep thinking.

Consultee: Well—[pause] maybe I haven't been able to discipline him as consistently as I
would like.

Consultant: What are some examples of the difficulty with
consistent discipline?

By encouraging a more concrete description, consultant reinforces continued active input from consultee,
which consultant clearly values.

Consultee: Sometimes I am
too busy to give Frank my full
attention and I don't even notice his disruptive behavior. Instead, I hear about it from one
of his victims. Also, he receives
so much punishment, some-
times I ignore his behavior be-

Transcript	*Analysis of Collaborative Interaction*

cause I don't have the heart to punish him again.

Consultant: Have you considered any approaches to discipline, including positive approaches as well as aversive ones, which you could possibly implement more consistently?

Consultant wants to begin considering some interventions. Rather than present his own ideas, he asks consultee to think of some. This gives consultee credit for having some good ideas and maintains consultee's active involvement. In addition, by pushing consultee toward action with a question, consultant is tentative and implicitly offers consultee the opportunity to reject this change in direction.

Consultee: I suppose the behavioral approach I told you about that Andrea [a professional colleague of the consultee] was using might work. I don't like the idea of bribing [clients], but it does provide a way to focus on Frank's positive behavior, rather than putting so much emphasis on punitive measures and his negative behavior.

Consultant: That sounds like an idea we can work on together, and I agree it might work.

Consultant gives credit for a good idea and reinforces the collaborative relationship by suggesting they can work on it *together.*

Consultee: You have been bringing out good ideas more and more.

Consultee tries to place herself one-down to consultant.

Consultant: We have developed a number of ideas together, but

Consultant again reinforces the notion that this was the *consultee's*

| *Analysis of* |
| *Transcript* | *Collaborative Interaction* |

this was really your idea. Can we begin working on it some-time today?

idea. The collaborative nature is re-inforced by the suggestion that "we" begin working on it.

Consultee: Yes, we can do it over lunch if you are free.

Pertinent Research in Social Psychology

At first glance the concept of collaborative consultation may appear contradictory. Consultation is an influence process directed toward specific goals involving the consultee and the client—and yet the collaborative nature of the interaction re-quires a collegial process in which both consultant and consultee exercise influence. Three social psychology theories provide a framework indicating how consultation can be a directed influ-ence process that is implemented collaboratively: French and Raven's theory of social power, Bateson's theory of relational communication, and Deutsch's conflict resolution theory.

Social Power as Influence. Regardless of theoretical per-spective, almost all professionals writing about consultation view it, in part, as an influence process. The consultant has cer-tain perceptions of the situation and certain ideas for action, and his or her goal is to influence the consultee to adopt these views. Although authors disagree about whether influence is exercised only by the consultant or whether it is bidirectional, there is consensus that the consultant seeks to exercise influ-ence in consultation.

Martin has identified various forms or sources of power that are legitimate in consultation (Martin, 1978; Meyers, Par-sons, and Martin, 1979). That discussion was based on early work by French and Raven (1959), who described five types of power that form the basis for exercising control in social situa-tions: legitimate power, coercive power, reward power, expert power, and referent power. Later, a sixth type, informational power, was presented (Raven, 1965). These authors argue that these six types of power account for the social change that derives from human interaction.

Reward power exists when one person provides a resource contingent on specified behaviors of another, whereas *coercive power* exists when a person withholds or removes a resource in response to the behavior (or the lack of behavior) of another. *Legitimate power* exists when one person (such as a parent, guardian, or public official) is viewed as having the right to control the attitudes or behavior of others. In *expert power,* one person is thought to have the knowledge or skill necessary to help another achieve his or her goal. In *referent power,* one person is viewed as having characteristics similar to the second person's, and as a result the second person identifies with the first. This identification serves as the source of influence over the second person. *Informational power* is seen when the information provided by one person is viewed as highly relevant and useful by a second person. Though clearly related to expert power, informational power is a characteristic of what the person says, whereas expert power is conceptualized as a characteristic of the person (for example, experience, advanced degree).

Three of these power sources do not belong in a collaborative model of consultation: reward, coercive, and legitimate power. The direct control characteristic of reward and coercive power reduces the consultee's active involvement and undercuts the potential for collaborative influence. Similarly, legitimate power, giving the consultant the implicit right to control the consultee's attitudes and behavior, is inconsistent with the collaborative model.

The three remaining types of power are appropriate for the collaborative model. The consultant who is asked to help solve a problem has the expertise (expert power) desired by the consultee. When the consultant and consultee are similar in age or when they share common interests, experience, or background, referent power might be established readily (see Exercise 2-1). Informational power can be used in consultation when the consultee views as relevant and potentially effective the information provided by the consultant.

Until recently, the consultation literature has devoted

Exercise 2-1
Dimensions of Similarity Between Consultant and Consultee

Part I

Below you will find a number of dimensions on which to compare/contrast yourself with the consultee with whom you are currently working. The dimensions listed are neither exhaustive nor exclusive but may provide a basis from which to evaluate and maximize the similarity factor. First, characterize yourself along the demographic, personality, and likes/dislikes dimensions and then contrast your profile with that of the consultee.

	Consultant	*Consultee*
Demographics		
Sex		
Race		
Ethnicity		
Age		
Other		
Personality		
Extroverted/introverted		
Emotional		
Intuitive		
Rational		
Spontaneous		
Reflective		
Assertive		
Passive		
Other		
Likes/Dislikes		
Sports		
Politics		
Religion		
Work		
Children		
Location/Area		
Other		

Exercise 2-1
Dimensions of Similarity Between Consultant and Consultee, Cont'd.

Part II

Select one dimension of similarity and one dimension of dissimilarity and develop plans for maximizing points of similarity and minimizing points of dissimilarity.

considerably more time and energy to referent power than to expert power, even though both can facilitate social influence. Although French and Raven's terms have not been used, it is clear that the notion of referent power runs throughout the consultation literature. Caplan's notion of a collegial relationship, the widespread reliance on the concept of empathy (for example, Meyers, Parsons, and Martin, 1979; Schowengerdt, Fine, and Poggio, 1976), the focus on the voluntary nature of consultation, and the special emphasis given to rapport and the use of indirect, rather than direct, confrontation techniques (Caplan, 1970) all point to the importance of referent power in consultation.

The consultant can also maximize influence using expert power, although this form is little discussed in the consultation literature. A variety of conditions that support expert power have been identified in the literature on attitude change (for example, McGuire, 1969). Age, social status, educational level, and evidence of relevant experience all contribute to expert power. Providing the consultee with clear, objective evidence of one's specialized training (titles, diplomas), using "testimonials" from satisfied clients and other indications of a positive reputation, and demonstrating control, direction, and vision regarding consultation can enhance expert power.

One reason some professionals deemphasize expert power is that it can act as a constraint (Martin, 1977). Often expertise implies that the consultant can be quite helpful but only in a limited number of specific problem areas. However, expertise can be more varied if based on knowledge of principles that ap-

ply in a variety of situations. For example, knowledge of oper-
ant techniques has particular value in one specific form of behavior modification, but it is also generalizable to a broad class
of problem situations. Thus, expertise need not narrow the consultant's power to a single set of conditions.

Expert and referent power might appear incompatible,
since it is difficult to emphasize one's unique expertise and re-
tain a sense of similarity or reference. However, the consultant's
goal is to blend expert and referent power. In one instance this
balance was attempted by a consultant to a group home for retarded adults. When introducing himself to the staff, the consultant described previous successful consultations with group
homes (expert power). Simultaneously the consultant indicated
that successful consultation would require expert input from
the consultees (referent power). Because he was contracted as
an external consultant, had advanced degrees, and had previous
experience consulting with group homes, expert power was high
at the outset. Referent power was therefore sought early in consultation through frequent efforts to have coffee and chat informally with the staff.

When the consultant is internal to the system, referent
power may be established more readily. In these circumstances
the consultant may be more effective by emphasizing his or her
expert power—for example, by publicizing scholarship, professional involvement, recent successes, or knowledge of relevant
information.

Cienki (1982) has investigated the blending of expert and
referent power in consultation. She found that expert power
was correlated with successful problem definition and production of an effective plan. Referent power was correlated with
the consultee's perception that the solution was effective. However, the consultant who blended expert and referent power was
perceived as most willing to help. Although much more research
is needed, it is suggested that the most efficient consultant
blends expert with referent power. Exercise 2-2 is designed to
help develop skills needed for such blending.

Relational Communication Theory. Relational communication theory has its origins in Gregory Bateson's work (1935,

Exercise 2-2
Balance of Powers

This chapter has indicated several concrete ways the consultant can use expert power and referent power. When applying these concepts, the consultant needs to assess the degree to which he or she has both expert and referent power. If there is an imbalance between these two sources of power, the consultant should seek a balance. This balance can be achieved by increasing the weak source of power and/or deemphasizing the strong one.

Consider your most recent consultation and assess your expert power and referent power in that relationship. List separately the sources of each type of power that are available to you and indicate how potent you think each source is. Following this evaluation, assess the degree to which a balance of expert and referent power exists.

If there is an imbalance, develop a plan to create the desired balance between these two types of power. Implement this plan in your next consultation and analyze the results. Discuss the effects with a colleague and/or supervisor in order to receive corrective feedback.

1958). Bateson observed communications to occur in two patterns. In *symmetrical* communication patterns, the relationship is equalized through equivalent behavioral exchanges. For example, in consultation, the consultant's dominance may be met with assertive responses from the consultee. *Complementary* interaction, the second form noted by Bateson, is characterized by relational exchanges that are dissimilar in terms of control. In a complementary exchange, one person's efforts to control are accepted by the second person, so that a consultant's dominance will be met with submissiveness by the consultee.

One derivative of Bateson's work has been the development of coding systems to assess the control aspects of communication. Sluzki and Beavin (1965, cited in Erchul, 1981) were the first to develop such a coding procedure. They operationalized symmetry and complementarity and developed an approach to assess how control was exercised during verbal communication. These authors classified statements as one-up or one-down to indicate whether the person was trying to exercise dominance or submissiveness in the relationship. The basis for such assignment was the grammatical form of the statement (that is, whether it was a question or an assertion) and its purpose (that is, whether it reflected agreement, disagreement, acceptance, and so on). This work was followed by sophisticated coding systems designed to assess relational control (Mark, 1971; Ericson and Rogers, 1973). The coding system described by Ericson and Rogers (1973) is particularly applicable to evaluate control in the consultation relationship.

There are three steps in using this system. First, each statement is described by a three-digit code. Table 1 shows the

Table 1. Categories for Ericson and Rogers' Three-Digit Coding System.

Digit	Meaning
1st	1. Speaker A
	2. Speaker B
2nd	1. Assertion
	2. Question
	3. Talkover
	4. Noncomplete
	5. Other
3rd	1. Support
	2. Nonsupport
	3. Extension
	4. Answer
	5. Instruction
	6. Order
	7. Disconfirmation
	8. Topic change
	9. Initiation-termination
	10. Other

categories coded by each digit of this system. The first digit indicates who the speaker is; for example, speaker A might be the consultee and speaker B might be the consultant. The second digit refers to the grammatical form of the statement. An assertion is defined as any completed referential statement that is not a talkover. A question is defined as any interrogative statement that is not a talkover. A talkover is defined as any effort to enter the conversation by interrupting the other person's speech. Finally, a noncomplete is defined as any grammatical form of speech that is started but not completed.

The third-digit codes in Table 1 refer to the purpose of the message. Support refers to communications that give or seek agreement, assistance, acceptance, and/or approval. Nonsupport refers to communications that provide disagreement, rejection, demands, or challenges. Extension refers to a noncommittal response that maintains the flow or content of speech by the other person. An answer is defined as a definitive reply to a question. An instruction is defined as a suggestion, whereas an order is defined as a command. A disconfirmation is a statement in which the speaker ignores what the other person has just said. Topic change occurs when a new idea is presented *without ignoring* the previous statement by the other person. An initiation-termination is a message that begins or ends an interaction.

Once each statement has been coded, the second step is to assign a control code to each statement. There are three possible control codes: one-up, one-down, and one-across. A message that is one-up is an attempt to assert dominance. A message that is one-down is one that attempts to place its sender in a submissive position. A message that is one-across seeks to neutralize control in the relationship. Tables 2 and 3 show how messages are assigned such control codes.

The third step in using Ericson and Rogers' coding system is to apply a *transaction code* to each pair of sequential messages in the interaction. This provides a vehicle for operationalizing two key theoretical principles derived from Bateson's work (symmetry and complementarity) along with a new notion called *transition*.

A *symmetrical interaction* occurs when the two messages have the same control direction (one-up, one-up; one-down, one-down; or one-across, one-across). A *complementary interaction* occurs when the control directions for the two messages are opposite (one-up, one-down; or one-down, one-up). A *tran-*

Table 2. Control Direction for Each Message Type.

Third-Digit Category

Second-Digit Category		Support	Nonsupport	Extension	Answer	Instruction	Order	Disconfirmation	Topic change	Initiation-termination	Other
		1	2	3	4	5	6	7	8	9	0
Assertion	1	↓	↑	→	↑	↑	↑	↑	↑	↑	→
Question	2	↓	↑	↓	↑	↑	↑	↑	↑	↑	↓
Talkover	3	↓	↑	↑	↑	↑	↑	↑	↑	↑	↓
Noncomplete	4	↓	↑	→	↑	↑	↑	↑	↑	→	→
Other	5	↓	↑	→	↑	↑	↑	↑	↑	↑	→

↑   = one-up

↓   = one-down

→   = one-across

Source: From Rogers and Farace (1975).

sitional communication occurs when the paired messages have different directions that are not opposite—that is, one of the messages is coded as one-across.

Relational theory and the Ericson and Rogers coding system have multiple uses in consultation research (see Erchul, 1981). Two uses are of special import for the current discussion. First, this scale assesses the *interaction* between two persons. Most process scales discussed in the consultation literature

Table 3. Assignment of Control Codes to Second- and
Third-Digit Code Combinations.

Second- and Third-Digit Code Combinations	Type of Control
12, 14, 15, 16, 17, 18, 19	one-up
11	one-down
13, 10	one-across
22, 24, 25, 26, 27, 28, 29	one-up
21, 23, 20	one-down
32, 33, 34, 35, 36, 37, 38	one-up
31, 30	one-down
42, 44, 45, 46, 47, 48	one-up
41	one-down
43, 49, 40	one-across
52, 54, 55, 56, 57, 58, 59	one-up
51	one-down
53, 50	one-across

Source: From Rogers and Farace (1975).

are not interactive. Typically, they are used to assess the consultant, the consultee, and/or both, but not the interaction between the two. For example, measures of accurate empathy (Carkhuff, 1969), accurate reflection of feelings (Ivey, 1971), and open invitation to talk (Ivey, 1971) can be used to assess elements of the consultant's style independent of the consultee's behavior. Although it is important to know the extent to which a consultant uses these communication skills (a point developed in Chapter Three), such scales ignore the notion that consultation is a *process,* an interaction of consultant and consultee. Ericson and Rogers' system provides a framework for assessing the paired sequential messages between consultant and consultee that provides a direct assessment of their interaction.

Second, the scale provides a measure of the degree to which consultation is a collaborative interchange between colleagues. It indicates who exercises control, in what ways, and at what times during the consultation process. In describing how this scale can be used in consultation, Erchul has identified several signs of dominance and submissiveness that the consultant and consultee can show. They can be used to determine the extent to which collaborative and noncollaborative approaches to

relational control are used in consultation. Consultant facilitativeness can be measured in at least two ways: (1) based on the
extent to which the consultant uses one-across statements,
which do not assert dominance, and (2) based on the balance
between consultant dominance and submissiveness. The following are some of Erchul's measures of relational control.

1. *Consultant domineeringness:* Number of one-up statements
    by consultant divided by total number of consultant state-
    ments.
2. *Consultee domineeringness:* Number of one-up statements
    by consultee divided by total number of consultee state-
    ments.
3. *Consultant dominance:* Given one-up statements by consul-
    tant, the percentage of one-down statements by consultee.
4. *Consultee dominance:* Given one-up statements by consul-
    tee, the percentage of one-down statements by consultant.
5. *Consultant submissiveness:* Number of one-down statements
    by consultant divided by total number of consultant state-
    ments.
6. *Consultee submissiveness:* Number of one-down statements
    by consultee divided by total number of consultee state-
    ments.
7. *Consultant facilitativeness:* Number of one-across state-
    ments by consultant divided by total number of consultant
    statements.
8. *Deference to deference:* Given one-down statements by
    consultee, the percentage of one-down statements by con-
    sultant.
9. *Transition to deference:* Given one-down statements by
    consultee, the percentage of one-across statements by con-
    sultant.

This system also provides a way to operationalize and test
Caplan's (1970) notions about one-downsmanship. In Caplan's
view, the consultee is likely to test the collegial nature of the relationship by making statements that place the consultant in a
superior position relative to the consultee. According to Caplan,

the consultant can maintain the collaborative relationship by responding in kind. The consultee's one-down statements should be followed with one-down statements from the consultant. Tying Caplan's work to the present discussion, the consultee's one-down statements should be followed by either one-down statements or one-across statements by the consultant.

The following transcript illustrates a collaborative consultation interaction in which the consultee is a first-grade teacher. The teacher requested help with a youngster who had socioemotional problems and was making very little academic progress. This transcript has been coded using Ericson and Rogers' system, to help the reader learn how to use the scale. The score for each utterance is recorded in the middle column, along with a brief explanation of the third digit. This digit reflects the purpose of the communication and is sometimes difficult to score. It is suggested that the reader cover the scores given beside the transcript and try to code each utterance. The scores accompanying the transcript can then be used as a basis for comparison. Table 1, along with the text explaining that table, will help the reader score the three-digit code for each utterance. Tables 2 and 3 provide the control codes.

Transcript	*Three-Digit Code*	*Control Code*
Consultant: Let me ask you another question. Do you feel that the teacher who taught James last year failed him?	1, 2, 8 The number 8 reflects that this is a topic change.	↑
Consultee: [Laughing] Oh, Lord—wow—I don't think it would be fair—but I would have to say yes.	2, 1, 4 The number 4 reflects that this is a direct answer to a question.	↑
Consultant: Okay, let me ask you, how did that teacher fail him?	1, 2, 0 The number 0 reflects that this question is simply asking for information without having any of the nine other purposes indicated in Table 1.	↓

Transcript	Three-Digit Code	Control Code
Consultee: He doesn't know his ABCs, you know, and there was a problem with recognizing his name, and he didn't know the concept of letters.	2, 1, 4 The number 4 reflects that this is a direct answer to a question.	↑
Consultant: So James did not learn these academic things, and therefore [voice softens] are you going to take it a step further and say the teacher was at fault if he didn't learn these?	1, 2, 2 The number 2 (third digit) reflects that the question was designed to challenge what may be an important underlying assumption of the consultee.	↑
Consultee: I can't say, it might depend on how many others in the class reached their goal.	2, 1, 2 The number 2 reflects the consultee's refusal to answer the challenge.	↑
Consultant: Okay—do you feel that academic achievement is the most important goal for a kindergarten teacher, like number or letter recognition?	1, 2, 0 The number 0 indicates that this is a question that is simply seeking information, with none of the additional nine purposes reflected in Table 1.	↓
Consultee: No. That is my priority number two. But number one would be to help the child develop self-confidence and work to potential.	2, 1, 4 The number 4 indicates that this is a direct answer to a question.	↑
Consultant: Then how would you evaluate James, this year, in terms of that goal?	1, 2, 1 The number 1 indicates that the consultant's question seeks agreement from the consultee.	↓

Control
Transcript	*Three-Digit Code*	*Code*

Transcript	*Three-Digit Code*	*Control Code*
Consultee: He's getting there [said in wonderment]. We're getting there. His self-confidence is 100 percent better than it was. He responds, he participates, and he even asks questions.	2, 1, 4 The number 4 indicates that this statement provides a direct answer to a question.	↑
Consultant: Do you see that as an achievement with James?	1, 2, 1 The number 1 indicates that this question is seeking agreement from the consultee that something has been accomplished with James.	↓
Consultee: Well, not until we started talking about it. I hadn't really thought about it, but I suppose it is.	2, 1, 1 The number 1 (third digit) indicates that the consultee's statement reflects her agreement with the consultant.	↓
Consultant: Try to think about what you are giving that child if you can help him build his self-confidence and feel good about himself.	1, 1, 5 The number 5 indicates that the consultant makes a suggestion to the consultee.	↑
Consultee: He does feel good about himself. I believe he knows I care about him— even when he fails.	2, 1, 1 The number 1 (third digit) indicates that the consultee's statement reflects her agreement with the consultant.	↓
Consultant: So, even though you said you were unsuccessful in helping him reach academic goals, do you feel he is making progress toward your most important goals?	1, 2, 1 The number 1 indicates that the consultant's question seeks agreement from the consultee.	↓

Transcript	Three-Digit Code	*Control Code*
Consultee: Yes, yes!	2, 1, 4 The number 4 reflects that this is a direct answer to a question.	↑
You are helping me to re-assess my work with him.	2, 1, 1 The number 1 (third digit) indicates that the second portion of the consultee's comment is a statement indicating acceptance of the consultant's help.	↓
Consultant: I'm feeling excited about the progress you have made in terms of this goal—that you have seen this much improvement in only two months.	1, 1, 1 The number 1 (third digit) indicates that the consultant is offering acceptance and approval to the consultee.	↓
Consultee: Yes, yes. Let's get up and dance! [Both laugh]	2, 1, 1 The number 1 (third digit) indicates that the consultee agrees with the consultant.	↓
So what do we do next?	2, 2, 8 The number 8 indicates that this question seeks to change the topic.	↑
Consultant: Well, we can still work on improving his academic skills. I agree that this is also an important goal for James.	1, 1, 4 The number 4 indicates that this is a direct answer to a question.	↑

A summary of the coding for the transcript reveals several interesting points. First, seven of the consultant's ten utterances were questions, while one of the consultee's utterances was a question. Consistent with this observation, six of the consultant's ten utterances (60 percent) were coded one-down, and seven of the consultee's eleven utterances (64 percent) were coded one-up. Consultant dominance was relatively low, as only one of the consultant's two one-up statements was followed by a one-down statement from the consultee. Conversely, consultee dominance was relatively high, as four of the consultee's six one-up statements were followed by one-down statements from the consultant. The consultant did conform to Caplan's suggestions by responding to deference with deference. Two of the consultee's one-down statements were followed by one-down statements from the consultant.

Exercise 2-3 is designed to facilitate the consultant's skills using the relational communication scale to determine how control can be exercised in collaborative consultation.

Exercise 2-3
Message Types and Control Directions

Using the consultation tape you have made to accompany this text, play back any five-minute segment and rate it with the scale provided in Table 1. To use this scale in rating the tape, each statement by the consultant or consultee must be rated separately. The rating for each statement is then listed sequentially as a three-digit code, and next to this rating the control code for each statement (one-up, one-down, or one-across) is recorded.

Next calculate some of the nine summary scores listed on page 30. Consider the implications of your ratings and list the modifications you will consider making in your consultation style. This exercise should be repeated with future consultation tapes and discussed with a colleague, consultee, or supervisor.

Conflict Resolution. Anyone who has worked as a consultant is aware of destructive effects that consultee resistance can have. Frequently the term *resistance* connotes that something is wrong with the consultee and that the consultee should accept the consultant's viewpoint and/or recommendations. We prefer to see resistance as an indication that there is a problem in the relationship. Regardless of who is "right," the consultant needs to know how to respond, and one useful approach is Deutsch's (1973) conflict resolution model.

Deutsch posited that interactions in which both parties act in a "cooperative" (congruent with our use of the term *collaborative*) manner are those in which conflict is most likely to be resolved successfully. In contrast, he found that conflict in "competitive" interactions is less likely to be resolved. A cooperative interaction is an exchange in which each person expects and depends on rewards mediated by the other person. Competitive interactions are those in which each person expects and fears punishment or loss mediated by the other person.

A variety of behavioral styles and personal characteristics can be used to describe cooperative and competitive modes of interaction. For example, a cooperative style would be implemented by a person who tends to be egalitarian, trusting, open-minded, and tolerant of ambiguity and who has a favorable view of human nature. In contrast, a competitive style is likely to be found in people who are authoritarian, aggressive, suspicious, exploitive, and derogatory and who have a need to dominate coupled with a negative view of human nature.

Persons characterized as cooperative and competitive may vary across the dimensions of task orientation, attitudes, perceptions, and communication. Regarding *task orientation,* cooperative interactions emphasize mutual interests and coordinated efforts, whereas competitive interactions stress competing interests and exploitation. Competitive approaches seek to minimize the other's power. As for *attitudes,* cooperative interactions highlight mutual trust and positive interest in the other, while competitive interactions involve suspicious, hostile attitudes. The *perceptions* of those involved in cooperative and competitive interactions also differ. Those in cooperative interactions show an increased sensitivity to areas of common interest, while competitive interactions are characterized by heightened sensitivity to opposing interests. Finally, concerning *communication,* cooperative interactions tend to be open and honest, with persuasive, rather than coercive, efforts to influence. Competitive interactions, in contrast, involve little communication or misleading communication and coercive tactics.

The following four factors may be particularly important in applying conflict resolution theory to collaborative consultation: (1) when a competitive style is matched with a competitive style, conflict resolution is not likely to occur, and rejection, verbal attack, and aggressiveness are possible outcomes, (2) when a cooperative style is matched with a competitive style, conflict resolution is not likely, (3) when a competitive style is matched with a cooperative style, resolution is likely after some time, and (4) when two cooperative styles are matched, conflict resolution may occur most quickly.

It follows that, when faced with resistance, the consultant should try all the more to implement a cooperative (collaborative) mode of consultation. Such attempts might be accomplished by using increased levels of empathy. This notion was confirmed in a consultation program designed to increase positive reinforcement and decrease the negative verbal behavior of three consultees (Meyers, 1978). It was found that consultation was successful with two of the three. Transcripts of the consultation sessions were analyzed to determine consultee resistance and consultant empathy (measured by the Accurate Reflection of Feelings Scale, Ivey and Gluckstern, 1974). It was found that accurate reflection of feelings varied systematically with the level of resistance in the two successful consultation cases, whereas no such relation existed in the third (ineffective) case. During effective consultation the relation between these variables was as predicted: As resistance increased, so did the consultant's use of accurate reflection of feelings. The successful consultant, when faced with resistance, made an increased effort to understand what the consultee was trying to say and how the consultee felt.

Conflict resolution and relational communication theory both provide direction for the consultant seeking to develop and maintain a collaborative relationship. The cooperative mode of interaction emphasizes an egalitarian interaction in which power and influence are exercised in a nonauthoritarian and noncoercive manner. Further, the cooperative mode is consistent with "transitional" interactions as well as a balance between "consultant dominance" and "consultant submissiveness." The emphasis is on mutual power to influence rather than unidirectional influence. In collaborative consultation the cooperative mode requires an egalitarian and trusting relationship; the use of empathy, respect, and genuineness as collaborative attitudes; and a focus on mutual interests and open, honest communication that is persuasive rather than coercive.

Toward a Collaborative Model

As noted at the beginning of this chapter, one of our goals is to present an integrated set of principles and techniques that can be used to implement collaborative consultation. These techniques, based on the theories reviewed in this chapter, are presented in two groups: (1) techniques that emphasize the consultee's role and (2) collaborative techniques to stimulate behavioral change. Although presenting these techniques is a useful step in generating research hypotheses and guidelines for the practice of consultation, that work is not complete or definitive. Research and model building will be necessary to generate a unified model of collaborative consultation.

Techniques Emphasizing the Consultee's Role. The consultation literature has emphasized the consultant's role. However, the collaborative notion of consultation as a bidirectional influence process suggests that more attention be paid to the role of the consultee. Several techniques facilitate the consultee's role in a bidirectional influence process.

1. *Allow the consultee freedom to accept or reject.* Consultation must be a voluntary relationship in which it is clear that the consultee is free to accept or reject the consultant's ideas. It is important for the consultant to communicate clearly that it really is acceptable for the consultee to reject his or her ideas. Doing so helps to neutralize the hierarchal power relationship that can arise between the consultant and consultee (relational communication theory). Similarly, it helps to maximize

the consultee's choice regarding consultation, and it is consistent with a cooperative, rather than competitive, model of interaction (conflict resolution theory).

2. *Encourage the consultee to contribute suggestions.* The consultant needs to request that the consultee contribute ideas in consultation. This does not mean that the consultant does not contribute ideas as well, but it is often necessary to take steps to ensure that the consultee will make suggestions, rather than allowing a passive stance. If consultation requires effort from the consultee, an egalitarian relationship (conflict resolution theory) is more likely, in which the consultant does not exercise hierarchal power over the consultee (relational communication theory).

3. *Encourage the consultee to make decisions.* The consultee must make some of the decisions about the course of consultation—for example, whether consultation should continue, which intervention plans to implement, and what assessment techniques to use. By making decisions, the consultee increases his or her commitment to consultation, which facilitates attitude change. Decision making also increases the consultee's power in the relationship (relational communication theory and conflict resolution theory).

4. *Emphasize the consultee's contributions.* The consultant should seek opportunities to give the consultee credit for any contributions to the consultation process, in particular acknowledging how the consultee has influenced the consultant. This deemphasizes the hierarchal power of the consultant (relational communication theory) while emphasizing cooperative, rather than competitive, interaction between the consultant and consultee (conflict resolution theory).

5. *Encourage consultee responsibility.* The consultant should try to ensure that the consultee feels responsibility for the outcome of consultation. To maintain a balance between expert and referent power, this responsibility should be shared by the consultant.

6. *Require effort from the consultee.* The consultee's active involvement in consultation will be ensured if effort is required of the consultee. It is important for the consultant to

make clear from the outset that consultation will require effort and investment from the consultee.

Techniques to Stimulate Behavior Change. The primary goal of consultation is to influence the consultee in order to effect behavioral and/or attitudinal change. Focusing explicitly on this goal, however, heightens the expert power of the consultant. Since the collaborative model seeks to balance expert and referent power, during the action phases the consultant must emphasize referent power.

1. *Use nonauthoritarian and noncoercive means of control.* There are at least three ways the consultant can emphasize nonauthoritarian approaches to control. First, consultant dominance can be balanced by consultee dominance. Second, deference by the consultee can be followed with deference by the consultant. Third, transitional modes of interaction can be emphasized, in which the consultant uses one-across statements to neutralize the hierarchal relationship.

2. *Use cooperative modes of interaction.* It is important that the consultant rely on cooperative, rather than competitive, approaches (conflict resolution theory). These include empathy, genuineness, and respect; open, honest communication; and efforts to develop and maintain trust (for example, being clear about confidentiality, availability for follow-up, and the use of recommendations that will not be forced on the consultee).

3. *Respond to resistance with cooperative behavior.* The consultant must make every effort to respond to consultee resistance with cooperative interaction, avoiding the temptation to use coercive and competitive approaches. This is consistent with both conflict resolution and relational communication theories.

4. *Ask questions.* The consultant should ask questions during all phases of consultation. Table 2 illustrates that questions can be used to achieve either a one-up or a one-down position in the relationship. For example, when a question is used to provide support, it places the questioner in a one-down position, but when used to issue a command, it places the questioner in a one-up position. In either instance, however, the grammatical form of the question allows the consultee to exert

the final control through the answer, thus reducing the hierarchal nature of the relationship.

In addition to the purposes of questions listed in Table 2, questions in consultation may have three major goals: to facilitate discussion about some aspect of the consultation problem, to facilitate discussion of interventions that the consultee can implement, and to confront the consultee with some aspect of his or her behavior. For each of these three goals, questions can be asked in an open or closed manner. Open questions encourage the consultee to generate a variety of additional ideas; closed questions tend to focus discussion more narrowly.

Generally it is useful to ask open questions, which encourage more active input from the consultee and which can generate many useful ideas about the consultation problem, the interventions, or even the confrontation. However, there are times when the consultant wishes to focus consultation on a particular aspect of the problem, a particular intervention, or a particular confrontation. It will then be important for the consultant to formulate a closed question.

Closed questions are asked using such words as *are, do, have, should, will,* and *can*. They are questions that can be responded to in yes-or-no fashion. Open questions use words like *how* and *what*. They require more elaborate responses and encourage self-exploration by the consultee.

In addition to knowing how to differentiate between open and closed questions, it is important to recognize when questions can be used to confront. This is accomplished when the question challenges a basic assumption of the consultee. By phrasing a confrontation as a question, the consultant can make the confrontation more acceptable to the consultee, who still has potential control in providing the answer to the question.

5. *Make suggestions tentatively.* The consultant should make suggestions and confrontations in a tentative manner that will emphasize cooperative interaction (conflict resolution theory) and will deemphasize the consultant's hierarchal power (relational communication theory). This can be done by phrasing the recommendations as questions (for example, "Do you think it would help if we . . . ?") or by communicating uncertainty

about the recommendations (for example, "I'm not certain, but I think it might work if we . . .").

6. *Do not oversell consultation.* The consultant should avoid the temptation to oversell consultation or the recommendations. Rather than promising success, the consultant must be more realistic and point out the problems that might occur. The consultant's goal is to provide enough reason to stimulate the consultee to engage in consultation without providing too much justification. By being realistic about the possible problems and the difficulties achieving success, the consultant reduces the hierarchal power relationship and reinforces the collaborative relationship (relational communication theory).

Perhaps the most important factor is that the consultant must "believe" that a collaborative relationship is not only desirable but also possible. The consultant must consider the consultee his or her equal in the task of consultation. This issue of consultation will be addressed in Chapter Five.

ᴥ CHAPTER THREE ᴥ

Understanding Relationships

The approaches used to exercise influence in collaborative consultation were delineated in Chapter Two, and certainly these can increase the probability of an effective consultation relationship. The communication skills and attitudes discussed in Chapters Four and Five, respectively, also can facilitate a productive consultation relationship. This chapter presents a framework with practical implications for the consultant and helps to develop the skills needed to understand relationships.

As people working with people, we may make literally hundreds of social contacts each day. Some of these casual contacts will develop into meaningful productive personal and professional relationships. Others will fail to progress beyond a pleasant smile and hello or even become antagonistic and destructive. What distinguishes these contacts? What accounts for relationships that develop positively? What can people do to facilitate positive relationships? The first step in answering these questions is to develop a framework for understanding the relationship. This requires knowledge of *what* constitutes a relationship and *why* relationships develop.

43

What Constitutes a Relationship?

Two structural features form the basis for any relationship: norms and roles.

Norms. Any relationship, whether a large organization or the dyad of a husband and wife, is affected by the norms of the setting where it takes place. Norms may influence who is sanctioned to interact with whom and for what purposes. Norms may define both the "what" and the "how" of communication within a relationship. To ensure a successful relationship, therefore, it is important to learn the norms operative within the relationship and to act on the basis of this information.

In consultation it is particularly important that the consultant identify the norms that operate within the systems affecting the consultee. The norms can be used to guide the consultant through the various interactions he or she encounters. Further, knowledge of the institution's norms may prove essential for selecting diagnostic and intervention techniques acceptable within that setting. One example occurred when Parsons (1976) recommended that a teacher use extinction procedures as part of a program to reduce a student's negative attention-seeking behavior. The consultant had not assessed whether extinction procedures were consistent with the school's norms. It happened that this school valued teacher control, order, and quiet in the classroom. The consultant's advice thus created conflict for the teacher, who risked violating school norms if she were to follow it. The results were that the teacher was placed under additional stress, the intervention proved ineffective, and it almost eliminated the possibility of future consultation contracts.

Roles. Any relationship consists of at least two persons, each with a role defined for that particular relationship. The same person will generally have different roles in different relationships. A relationship can be conceptualized clearly by starting with a definition of the role of each participant. Both consultants and consultees—be they nurses, teachers, supervisors, middle-line managers, business executives, or whoever—have a variety of roles. Such roles as provider, disciplinarian, leader, follower, or lover are but a few that one may play, and the roles enjoyed most are those free of conflict. To facilitate interaction with a consultee, the consultant should be aware of roles played by consultants and consultees. Further, the consultant must be sensitive to possible conflicts for the consultee's roles and must develop procedures to reduce such conflicts.

Consultees generally exhibit two types of conflict associated with roles. *Interrole conflict* exists when a consultee occupies two or more roles that impose contradictory expectations about a given behavior. In the collaborative consultation relationship, for example, the consultee (a role of helpseeker) is called on to provide solutions, in conjunction with the consultant. This expectation places both the consultant and consultee in the role of helpgiver at the same time as helpseeker. The conflict between these two roles can cause confusion for the consultee and can be destructive to the relationship. A consultee may try to resolve this conflict by attempting to occupy the role of helpseeker exclusively, relinquishing all responsibility for problem solving, or else by moving to a position of control and absolute decision making independent of the consultant's advice. Either position is detrimental to the consultation relationship, so the consultant provides a third approach by trying to help the consultee redefine the consultation relationship in collaborative terms—the consultant's role is not to provide all the answers, and the consultee is to be actively involved in joint problem solving, involving sharing and interdependence in creation and implementation of intervention plans. This redefinition may help to reduce the consultee's interrole conflict. Redefinition may be an ongoing process occurring throughout the various phases of consultation.

A second form of role conflict is *intrarole conflict*. As with interrole conflict, a consultee experiencing intrarole conflict will behave in ways that are destructive to the outcome of consultation. Intrarole conflict emerges when expectations and guidelines for appropriate behavior in *one* role create conflict for a particular person. For example, Mr. Anderson, as chief executive for the Z-Company, may feel that seeking consultation is completely congruent with that portion of his role that

calls for facilitating company operations. The help-seeking role
of the consultee, however, requires that this executive present
the current work problem along with his own unsuccessful attempts at resolution. Such a role may be incongruent with Mr.
Anderson's perception of a chief executive, which includes
being a competent, self-sufficient, authoritative problem-solver.
This role of consultee may create significant conflict for him.

The importance of understanding the role expectations
of all participants in consultation, along with developing the
tools for redefining roles so as to diminish role conflict, cannot
be overemphasized. Exercise 3-1 illustrates a number of roles

Exercise 3-1
Identifying and Ameliorating Role Conflict

For each of the scenarios described, identify (1) the roles
the consultee exhibits, (2) the existence and type of role conflict, (3) the negative impact of the role conflict, and (4) techniques for redefining the roles in order to reduce the strain.

Scenario I

J. L. Smithbridge, the consultee, is the corporate president of LZX, Inc. He contacts you in order to discuss possible
solutions to the current stress manifested within his company
around the issue of sexism and promotions. Mr. Smithbridge
has served as an expert in Washington on the formulation of legislation on sexism in the business place and has consulted with a
number of national and international firms on the development
of policy statements on the issue of sexism within their busi-
nesses.

Consultee role(s): _____

Type of role conflict: _____

Possible impact: _____

Steps to reduce role conflict: _____

Exercise 3-1
Identifying and Ameliorating Role Conflict, Cont'd.

Scenario II

Dr. Laura Hewstone, the academic provost of a small New England liberal arts college, has requested your services. Dr. Hewstone has served in her post for two years and has prided herself on using a humanistic Theory Y approach to administration. In your first interview Dr. Hewstone discusses how she has resolved all the difficulties she has faced by employing consensus and group process decision with her faculty. She hastens to add that such group consensus is better than being "one of those damned autocratic administrators." The presenting problem concerns the fact that the board of trustees has established that, for cost-efficiency, 15 percent of the current faculty must be let go. Dr. Hewstone felt that a consultant might be able to "do" this more "humanely."

Consultee role(s): _____

Type of role conflict: _____

Possible impact: _____

Steps to reduce role conflict: _____

Scenario III

Describe your most recent consult in which you felt there was consultee role conflict. Follow the same format for responding as was used for Scenarios I and II.

Consultee role(s): _____

Type of role conflict: _____

Possible impact: _____

Steps to reduce role conflict: _____

associated with a variety of potential consultees and demonstrates the possible impact of role conflict. This exercise seeks
to develop the consultant's skills for reducing role conflict.

Why Are Relationships Formed?

The previous section gave several important characteristics of relationships; this section discusses the reasons that relationships are formed. One characteristic of most consultation
relationships provides the primary motivation for consultation.
Invariably the consultee perceives himself or herself to be in *crisis,* and this crisis provides impetus for seeking assistance. If the
anxiety resulting from the crisis is too intense, it may interfere
with the consultation relationship. That is, extreme anxiety
may encourage the consultee to seek immediate relief, and this
priority can block the critical thinking processes required for
long-term effectiveness. Similarly, the consultee in a state of extreme anxiety may attempt to avoid the problem and all the
stimuli associated with it and thus either avoid consultation or
resist gathering and presenting needed information about the
problem.

Consultants must learn to respond to consultee anxiety.
A consultant can alleviate some of the consultee's anxiety by
examining the facts surrounding the problem and showing a
shared concern for the possible impact of the problem. Once
the consultee feels that the consultant understands the complexity of the problem and is concerned about its amelioration,
a sense of relief may follow. However, the consultant must
avoid the temptation to reduce anxiety by reassuring the consultee that "all will be well" and the problem will be "solved."
Such rapid reduction of the consultee's anxiety may undermine
the consultee's self-confidence (for example, "Why was I making such a big deal of the situation?" or "Why didn't I see the
solution so easily?"). Furthermore, anxiety may be reduced to
the point that the consultee feels no need for consultation.
Either reaction would be counterproductive.

The consultee's anxiety can be viewed as consisting of

two distinct components: anxiety about the presenting problem and anxiety about the consultant. Often consultees view the decision to use a consultant as an admission of inadequacy. There is also an underlying worry that the consultant might discover the consultee's work deficiencies and share this knowledge with the consultee's supervisor. It is important for the consultant to assure the consultee about confidentiality of consultation to reduce this unnecessary source of anxiety. It is also important to provide support and reinforcement for the consultee in order to reduce feelings of inadequacy in the relationship with the consultant.

Among the many other theories that explain why relationships are formed, two are particularly applicable to consultation—exchange theory and need-fulfillment theory. These approaches are described briefly with reference to consultation. The reader interested in more detailed discussion of the theories is referred to the original sources cited.

Exchange Theory. Originally proposed by Thibaut and Kelley (1959), exchange theory is a functionalist approach that assumes that a relationship is based on the satisfaction of the participants. It posits that all relationships are selective both with respect to who interacts with whom and with respect to what behavior sequences will be enacted. Thibaut and Kelley suggest that people seek relationships in which the *rewards* outweigh the *costs*.

Rewards include any aspect of the relationship that is enjoyable, gratifying, or otherwise satisfying. Such rewards may be either "exogenous" or "endogenous" to the relationship. Often rewards are accrued because of the *individual* aspects, talents, or resources of one or both participants. Since these are brought to the relationship from the outside, they are called "exogenous." Several types of exogenous rewards exist in consultation. For example, the consultant's expertise about the consultation problem or the consultant's apparent self-confidence when interacting with the consultee can be a source of exogenous rewards. (See our description of expert power, in Chapter Two, for a discussion of these types of exogenous rewards.) Another source of exogenous rewards is referent power. For example, similarity of consultant and consultee in values or backgrounds can produce exogenous rewards in consultation.

Other rewards are inherent in the relationship itself, coming from the interaction of the participants. These are called "endogenous" rewards. Though not discussed much in the literature, they can have important effects on the consultation relationship. Many things can occur during consultation to produce endogenous rewards for the consultee. An example occurs when the intervention strategy developed results from a brainstorming session in which the consultant and consultee continue to build on each other's ideas until the final strategy is derived.

The costs in a relationship can also be exogenous or endogenous. An exogenous cost may result from any preliminary demand placed on the consultee that requires a major modification of his or her response pattern. Scheduling meetings with the consultee at inconvenient times or requiring the consultee to fill out too many forms will act as an exogenous cost of the relationship. Another exogenous cost occurs when the consultee is criticized by peers or supervisors for seeking consultation.

Endogenous costs develop during the consultation relationship and can harm it. Once contact has been made and the current work problem is discussed, the consultee may experience anxiety about confronting his or her inadequacies. An endogenous cost occurs when these feelings of inadequacy are exacerbated by the consultant's response. Another endogenous cost can occur if the consultant observes the consultee at a time when the consultee feels particularly inadequate.

Endogenous and exogenous costs and rewards are all available to both the consultant and the consultee during consultation. Exercise 3-2 will help the consultant learn to identify the rewards and costs occurring during consultation and to increase rewards and minimize costs, thus maximizing the probability of an effective relationship.

Exchange theory suggests that each individual enters a relationship with a minimum level of rewards minus costs set as a

Exercise 3-2
Identifying the Rewards and Costs of Consultation

In Part I of this exercise you are asked to identify endogenous and exogenous rewards operating in your most recent consultation relationship. Further, you are asked to identify possible strategies for increasing these rewards. Part II asks you to identify costs operating in the relationship and develop strategies for reducing these costs. After completing this task, discuss your results with your colleague, consultee, or supervisor.

Part I: Reward Identification

Strategies for Maximizing Rewards

Exogenous
Endogenous

Part II: Cost Identification

Strategies for Minimizing Costs

Exogenous
Endogenous

bottom line. This is the *comparison level* against which the current relationship is assessed. It is generally established from experience in previous relationships and often acts as the criterion for deciding whether to continue the current relationship or pursue another. If a consultee has experienced an extremely costly consequence when relying on self or peers for solving the current work problem, a minimum of success (reward) experienced early in the consulting interaction can help to ensure and maintain the relationship. However, if the consultee has a history of successfully solving professional problems independently, the consultant's entry into and maintenance of a relationship will demand a high reward-to-cost ratio for the consultee.

Need-Fulfillment Theory. People seek each other out because relationships help meet many needs, and particular people are sought to fulfill particular needs. It is important to develop a frame of reference that can help consultants understand their own needs operating within the consultation along with those of the consultee. The FIRO (fundamental interpersonal relations orientation) theory of William Schutz (1967) provides one such approach. FIRO posits that individuals orient themselves toward each other in an attempt to satisfy three basic interpersonal needs: the inclusion need (the need to associate), the control need (the desire to dominate others), and the affection need (the desire to share close personal and emotional feelings with another).

It is important to know which of these needs is most important to you and particularly which needs are satisfied during consultation. By reflecting on a recent experience in which you entered a room full of strangers and recalling how you felt (tense, anxious, hopeful, as if on center stage) and what you did (introduced yourself, tried to blend, waited for someone else to approach), you can begin to sense your need for inclusion. Similarly, consider how you feel and act when placed in a situation calling for decision making. Do you sit back and "let George do it," or do you try to influence the decision? When being controlled or influenced by others, do you relax and enjoy the vacation from responsibility, or do you feel tense and uncomfortable and try to resist or acquire control? In decision-making situations, do you feel more comfortable "on top," "at the bottom," or in a coequal position? Answering such questions will give you insight not only into your interpersonal need for control but also, perhaps, into the way a situation or relationship is flavored by your ability to satisfy that need. Finally, the affection need is manifested to the degree that one likes others and feels comfortable sharing and receiving feelings. People with a high need for affection enjoy close interpersonal relationships.

Although there is no right or wrong need profile or level of need, the FIRO theory posits that a relationship will be functional if the participants' need states are compatible. There are two ways that compatibility can occur. *Interchange compatibility* is based on the mutual expression of the three need states. This occurs when the two persons interacting are similar in each of the three need areas. For example, a consultant who has a high need for inclusion, will inquire, prod, and ask to be included in the consultee's activities while similarly inviting the consultee to participate in the varied activities of the consultant (before, during, and after work), and is likely to be successful with a consultee who has a similar desire for inclusion. However, this same consultant may conflict with consultees who have a low need for inclusion. Similarly, when the consultee prefers minimal inclusion, a consultant who is objective and businesslike, who encourages only minimal personal involvement around the work-related topic, is more likely to be successful.

Interchange compatibility can occur with any of the three basic need states, but it is most likely with the need for inclusion and the need for affection. When the consultant and consultee both have a high need for control, conflict results as the two begin to compete for power and control in the relationship.

The second type of compatibility (Schutz, 1967) is more likely to be effective with the need for control. *Originator compatibility* exists to the degree that one person's expression of a need (that is, inclusion, control, or affection) corresponds to that which the other person wishes to receive. For example, if the consultee feels extremely anxious and insecure and is seeking professional guidance and direction from the consultant, the consultant can be compatible by exhibiting a high need to control in that particular situation.

To determine whether need compatibility exists between the consultant and consultee, the consultant must first assess the needs of both the consultee and the consultant in the relationship (inclusion, control, affection) and then compare each need for the consultant and consultee to determine whether either of the two types of compatibility exists (interchange or originator). If compatibility does not exist, the consultant can develop strategies to increase need compatibility for a more effective relationship.

Other needs besides inclusion, control, and affection can have an important bearing on consultation. These can be conceptualized using Maslow's (1970) hierarchy of needs: physiological needs, safety needs, esteem needs, and self-actualization needs. The last three are particularly relevant to consultation.

The safety need may be involved when the consultant is viewed as the person who will provide security and protection against failure by solving the problem. The need for esteem can involve both the consultant and consultee. Often the consultant can help satisfy this need for the consultee by supporting the consultee's feelings of competence and self-worth and by providing reinforcement. Consultation may also meet the consultant's esteem needs. This occurs when the consultant is afforded special professional status because of the consulting role, when the consultant is able to exercise power effectively during consultation, and, in particular, when the consultant does a good job in working with the consultee to develop productive intervention plans.

Finally, self-actualization can be an important motive in the consultation relationship. This occurs for the consultee when the preventive goals of consultation are in force and the consultee seeks professional growth and development. The consultant can similarly begin to satisfy his or her self-actualization needs by benefiting from the evaluative feedback provided by the consultee on both the intervention plan developed and the consultant's style (see Chapter Eleven).

Although it is clearly important to understand consultees' motivations for participating in consultation, it is equally important for consultants to understand their own motives. Exercise 3-3 is designed to help the consultant develop an awareness of his or her motivations during consultation.

Exercise 3-3
Identifying Consultant Motivations

Spend some time thinking about what satisfactions you get from engaging in consultation. Use the discussion of needs from this chapter to help generate ideas, but feel free to add any motivations not mentioned that are important to you. Next

Exercise 3-3
Identifying Consultant Motivations, Cont'd.

take a sheet of typing paper and draw a map reflecting the
needs that you satisfy by engaging in consultation. Draw lines
to produce a separate space to reflect each of your needs, and
be sure that you plan the map so that the relative size of each
space reflects your view of the importance of that need. Ask
one or more of your colleagues to do the same, and then discuss
your motivation maps with each other, trying to identify the
specific ways such motives may affect your consultation styles.
    One sample of a consultant's motivational map follows:

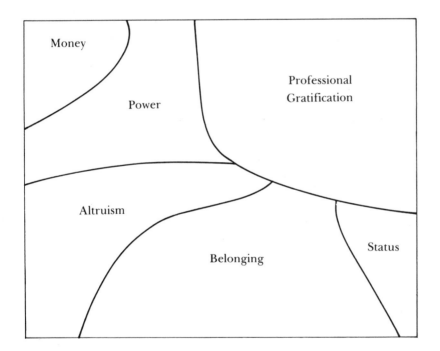

    A final worksheet, Exercise 3-4, is presented for use be-
fore consultation in order to identify variables that might be
effective in developing the consultation relationship.

Exercise 3-4
Effective Relationship Checklist

After the initial interview with your next consultee, complete the following checklist. Use this checklist periodically to maintain sensitivity to the factors that influence your consultation relationship.

Checkpoints

1. What needs do I hope to satisfy?
2. What needs does the consultee manifest?
3. Describe the types and levels of personal need compatibility.
4. What are the potential rewards and costs to the consultee?
5. What is the consultant's potential power profile (that is, expert and referent power)?
6. What might the consultant do to maximize the blend between expert and referent power?
7. What are the unique norms for this setting?
8. Describe any consultee role conflict.
9. Does the consultee's level of anxiety need to be raised? lowered? maintained?
10. Does the consultee's self-esteem appear optimal for coordinate participation?

❧ CHAPTER FOUR ❧

Improving
Communication Skills

The effective consultant must have interviewing and communication skills (Alpert, 1977; Bergan and Tombari, 1976). Regardless of the content or focus of consultation, it is first and foremost a helping interaction. Thus, consultation is highly affected both by the factors known to facilitate or inhibit creation and maintenance of a helping relationship and by the skills needed to transmit and receive effective communication. This chapter addresses these factors and suggests a number of activities for self-assessment and skill development in the process of communicating as a helping consultant.

Although communication may be defined in various ways, one definition is offered by Tubbs and Moss (1977, p. 6): "Human communication is the process of creating a meaning between two or more people." *Effective* communication is more involved and can be difficult to achieve. We can think of effective communication as creating a condition in which the message perceived and responded to by the receiver corresponds to the one intended by the sender. Research has shown that achiev-

ing such correspondence between intended and perceived messages is strongly affected by a number of personal, interpersonal,
and environmental factors. A consultant must be skilled at recognizing these factors that support effective communication
and must also be competent in manipulating them.

The importance of effective communication is obvious,
but its attainment is not always a certainty. One need only review media coverage of political speeches to appreciate the impact of an ill-chosen word or phrase or of a poorly timed inflec-
tion in one's delivery. How different it might have sounded if
former Secretary of State Alexander Haig, when facing the cam-
eras after the shooting of President Reagan, had said, "For the
moment, I am in charge," or simply "I am in charge," rather
than exclaiming, "*I'M* in charge!"

Similarly, it should be apparent that the ill-chosen word,
poor timing, confused mixture of verbal and nonverbal signals,
and poor listening skills exhibited by the consultant in the following hypothetical transcript not only will inhibit the successful orchestration of the consultation contract at hand but will
likely interfere with future referrals from that consulting source.
In this illustration the consultant is called in to analyze the formal institutional communication processes and patterns in a religious community because of the perceived negative feelings
shown by the members and their expression of feeling overwhelmed, underprized, and dehumanized by the "decision
makers."

Consultee: As with most religious orders, this is a time of crises
—dwindling numbers of new recruits, more work for fewer people, and generally more emphasis and focus being placed on
secularism. We—

Consultant: [Interrupting] Well, you called the right person.
Doesn't sound like a big deal—little communication difficulty,
I've done a number of these things before.

Consultee: But I hope you understand the sense of value and
commitment which is being shaken and the—

Consultant: [Ignoring the consultee's obvious concern] My fee is generally $300 a day plus expenses, and if we will be doing any workshops, which is very likely, I will need one day prep time at the same rate.

Consultee: [Somewhat flustered] Well, well, I'm just the director and must confer with the community advisory board—but we are not really sure what we need to do [anxious and with a sense of desperation].

Consultant: [Smiling and somewhat patronizingly patting the consultee on the back] I can see this is a problem for you—so leave it to me. You talk to the people controlling the purse strings, and I'll take care of the nitty-gritty.

Although this scenario is a caricature of what not to do, the sad reality is that many "consultants" use this style and believe it to be appropriate to the professional contract. After all, "We are the experts, and we need to discuss fees and contracts on entry, don't we?"

To be effective, the mental health consultant must be aware of the intricacies and pitfalls of effective communication. The consultant must also be able to receive the intended message from the consultee and to formulate communication in such a way that the consultee can properly receive and respond to the message.

A Model for Communication Skills

Consultation, at its very basis, involves the consultant's reception and accurate understanding of the consultee's problem, followed by the consultant's effective transmission of an intervention plan back to the consultee. Such an exchange occurs over a number of contacts and involves a series of interdependent and interrelated processes. Each step has the potential for distorting the intended message. For example, the well-intended message of our consultant in the preceding illustration, "I do have some experience and expertise with this type of situation, and I think I can help resolve it; let me help you; try to relax," certainly is well disguised or actively distorted. Poor timing (interrupting), poor selection of words ("Doesn't sound like a big deal"), and mixture of an oral expression of care and concern with a nonverbal (with superficial smile and pat) suggestion of a patronizing desire to rush off—all acted to inhibit accurate reception of the basic helping message. The same consultant would have proved much more effective by empathically reflecting the consultee's concern (for example, "You seem to be feeling that this is extremely urgent?"), affirming the noncatastrophic nature of the situation ("I think perhaps you have taken the right initial step"), and offering some sense of hope and support ("I am familiar with this situation, having worked with a number of religious orders in the past. Perhaps my experience with these other groups will help").

To remedy such problematic communication, one needs to be aware of the many factors involved in the communication process. Figure 2 diagrams the process for a one-way communication. This simplified model represents a one-way communication with a specified sender and a specified receiver. In reality, communication is bidirectional, involving the ongoing sending and receiving of messages by both consultant and consultee. This bidirectionality further compounds the process because of the demands of shifting between the roles of receiver and sender. Nevertheless, Figure 2 does incorporate the basic elements of dyadic interactions. These elements are described below.

Identifying the Intended Message. As the initial step in creating and delivering a message, the consultant/sender scans all the sources of information, past and present, that may have relevance to the current consultative situation. After scanning the potential inputs, the consultant can determine the intended message. Effective communication and the consultative process may begin to deteriorate even at this early stage. This can occur when the consultant gives premature closure to the situation so that, rather than scanning all the relevant data, the consultant simply concludes: "This is just like the last time" (or "just like Case B"). Further, consultants may restrict the inputs to the potential message because of their own selective attention, or fil-

Figure 2. Simplified Model of One-Way Communication.

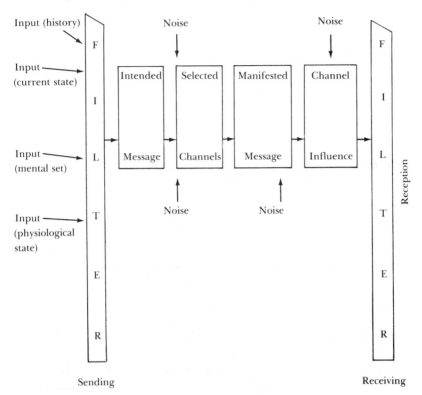

tering, process. Filtering—blocking the reception of some inputs while highlighting others—often occurs when the consultant enters the consultation with a preconceived idea about the nature of the problem or remedial strategy. Suppose, for example, that the consultant in our illustration a few pages back had received notification of another client's refusal to pay for services rendered just before meeting with the new consultee. That occurrence might have sensitized him to the money agenda, so that he processed all the information from the consultee through an "I have to be clear about my fee" filter. This filtering process could impose restrictions on the type of information to which the consultant would attend (for example, "She can't make the decision, so send her back to the advisory body") or even reshape or misshape the message so that it would fit into his cognitive set (for example, "Dwindling numbers, probably less income").

Similar types of filtering and restriction of inputs are evident when a consultant offers pat remedial suggestions or end-all solutions. The consultant has filtered the received message so that it fits into his or her favorite ideas of problem definition and remediation. Alternative and supplementary procedures are most often overlooked. The strict and narrow focus that shapes the message sent lends an authoritative overtone that this recommendation is the one and only approach to take, leaving little or no room for the consultee's contribution to or involvement in the process.

Encoding the Message. After identifying the intended message, the consultant must decide on the form the message will take in order to be transmitted, as well as the channel (oral, visual, tactile) to be used. The channel and form are selected to maximize the probability that the message will be accurately received. This is not always easy to achieve.

For example, the consultant using oral channels without visual cues (that is, speaking with little or no animation or visual prompts) with a consultee who is deaf will be ineffective in communication regardless of the merits of the intended message. Similarly, use of multiple channels (voice, gesture, touch, and so on) can increase the potency of the message, but it may detract from or interfere with the intended message. In our illustration, for example, the pat on the back may have distorted the intended message so that it was received as superficial, patronizing, and uncaring. Another example is found when a male consultant, trying to communicate his genuine professional and human concern for a female consultee, chooses to smile warmly (facial), lean forward (body orientation), touch the consultee's arm (tactile), and say (oral), "I really do care about you." Although each of these conditions can act as a channel for the expression of the "caring" message, each might be misinterpreted —depending on the context, the nature of the relationship, and the consultee's own mental set—as seductive, threatening, or simply presumptuous. If a particular channel employed (oral, tactile, body orientation, facial) provokes anxiety or defensiveness in the consultee, it may interfere with reception of the intended message.

Noise. Once the consultant/sender has encoded the message in a channel that appears appropriate to the conditions, its transmission becomes open to a number of sources of interference, or "noise," existing in the environment. Anything that distorts the message or distracts the receiver from the reception of the message is noise. Environmental distractors such as telephones ringing, babies crying, and class dismissal bells sounding are examples. Environmental noise is experienced daily in our professional and personal interactions and can generally be remedied rather easily (take the phone off the hook, feed the baby, reschedule after dismissal), but consultants often fail to implement such remedies.

To compound this problem, noise can also originate within an individual and thus be harder to recognize and ameliorate. The filtering and channel interference discussed earlier can be sources of internal noise. For example, the consultee experiencing concern over the classroom that she left unattended while discussing the case with the consultant in the hall will split her attention and energies between "being with" the consultant and "being in" the classroom. Such concern interferes with her accurate reception of the consultant's message. Similarly, the consultant discussing human relations training with a firm's director of personnel might find his messages poorly received should the consultee have psychological noise originating from his concern for the child he left at home that morning with a 102-degree temperature or from his displeasure with the memo about morale that he received from the president earlier that day. Such psychological sources of noise, like their environmental counterparts, need to be identified and then reduced or avoided if the consultant's intended message is to be received as desired.

Receiver's Channel Effects. Continuing along in the process of communication, we find our message impinging on the senses of the receiver, wherein the effects of the receiving channel will be incorporated into the reception of the message. For example, a receiver with a bad case of sunburn might find it difficult to "receive" an intended message of care and concern that is channeled through a gesture of hugging. Similarly, a memo that is sloppily written and therefore visually displeasing to the receiver will influence the reception of the written message. Thus, one more challenge to the effective communicator is to overcome any potential distortions of the intended message by the receiver's channel effect.

Reception Filters. As the last step before reception of the intended message, the receiver will actively process the information through his or her own set of filters and thus may modify the message. One such modification occurs when the receiver has a limited capacity for stimulus reception or message retention. This limitation (reception filter) is attributable both to physiological constraints (for example, limited short-term memory, sensory gating by the reticular system, perceptual limitations and weaknesses) and to psychological constraints (for example, bias, expectations, mental sets). Long-winded messages—chained, unending series of information—may be filtered down to a less than complete condensation for simplified (but less accurate) reception. The consultee, for example, who enters the communication expecting to hear the worst might bring with him a negative set that cognitively filters incoming information so that all the negative, critical comments are received while positive communications are discounted or discarded.

It is clear, even using such a simplified model of communication, that although communicating may be perfectly natural, it is not perfect naturally. Communicating effectively is neither an automatic nor a simple process, and formal training is essential for all aspiring consultants. The orientation that follows within this chapter, as in the entire book, is that of a skill approach. The rest of this chapter is designed to help the consultant develop the skills essential to receiving, sending, and clarifying messages.

Skills of Reception

One of the consultant's most important roles is to be a receiver of information. The consultant must accurately receive the consultee's description of the problem, the consultee's presentation of the previously unsuccessful remedial tactics, the consultee's concerns about new methods, and the consultee's apprehension about being in a consulting relationship. To receive this information accurately and effectively, the consultant must open all channels to the information presented. The consultant must be ready to receive information with his or her eyes, ears, and very being. Further, the consultant needs to reduce noise and filter effects as far as possible and provide the sender with evidence that the information was accurately received. Such effective and facilitative reception can occur only when the consultant takes an active role in the exchange and demonstrates facilitative *attending behavior.* Attending not only sets the stage, physically and psychologically, for reception but also gives the sender/consultee evidence of the consultant's accurate understanding and willingness to continue to receive.

Physical Attending. Attending, or "being with" another, requires both a physical stance, or position, and a psychological orientation. Gerard Egan (1977) discusses the importance of body orientation in setting the physical stage for attending. Egan characterizes proper attending behavior as being face to face, with a straight body orientation, openness in body posture, a comfortable, slight forward lean to the body, and maintenance of eye contact. Support for the effectiveness of Egan's SOLER (straight, open, lean, eye contact, relaxed) attending posture is abundant. Many authors (for example, Argyle, 1967; Mehrabian, 1967; Reece and Whitman, 1962; Steinzor, 1950) have found an increased potential for communicating and a perception of increased warmth when the communicator uses this posture.

The SOLER position has two purposes. First, this posture places the receiver in a body orientation that facilitates reception by "opening" the receiver to a number of channels and narrowing the band of potential noise and interference. Second, SOLER allows the receiver to convey (by means of body language) that he or she is attending to the sender. To attain such a positive effect, the position assumed and the degree to which each component of the SOLER orientation is used must be dictated by the consultant's personal style. For example, although spontaneous, relaxed, and frequent eye contact is effective, staring may be perceived as threatening and may act as a major source of distraction or noise.

In addition to a SOLER position, attending behavior requires that the helper be aware of any interference created by his or her personal habits that might suggest inattentiveness to the consultee. One need only consider the difficulty one has staying on topic while someone twirls a strand of hair, files fingernails, or straightens a desk of papers to appreciate the detrimental effects of such personal habits on the communication process. Exercise 4-1 provides a checklist for recording such personal habits.

Exercise 4-1
Interference from Personal Habits

This exercise will require "objective" feedback of information to you about your personal habits and idiosyncrasies manifested during interviewing or consultation. Video equipment might prove most efficient, but an audiotape can be used.

After your next consultation interview, review the session and take special notes of the frequency of any distracting behaviors, along with the apparent effect on the consultee. The following checklist includes sample distracting behaviors that may be observed.

Behavior	Frequency Count	Impact
Repetitive sounds (clicks, sniffles, and so on)		
Voice quality (clarity, tone)		
Behavioral twitches		
Extraneous movements (head bob, bouncing hand movement, and so on)		
Use of objects (pencil drumming, doodling, and so on)		
Lapses from SOLER attending position		

Psychological Attending. In addition to using body position as a form of attending, the consultant needs to use psychological attending skills. The consultant must place himself or herself in a position of psychological readiness to receive information accurately and must communicate this state of readiness to the consultee.

Many of us, as children, were schooled in the notion that when others speak, we should be polite "good" listeners—non-interruptive, docile, and silent. Effective listening, however, is far from a passive process. One cannot simply sit back and passively record the messages sent. Effective reception requires us to reach out psychologically and step beyond the noise and filter effects in order to enter into senders' phenomenal fields so that we can experience their worlds as they do and their messages as intended. Such reception requires the skills of active empathic listening.

Active listening is a total listening—a reception of all the cues (verbal and nonverbal) being sent from the consultee, from the environment, and from within oneself. These signals are then accurately identified in order to focus on the intended message. Active empathic listening demands that the consultant stop talking internally and quiet the voice inside that argues mentally, passes judgment, and races to conclusions or points of rebuttal. It requires us to concentrate not only on what is being said but on how it is said and to check our reception for its accuracy. Although this sounds simple, it is difficult in practice.

Often a consultee's long-windedness inhibits active empathic listening. The consultant's limited capacity for storing information in short-term memory and the tendency to sensory-gate (that is, neurologically "ignore") repetitive, nonnovel stimuli make such long-winded statements hard to receive. As a result, all consultants at times daydream and fail to listen carefully to the consultee. The consultant's goal is to become aware of these incidents and to reduce them. Exercise 4-2 is offered to assist in reducing inattentiveness and developing active listening skills.

In addition, many of us are prevented from being good listeners because we have developed a series of poor listening

Exercise 4-2
Active Listening

This exercise requires three persons—one acting as consultee, one as consultant, and one as referee. Before starting the discussion, have each player select one of these three roles and stick to it. Select a "problem" that the consultee is presenting for the first time to the consultant.

Step 1: The consultee is to begin discussing his or her position on the topic chosen. For Step 1, the consultant, in the role of the listener, will respond as he or she typically would. The referee is simply to observe and note the effectiveness of the discussion. The referee should stop the discussion after five minutes.

Step 2: Continue the discussion, with one major change: Our consultant will now have to follow a simple procedure before responding to the consultee. After listening to the speaker and *before* responding, the listener must "repeat," or paraphrase, the explicit content of the speaker's message. The referee is asked to prevent the consultant from responding without this step. If the consultant's perception of what was said is wrong, the consultee needs to correct it. The consultant must repeat the corrected version and then respond. This procedure is to continue for five to ten minutes.

Step 3: In Step 3 the consultant and consultee will take on the duties of both speaker and listener, using active, reflective listening. The referee will again prevent anyone from speaking without first reflecting accurately the message just received. Continue for five to ten minutes.

Step 4: Analyze and discuss the experience of active listening. Hard? Easy? More or less energy required? More or less attentive? Less time and freedom for internal discussions? Other comments?

habits. Adler, Rosenfeld, and Towne (1980, p. 202) identify a list of negative habits that will interfere with accurate empathic reception. Table 4 presents our version of these poor listening

Table 4. Poor Listening Habits.

Habit	Description	Example
Pseudo listening	Providing the outward appearance of attending while internally becoming self- rather than other-focused. One finds oneself beginning to plan new agendas, seeking extraneous stimuli from the environment, carrying on internal conversations, daydreaming, or just going numb.	*Consultee* (I. M. Boring): "Oh, hi, Dr. Goodman, am I glad I bumped into you— you know Jimmy, the one I'm always telling you about . . ." *Consultant:* "Oh, hi—Jimmy—yes." Internal conversation begins while maintaining external listening appearance ("Gads, why me— Jimmy's only problem is this guy—let me out of here").
Selective listening	Having a brief set of criteria that will be used for processing the information one is about to receive. Information falling within the parameters of the criteria will be attended to, all else ignored or dumped (sensory-gated).	Consultant is trying to give feedback to a teacher (consultee) about her use of extinction. Consultee is anxiously expecting negative feedback, "knowing" she "did it all wrong." What she hears is in capital letters. *Consultant:* "Well, DE-LORES, extinction with a kid like Joe is really TOUGH, but you did a fine job. THERE WERE a few MISTAKES, but overall you did it just as we discussed . . ."
Stage hogging	Using each speaker's statement as a cue for oneself to take control and occupy center stage. Stage hoggers are listeners only briefly, since their goal is to dominate the airwaves with their presentations.	*Consultant:* "Could you describe the group you are referring to?" *Consultee:* "Group! I'll describe them and the whole damned company . . ." *Consultant* (interrupting): "Let me see if I got this—" *Consultee:* "I'm sure you did, but there is more . . ."

(continued on next page)

Table 4. Poor Listening Habits, Cont'd.

Habit	Description	Example
Assimilation to prior messages	Filtering new incoming information through an old schema. Encounters with a particular person or topic often provide one with a schema for organizing the information into a meaningful whole. Once the schema is formed, it is psychologically much easier to force-fit all new data into the existing pattern set by prior messages, thus often distorting the new information.	After successfully working with a number of consultees on developing a token economy system for their disruptive clients, in a new consult the consultant forces the new data into the old set and therefore immediately plans another token system even though on closer inspection it appears inappropriate.
Insensitive listening	Being unable or unwilling to look beyond the explicit words or behaviors and responding only to the face value of the message.	Our consultant in the illustration early in this chapter, who heard only that there was a problem without listening to the sense of devastation and urgency expressed.

habits as they apply to consultation. Check your own listening style for evidence of these sources of poor listening, using the audiotape that you have prepared to accompany this book (as suggested in the Preface). Note any of the poor habits that occur in the tape.

Skills of Sending

Facilitative Messages. To remain psychologically and socially alive and active in a conversation with a consultee, the consultant must be able to provide evidence of his or her understanding while facilitating the consultee's effort to provide further information. One technique that may provide the consultee with this sense of being attended to is the use of "minimal encourages to talk" (Ivey, 1971)—brief utterances or expressions, verbal or nonverbal, that indicate continuing interest in the con-sultee's statements. An appropriately timed "Oh?," "So?," "Then?," "And . . . ," "Um," or "Uh-huh," along with repeti-tion of one or two of the consultee's key words and a nod of the head, will help to convey that the consultant is actively en-gaged in the exchange and is "with" the consultee. The skills of minimal encourages can be clarified by analyzing the audiotape of your own consultation interaction for the appearance of minimal encourages. Exercise 4-3 is presented as a simple check-list to assist you in this analysis.

Exercise 4-3
Checklist of Minimal Encourages

Listen to a tape recording of a recent consultation session and, using the following guidelines, record the frequency of your use of minimal encourages. Then summarize your feelings about the apparent impact of these minimal encourages on the consultee and on your interaction. Finally, identify areas in which minimal encourages might have proved effective but were absent in this exchange.

Minimal Encourage	Frequency Count	Impact
"Tell me more" (or some such request)		
"Um-hum" (or "Uh-huh")		
"Oh?"		
"So?"		
"Then?"		
"And?"		
Repeat one or two key words		
Echo consultee's last statement		

Notes on where minimal encourages might have proved facilitative: _____

Often the consultant desires not only to convey "with-it-ness" to the consultee but also to help the consultee clarify the problem. To achieve these goals, appropriate use of *open questions* is facilitative. Special emphasis is given to the *appropriate* use of questions because unskillful use of questions may create a feeling of interrogation or challenge, which may give rise to defensiveness, resulting in justification, explaining and excusing, or some other form of defending by the consultee.

Questions need to be asked in such a manner that the consultee feels invited to expand and elaborate. This purpose is better served by open questions, often identified as those that begin with words such as *how* and *what,* than by closed questions, which call for yes-or-no responses or demand explanation (*why?*). Refer to Chapter Two for a more complete discussion of questioning strategies.

Influencing Messages. Consultation, like all helping interactions, is an influence process. The consultant has been called on to assist in remediating the consultee's work-related problem and, in doing so, will influence the consultee's perceptions, attitudes, and/or behaviors in relation to the handling of that problem. As discussed in Chapter Two, consultation is a bidirectional influence process in which consultant and consultee influence each other. However, this section focuses on the skills that the consultant can use to influence the consultee. Messages that can provide the consultant with the means for a helping influence need to be identified, and then the consultant's ability to use these messages needs to be nurtured. It is essential that the consultant remember that he or she must, first, attend to and accurately receive the consultee's messages and, second, provide evidence of this understanding to the consultee before attempting to influence the consultee.

1. *Paraphrase.* Paraphrase, in which a listener provides the speaker with the essence (not simply a regurgitation) of his or her message, may prove to be a simple yet potent influencing technique. Because it focuses on the essence of the message, the paraphrase proves highly selective. By deciding what information to paraphrase, the consultant will guide the consultee in selecting the next topic. Thus, selection of material to paraphrase

can influence the direction and focus of an interaction. Exercise 4-4 will help to clarify the power of the paraphrase to influence.

Exercise 4-4
Paraphrase as Influence

Below you will find one consultee statement, with two possible consultant paraphrases. After reviewing the paraphrases and their predicted impacts, generate at least two additional paraphrases along with their predicted impacts.

Consultee statement: "I spent one week taking baseline data on out-of-seat behavior, and here are the charts. Wow, that was a lot harder than I thought. It did give me a better focus on the conditions under which the behavior occurs. I think I see a pattern, but I would like to discuss it with you."

Consultant paraphrase #1: (Intention is to direct toward focusing on data.) "Taking baseline data is sometimes more difficult than one first expects, but the information we gather often seems worthwhile and educative once we examine it."

Impact: Consultee is directed toward the value of baseline data, the acceptability of expressing difficulty with procedures, and the importance of discussing data.

Consultant paraphrase #2: (Intention is to focus on lack of skill in observing, since it will be a subject of treatment.) "Baseline data are often difficult to collect, even after a week. It is often hard to predict how difficult it can be or the problems one can encounter."

Impact: Consultee hears that it is acceptable to have a problem and to discuss this problem and the possible need for skill development.

Consultant paraphrases #3 and #4: (Write paraphrases that focus on the value of collecting baseline data despite its difficulty.)

2. *Summarization.* To encourage the consultee to move on to another topic or into greater depth of a particular topic,

the consultant may use the technique of summarization. Summarization is the attempt to condense, or crystallize, a number of critical dimensions of the previous series of exchanges. Whereas ongoing inaccurate summarization can suggest the consultant's inattentiveness or ineptness in self-expression and thus act as a wedge in the facilitative relationship, accurate and timely summarization will act as a check on the accuracy of the consultant's perception. Further, by providing a sense of closure and accomplishment, summarization can move the consultee on to explore additional topics or act on those discussed.

Challenging Messages. As the consultant attends and facilitates the exchange, the consultee's concerns will become clearer, as will the nature of the presenting problem. At the point in the relationship when the consultant has a firm grasp of the nature of the problem and has begun to generate strategies for intervention, communication skills that are more directly influencing may be required. At this juncture the consultant may use the skills of confrontation, interpretation, and direction.

1. *Confrontation.* Too often confrontation is equated with a noncaring, destructive act, typically used to hurt or attack another. In the political arena, confrontation often implies an impasse or a standoff of a dangerous dimension. However, within a helping relationship such as consultation, it is—or can be—a constructive, growth-producing experience that occurs any time the helper/consultant causes or directs the consultee to reflect on, question, reconsider, or modify some aspect of his or her behavior, attitudes, or feelings. That is, whenever the consultant's behavior, deliberately or inadvertently, acts as a stimulus to challenge the consultee, confrontation has occurred.

How a confrontation affects the relationship (that is, whether it is growthful or destructive) appears to depend on the nature of the relationship, the motivation of the confronter, and the manner of the confrontation. Confrontation techniques are to be used only after a positive relationship has been established. Moreover, the consultant must be certain that his or her motives for confronting are clearly positive and meet the consultee's needs, rather than the consultant's. Assuming that these two conditions are met, then the form and manner of confrontation may be the crucial factor differentiating successful from destructive confrontation.

As Egan (1973, p. 108) notes, "If confrontation were merely the transmission of correct and meaningful information by a concerned observer to a willing listener in order that the latter might engage in and grow through self-examination and subsequent behavioral change, then the whole process of confrontation would be simple indeed." Such simplicity is not to be found, and in fact the predicted growth-producing effect of confrontation is mediated by a variety of intra- and interpersonal factors.

A comparison of the confrontation styles in the following illustration provides insight into the importance of the consultant's style. In particular, observe how the second approach uses a question by the consultant as part of an effort to present the confrontation in a tentative manner. The scene is the second consultation session with the director of personnel for a small advertising firm. The director of personnel presented the problem as a need to reduce staff dissatisfaction (evidenced by increasing absenteeism, staff turnover, reduced productivity). At the end of the first session, the consultant asked that the consultee (1) gather specific data reflecting the "symptoms" and (2) survey the staff for points of concern.

Consultee: Hi, Dr. Howards. Gads, things are getting worse! We had our layout man quit yesterday, and the man at the top is furious. It's been so busy that I really didn't get the data you wanted—you know, the numbers of absences and so forth—and I really haven't had the time to get the survey developed, but I will.

Consultant 1: What! How do you expect us to get anywhere if you either don't give a damn or are too incompetent to do a few simple tasks? It seems that I am just wasting my time and perhaps need to work directly with Mr. Hicle ["the man"]. At least then I will get some cooperation.

Consultant 2: It sounds as if things continue to be strained, and the layout man must really have been upset to quit. I can see the pressure you must be under now as the personnel director. I know you were unable to survey the staff this week, but do you agree it is important that we gather these data this week? Would it help if we brainstormed some possible ideas or perhaps developed the survey now?

It can be helpful to evaluate confrontation efforts. Whether or not one follows all the rules for appropriate confrontation, the true measure of its effectiveness is whether it leads to a closer, more accurate and productive relationship. A confrontation that elicits defensive reactions such as counterattacking the consultant, ignoring the confrontation, or distorting or devaluing the message is a confrontation better left undone. The consultant must be sensitive to these signs, and when they occur, it is important not to persist with the confrontation.

Several approaches to confrontation have been identified that are relevant to consultation; Berenson and Mitchell (1974) provide an excellent discussion of this topic. We shall consider three approaches to confrontation: didactic confrontation, experiential confrontation, and calling the game.

Didactic confrontation occurs any time the consultant gives the consultee information or corrective feedback. To be productive, a didactic confrontation should provide information which is new to the consultee and which the consultee views as important. For example, providing the information "You are late" to a consultee who comes rushing into the meeting room glancing at her watch will not be perceived as sharing information. It is more likely to be perceived as pointing out a weakness or failure.

In addition to providing new and desired information, the confrontation should be presented in a descriptive form rather than using commanding, judgmental, evaluative language. Effective didactic confrontation is not accomplished by labeling, name calling, or dictatorial presentations of "musts," "shoulds," or "have to's." A descriptive, nonjudgmental, tentative manner is applicable to each type of confrontation we discuss. In a didactic confrontation, for example, after observing a teacher's classroom manner, a consultant could say: "I noticed that when you began to discuss Whitman's work, your rate of speech seemed to become more rapid. I found myself beginning to attend to this rather than your content, and I didn't remember all that you had said about Whitman. I wonder whether some of the students experienced that same effect. Do you think it would be more effective if you spoke at the rate you used while reviewing the quiz this morning?"

Finally, in presenting a didactic confrontation, the consultant should be alert to the potential impact on the consultee. A consultee who has just experienced a lengthy didactic exchange may be in a position of "stimulus overload." The consultant who can view the exchange from the eyes of the consultee will realize that additional information can only prove unproductive at this time. Similarly, should the consultant perceive that the consultee is feeling a reduction in self-worth or self-esteem, the manner of didactic confrontation becomes especially important in order that the confrontation be viewed as a nonevaluative, specific description of a behavior, rather than a global negative evaluation of the self.

Experiential confrontation, the second type of confrontation, can be used when a discrepancy is perceived in the messages sent by the consultee. The discrepancy may be between what the consultee says and what he or she does. For example, while discussing a problem of the low morale of a group of production-line workers who, after hearing rumors of a possible shutdown, have begun to develop a "who cares" attitude about work, the middle-line manager says to the consultant: "You know, some of these guys just started work, they're young. They can find other jobs if they have to. How about me? I mean, look at me—after twenty-two years in the plant, almost fifty-eight years old. Hell, this is no big deal. I don't know what they're worried about. I keep telling them, just do your jobs. No big deal—stop worrying." The "no big deal" message and the attempt to present a nonplused attitude are incongruent with the concerned, somewhat hopeless feelings shown in "after twenty-two years, almost fifty-eight years old." An experiential confrontation would point out this discrepancy by stating: "First you seem to feel they need not worry. But at the same time you seem to be concerned yourself about the impact. Is that right?"

For such a confrontation to prove helpful, the consultant, in addition to being empathic and descriptive, needs to present the discrepancy in a tentative manner.

Calling the game is the last form of confrontation presented here. Eric Berne (1964), who popularized the Transactional Analysis notion of "games," defined a game as an ongoing series of transactions occurring at two levels (an overt, explicit social level and a more subtle psychological level) that progresses to a well-defined, predictable outcome of ill feelings for those involved. One such pattern is typified by the consultant who says to her consultee, with a patronizing smirk, "This is the correct procedure to use; however, it may be a bit overwhelming for someone like you." Although the consultant might be expressing a considered point of view (that the procedure is difficult for some to implement), this message is accompanied by an ulterior message—one implying consultee incompetence and challenging the consultee to prove otherwise. Consultants must avoid this sort of game if they want consultation to be successful.

Consultees can be game players as well. Most consultants are all too familiar with consultee-generated games, in which the consultee's true intentions take on the form of a hidden agenda and, if allowed to proceed unnoticed or unchallenged, prove destructive to the consultation outcome.

When games take place in consultation, it is essential that the consultant step back from the interaction—disengage, as it were—and call the game. Beier (1966) suggests that an "asocial response" that fails to reinforce the expected gamelike banter will force the consultee either to continue alone in a nonreciprocated exchange or to adjust his own interaction away from the game. Similarly, directly confronting (by didactic or experiential confrontation) the apparent hidden agenda—for example, the expression of feelings of hopelessness or the "yes—but" orientation—may act as a cross to further game playing. Moving the once-hidden agenda to a conscious, explicit level will put an end to the value of and need for continued "gaming."

For a confrontation to be productive and growth-producing, regardless of its type, the consultant must view it as an interactional process enacted to bring the consultant more closely in line with the consultee. Thus, the consultant should engage in confrontation for the purpose of mutual growth and should be aware of possible idiosyncratic and potentially destructive motivations, such as, expressing anger, attacking, projecting one's own insecurities, or demonstrating relational dominance and power. It is therefore helpful to become aware of one's biases toward the consultee before confronting, in order to be sure that such biases are not primary in the motivation for engaging in confrontation. The consultant must be certain that the motivation is to help, not to hurt, the consultee.

2. *Interpretation.* Many of us, with elementary and stereotypical views of analytical paradigms, may expect the act of interpreting to be a magical and mystical exposure of the deep and dark nature of the consultee's intrapsychic world. In fact, however, it is a far less magical and imposing process. Interpretation can be viewed as the creative act of redefining the reality at hand. It is the presentation of an alternative frame of reference or point of view from which to consider the consultee's expressed or implied feelings, attitudes, or behaviors. In discussing attending, we noted the value and importance of giving the consultee feedback that demonstrates the consultant's reception of the explicit message both in content and in feeling. When interpreting, the consultant goes beyond simple feedback and reflection of the explicit message to a level of connecting, concluding, and hypothesizing about the underlying nature of the message. Interpretation takes one past the understanding of the consultee's frame of reference, past the current exchange, and focuses on the manner, the tone, the intuitive sense about the underlying issue. It may take a variety of forms, such as a simple focus on what is implied ("I think what you are saying is . . .") or moving from the specifics to a global statement ("I can see how the work load, schedule, and type of tasks you are assigned are extensive. You really are feeling overwhelmed and used, aren't you?"). Finally, interpretation may take the form of identifying recurrent themes—themes of dependency, insecurity, concern for approval, and the like.

For interpretation to be effective and helpful, not only does the consultant need to be in touch with the consultee's world (that is, empathic), but the consultee must be open to an alternative perspective. If these conditions exist, the interpretation can help the consultee develop a new orientation from which action plans will flow.

3. *Direction.* A third procedure to challenge the consultee to a new position is to give directions. The consultant, being perceived as having some expertise, will be called on to tell the consultee what to do or try. When providing advice or direction, the consultant is also challenging the consultee in a "call to action" confrontation. Accordingly, the direction given must be clear and concrete. Facilitative directions are (1) concise, not given in complicated terms, (2) stated in ways that are understandable to the consultee, using descriptive terms rather than jargon labels, (3) appropriate to the consultee's reality, (4) presented in a tentative manner, and (5) delivered in a congruent manner in which the consultant's nonverbal behavior is consistent with the verbal direction given.

In addition to following the "rules" of direction giving, it is essential for the consultant to ascertain that the consultee clearly understands and accepts the directions provided, rather than assuming that the consultant's pearls of wisdom will be readily understood and accepted. In checking the accuracy of the consultee's reception, along with the acceptability of the direction, the consultant not only needs to give the consultee a chance to reply by openly inviting dialogue but may need to be sensitive to the subtle verbal cues ("Yes—but") and nonverbal cues (inquisitive or concerned look) that suggest the consultee's confusion or resistance to the direction given.

This chapter has pointed to the complexity of human communication in order to sensitize the consultant to the notion that hearing is not simply listening and expression is not simply talking. Further, although each of the phases and forms of the communication process discussed was presented in a static form, the real focus should be on communication as *process.* Communication is a process wherein the consultant must act as both a receiver and a sender who facilitates, influences, and challenges the consultee. There is no invariant order to communication (that is, message or influence? challenge? active listening?). However, attending skills and facilitative messages are most appropriate during early phases, influencing and challenging messages later in the relationship.

CHAPTER FIVE

Attitudes Needed to Maintain Collaboration

Consultation, like all relationships, involves interpersonal processes that mediate the nature and productivity of the interactions. The best recommendations are doomed to failure if the consultee fails to trust, like, and respect the consultant or does not feel like an alive and active participant in the process of consultation.

As we have stressed, the consultation process must be viewed as an interchange in which experts of diverse orientations view a problem through their respective prisms and share these viewpoints on the common reality of the problem, its definition, and its solution. In addition to using appropriate interpersonal and communication skills, the consultant interested in developing such a collegial relationship must assume an appropriate attitude toward the consultee and the consultation. The collaborative model requires that the consultant *believe* the consultee is a fellow professional with an equally important contribution to make to the consultation process. This *belief* is then evidenced by the consultant's willingness to allow the consultee the freedom to accept or reject the consultant's recommendations. Given the consultant's investment of time, energy, and self in the consultation, it is not easy to be accepting when the consultee rejects the consultant's ideas and recommendations about the case.

This chapter identifies an orientation, an attitudinal posture, that is essential for a collaborative consultation relationship. We discuss attitudes that facilitate the collaborative relationship and those that can inhibit it. Then we try to help readers identify their own attitudes relevant to consultation so that they can develop those that will prove most facilitative.

Attitudes That Facilitate Collaboration

Carl Rogers' ideas have had a pervasive influence on applied psychology, including his proposal of the core conditions necessary for successful psychotherapy—warmth, acceptance, genuineness, and respect. These conditions, defined initially by Rogers, have been elaborated operationally by Robert Carkhuff, Gerard Egan, and George Gazda. Although little research has examined these variables in consultation, their value to the development of intense, facilitative, and helpful relationships in other settings, such as psychotherapy and counseling, has received some support. We feel that consultation, like these other helping relationships, can be productive only when the consultant shows a genuine concern for the individual consultee and the situation at hand. It is difficult to maintain a relationship and involve oneself deeply in the consultee's situation without a basic interest in and concern for that consultee. The most productive consultant will be one who has a warm, accepting, genuine, and respectful attitude toward the consultee and who actively conveys these attitudes to the consultee.

Nonpossessive Warmth. Nonpossessive warmth, or unconditional positive regard, can be defined as the consultant's ability to accept the consultee without imposing conditions on the consultee for this acceptance. This does not mean unconditional approval of any behavior of the consultee's. Rather, nonpossessive warmth requires the consultant to separate his or her evaluation of the consultee's behavior from the intrinsic value of the person. Such nonpossessive warmth is manifested by (1) the consultant's undivided attention to the consultee, which communicates that the consultant is 100 percent with the consultee, (2) the consultant's demonstration of respect for the consultee regardless of what the consultee says or does, and finally (3) the exhibition of accurate empathy.

As might be apparent, warmth can be conveyed through verbal and physical expressions of understanding and empathy. Accordingly, the reader is referred to the exercises in Chapter Four pointing to the components of empathy and offering opportunities for further skill development.

Acceptance. Consultation requires a climate of mutual acceptance in which the consultant will not attempt to impose roles or norms of behavior on the consultee but will let the consultee be who he is. The consultant seeking to establish such acceptance must lay aside both formal status and informal social roles, which may interfere with an open relationship between consultant and consultee. Roles such as male/female, young/old, or even helper/helpee may set stringent demands on each participant and thus interfere with the honesty of the relationship. A facilitative consultant should be guided by the "here and now" of the interaction rather than being controlled by a priori role expectations.

Such acceptance requires that we refuse to exercise control over the consultee or even demand mentally that the consultee conform to our expectations. But this acceptance of others does not imply absolute approval. Wholesale approval of another is often a way of expressing radical noninvolvement or nonconcern (Egan, 1977). If I really do not care for you, then I can readily approve of whatever you do, because it costs me nothing to do so. An accepting consultant must not avoid educating, motivating, or encouraging the consultee to change. Even when the consultant has intentions of changing the consultee, however, he or she must actively allow the consultee the freedom not to change. That is, even when the consultant knows that the recommendations are excellent, he or she must avoid the temptation to demand or expect implementation.

Consultants (and other professional helpers) often assume that helpees/consultees *know* that we accept them. This assumption can interfere with the development of an accepting relationship. Rather than simply assume that such acceptance is understood, the consultant should actively encourage the consultee to express the ways in which he or she is different from the consultant, professionally, philosophically, and personally, and should make acceptance active by showing care, respect, and concern for the consultee and the consultee's problem.

Genuineness and Respect. Individuals involved in formally defined relationships, such as consultants, often find themselves acting in accordance with prescribed or expected roles. Genuineness within consultation is achieved when consultants (or consultees) are free to be themselves. The consultant who is genuine acts in an integrated, authentic fashion. With genuineness the individual shows congruency in his or her feelings, as revealed by both verbal and nonverbal cues. A consultant who is genuine is open, as opposed to defensive, and is real, as opposed to phony. The main ingredient of genuineness is congruence, or agreement, among one's words, expression, tone, actions, and feelings. Genuineness involves responding authentically to the consultee in both a negative and a positive manner, much as one would do in any human relationship (Carkhuff, 1969).

Although there may be instances when the consultant freely chooses not to express feelings during consultation, such a decision should be made in light of an active awareness of these feelings. The key to genuineness is that the consultant must remain nondefensive while avoiding a retreat behind the façade of a professional role.

Respect, like genuineness, can be communicated through one's behavior and response style. Respect is really a way of viewing another. Respect means appreciating the other simply because they are human beings. Respect implies that being human is an important value in itself.

Even though most people think of genuineness and respect as values or moral qualities, such qualities take on value only when translated into interpersonal behaviors. Exercises 5-1

Exercise 5-1
Identifying and Developing Behavioral
Manifestations of Genuineness

Below you will find a listing of behavioral dimensions that can be used to define "genuineness" operationally. Review the descriptions and then, using your tape recording of a consultation session, assess the degree to which each dimension was evidenced, on a scale of 1 (not at all present) to 5 (100 percent present).

Then select one or two of the dimensions and deliberately focus your attempts to increase their expression in your next session. Compare this second session against the tape of your previous performance.

Behavioral Descriptors

These are behaviors through which genuineness is expressed:

1. *Freedom from roles.* Consultant does not hide behind titles, labels, degrees, or roles; consultant resists using labels as justifications or disguises for manipulating the consultee.
2. *Spontaneity.* Though tactful and considerate, the consultant does not appear to be constantly weighing what he or she says, as if in a preplanned, manipulative exchange. The consultant appears responsive to the moment rather than rigidly set in a response pattern.
3. *Nondefensiveness.* When questioned or criticized by the consultee, the consultant shows accurate empathic listening and a willingness to consider the consultee's point. The consultant does not retreat or counterattack when challenged by the consultee.
4. *Congruence.* The consultant appears consistent in expressing his or her thoughts, feelings, and behaviors. No discrepancies are evident between what the consultant thinks or feels and what he or she does or says.
5. *Openness.* The consultant demonstrates a capacity for self-disclosure and mutual sharing within the relationship.

and 5-2 afford readers an opportunity to behaviorally define both genuineness and respect in order to evaluate their own on-going levels of expression of each of these attitudes and begin to increase the manifestation of such behaviors in their own practice.

Exercise 5-2
Recognizing the Manifestations of Respect

This exercise describes the types of behaviors suggestive of a "respecting" orientation. Analyze your taped consult for evidence of each of these dimensions (use a 1 to 5 scale, in which 1 = not at all present, 5 = completely present). Next, select one or several of the dimensions identified and consciously attempt to increase their manifestation in an upcoming consultation. Through such goal setting and self-monitoring, manifestations of respect will become a natural part of your consultation.

Dimensions

1. Is the consultant "attending"? Is there evidence that the consultant is actively and accurately listening?
2. Does the consultant actively encourage the consultee to contribute? to provide his or her own unique insight?
3. Does the consultant verbally state or behaviorally demonstrate a belief that the consultee is competent and can take care of himself or herself?
4. Does the consultant appear to enter the relationship assuming the good will of the consultee?
5. Does the consultant show appropriate warmth, closeness, and feeling within the relationship?
6. Does the consultant give evidence of spending time and energy to truly understand the consultee and his or her problem?
7. Does the consultant use descriptive language, as opposed to judgmental, evaluative language?

Attitudes That Hinder Collaboration

As a starting point for this discussion, let us digress into a more lighthearted discussion of the collaborative relationship. Returning to yesteryear and the era of the TV folk hero, we can identify the real prototype of collaborative consultation. The Lone Ranger, defender of justice and devotee of collaborative consultation, clearly knew the value of both interpersonal skills and attitudes for effective consultation.

Recall the typical ending of the *Lone Ranger* episode. The townspeople are milling about in front of the jailhouse and listening to the sheriff describe how he captured the dangerous criminal, who, he proudly points out, is now safely behind bars (mustache, black hat, and all). Then from the distance, the proud sheriff, the relieved townsfolk, and we, the informed viewers, hear hoofbeats whose thundering sound draws the attention of all to the cloud of dust followed by the hearty "Hi-yo, Silver—away." The sheriff asks, "Who was that masked man?," and often, after a pause, he adds, "I didn't even get a chance to thank him."

This example demonstrates the Lone Ranger's in-depth understanding of the collaborative process of consultation. Sometimes consultants believe they have difficult caseloads and job demands and therefore "deserve" some "special" recognition or sign of appreciation from the consultee or others in the organization. Under these circumstances, if consultees do not provide the consultant with this recognition, the consultant may become upset at them (since they are not doing what they are "supposed" to), depressed ("Nobody really cares!"), or hurt ("After all we did for them"). This attitude that we are due something special is not only unfounded but destructive to the maintenance of an effective consultation relationship. Although it is true that consultants often extend themselves and at times are given more than is possible to accomplish, the anger, depression, or hurt generated when the consultant thinks in this manner may destroy the collaborative nature of the relationship and interfere with the consultant's ability to move the consultee toward self-confident, autonomous problem solving in the future.

One need only consider the extensive work load of the Lone Ranger to appreciate his strategy of letting the sheriff take the credit, rather than staying around to take the thanks and credit himself. The Lone Ranger could not afford to solve a problem in South Texas, then travel to a crisis in Montana, only to be called back to the town in South Texas the following week. Therefore, in addition to helping the sheriff solve a problem, the Lone Ranger made every effort to deemphasize his own contribution. Consequently, the townspeople would give credit to the sheriff, whose credibility would increase so that he would be more likely to be able to solve the problem next time. In this manner, the Lone Ranger accomplished the same preventive/educative goal that exists in consultation. Demanding special recognition not only would have destroyed his modus operandi but might have encouraged unnecessary dependence and increased his already unrealistic work load.

The most effective consultant is one who, like the Lone Ranger, believes in the importance of collaboration and behaves so as to ensure collaboration. To attain these conditions, consultants need to develop *a set of functional and rational beliefs about consultation and a process for assessing their attitudes along this dimension.*

Often a consultant must work with an "ungrateful" consultee who clearly does not appreciate the hard work and expertise the consultant has put into the fine recommendations and intervention strategy. When faced with these conditions, or even the less threatening conditions of a "questioning" consultee, a consultant might become angry, sarcastic, and aggressive. These emotions and the accompanying behaviors are too readily attributed to the actions or the intent of the "ungrateful" or difficult consultee, who is easy to blame. "He makes me so mad. Gads, I explain and explain and he still screws it up!" However, as the Stoic Epictetus wrote in the first century A.D., "Men feel disturbed not by things but by the views which they take of them" (quoted in Ellis, 1962). Taking responsibility for one's own emotions, learning how one's beliefs create one's emotions, and developing strategies for modifying these beliefs and the resulting emotions can be invaluable tools for the consultant when his or her negative emotions of anger, guilt, and fear interfere with the maintenance of a supportive, collaborative relationship.

The writings of such theorists as Aaron T. Beck, Albert Ellis, Russell Grieger, and Robert A. Harper on cognitive psychotherapy provide the foundation for recognizing and challenging the dysfunctional beliefs of the struggling consultant. This fast-acting approach to handling emotional upsets has been termed "cognitive" because its focus is on identifying the way people think about events. The emphasis is on how one interprets experiences and how such interpretation forms the basis for feelings and behaviors. This model of therapy attempts to retrain the individual in his or her views or beliefs about life events, so as to create a more rational, functional feeling and behavioral response. Apart from the value of these principles in cognitive therapy or other cognitive restructuring techniques (assertiveness training, rational-emotive training), they can be beneficial for recognizing and ameliorating dysfunctional belief systems that inhibit the productive functioning of consultants, especially when they confront resistance.

The first principle of cognitive therapy is that *all moods are created by one's cognitions, or thoughts.* Thus, one's feelings at any moment are caused by one's thoughts. For example, when confronted with a new consulting contract (an event), the consultant might feel elated or depressed (consequence), depending on whether she believes (or says mentally): "Thank goodness, I've waited a long time for this contract" or "Damn, why is it always me getting the tough ones, never Harry!"

The second major principle is that *thoughts that lead to emotional turmoil and behavioral dysfunction nearly always contain gross distortions.* Although such a cognition might appear quite valid at the time, a closer, more objective analysis will reveal that it is irrational, dysfunctional, nonevidential—and just plain wrong. As Ellis (1962) posited, feelings have valuable goals or purposes (for example, survival and happiness), so that when they help us to achieve these goals, they are appropriate feelings, whereas when they act to block our basic goals, they are inappropriate. When the consultant believes the consultee should implement the excellent intervention plan that was developed and finds that the consultee does not like the idea and has not implemented it, the consultant may become angry at the consultee, the institution, and the world. If our goal is to create and maintain a helping, supportive relationship, clearly the belief that this consultee is an irresponsible, ungrateful person who does not do what he should is dysfunctional, as is the resulting emotional state of anger.

The intent here is not to argue for or to explain in detail the value of cognitive psychotherapy. Rather, our hope is to alert the consultant to the fact that often the emotions that lead to ineffective functioning during consultation are created by the consultant's distorted cognitions. Further, we hope to show that with some rapid training the consultant can learn to identify the distorted cognitions, challenge these distorted beliefs, and substitute a more functional way of interpreting the reality of consultation. This reeducation of the belief system not only provides significant relief from moments of depression, anger, or guilt but also allows the consultant to challenge the dysfunctional beliefs that interfere with maintenance of a collaborative relationship.

According to Ellis, Harper, Beck, and other cognitively oriented theorists, restructuring one's irrational or dysfunctional beliefs is the key to a happier, more functional life. The particulars of achieving cognitive restructuring vary across theoretical perspectives, but most agree that it requires attainment of three levels of "insight." First, one must realize that feelings are created by one's thinking. Second, the connection between one's distorted beliefs and one's dysfunctional feelings needs to be made clear. Last is the realization that replacing one's distorted beliefs and cognitive errors with more rational thinking will lead to more functional feelings and behaviors.

Insight 1: Connecting Thoughts to Feelings. The first step in learning to modify one's dysfunctional thinking is to appreciate the connection between what one is feeling at any moment and the interpretation, or self-talk, occurring then. Because most of us have been interpreting, without reflection, for many years, we often fail to discriminate between the "fact" of an event and the "belief," or opinion, that we add. Thus the belief often appears natural, or "automatically" tied to the event, as if it "had" to be there. For example, should someone thrust a pencil in your face (event) and say, "Stick 'em up!," you might very well become apprehensive ("What's this guy, crazy?") or amused ("This is funny"). However, should someone flash a gun in your face and say, "Stick 'em up!," your reaction (emotive and behavioral) would most likely be quite different. If asked to identify the real, factual difference between that pencil and that gun, most people would say something like "Are you crazy? The guy with the gun is going to kill me!" If pressed, some people might be able to recognize that the only *real, here-and-now* difference is that the gun is black, metallic, and so on. That it will kill is not a fact about the gun but only a prediction or belief, however well founded in personal or cultural history. We so often associate the event (gun) with the interpretation (it is going to kill . . .), though, that the two become treated as one.

Such a blending of fact and opinion may be drawn to our attention only when we overreact in response to an event. For example, should I immediately scream and lash out at the assailant, I may find that he backs off, saying, "What's wrong with you? I found this pencil and thought I'd tease you." In the same way, beliefs such as "It is horrible if things don't go the way I want" or "I am a failure" (when I failed at something) or "I deserve more than I am getting—I am entitled, after all I did" or "He, she, or they have no right to . . . " create unpleasant and dysfunctional emotional states and need to be separated from the facts of the events with which they are associated.

Exercise 5-3 is provided to help you develop insight into how your emotions result from your beliefs at any one time. Negative, self-defeating beliefs lead to negative, self-defeating emotions and behaviors.

Insight 2: Recognizing Cognitive Distortions. Becoming aware of the connection between one's thinking and the consequent emotional reactions is the first step toward rational thinking. The second step is to recognize one's cognitive distortions. When one's thinking and one's interpretations of events are accurate, the emotional reactions and behavior that result will most likely be functional. When a belief is distorted, however,

Exercise 5-3
Connecting Thoughts to Feelings

As noted in the text, the position taken here is that an individual's emotional reactions, which are usually identified as being caused by outside events, are really a consequence of one's thinking. To develop the skill of identifying the beliefs or thoughts that lie at the base of your emotional reactions, it is suggested that for the next week you keep the following "A-B-C" (antecedent-beliefs-consequences) diary.

Each time you find yourself experiencing a strong negative emotion (anger, fear, depression), even if for only a second (if, for example, a pencil point breaks and you toss the pencil and curse, feeling angry), complete the following form. "A" and "C" of the exercise are generally relatively simple to identify, but it will take some practice to become sensitized to the "B" of each situation. The purpose of this exercise is just that—to raise your awareness of and sensitivity to the beliefs that create your emotional reactions.

Step 1: Listing the consequences ("C"). What emotion do you feel, and how much (0–100 percent)?
Example: "Angry, 80 percent."

Step 2: Describing the antecedent event ("A"). Describe what external event or memory of an event or experience was occurring at the time you experienced the consequent emotion.
Example: "I was sitting in my office, having canceled a dinner appointment because the general manager had called me for an emergency after-work meeting."

Step 3: Pinpointing the belief or thought associated with the event ("B"). Go back to your memory or description of the antecedent event and listen to the interpretation or meaning you may be giving to it. Listen to the self-talk, the little voice in your head. Turn it up. What is it saying about "A"? Copy down this "self-talk."
Example: "Damn it—he has *no right* doing this. This stinks! I can't stand to be treated like a damned slave—do this, do that, I get absolutely no respect, *I can't stand it!*"

the reaction (emotional and behavioral) will be dysfunctional. Distortions of beliefs, or cognitive errors, can be created any time one overgeneralizes, personalizes, thinks only in terms of absolutes (black or white), or confuses fact with opinion. Under these conditions one's reaction (emotional and behavioral) will often be detrimental to goal attainment and thus must be considered dysfunctional. Elaborate, insightful discussion of such cognitive errors can be found in Ellis (1962) and Burns (1980). We have condensed this work and adapted it to the special dynamics of consultation. The following are cognitive distortions typically made by consultants.

1. *World according to . . . (WAT)*. Consultants who are well trained and experienced and who are viewed as the "experts" often forget that the world is just the way it is at any one time, regardless of what "we" feel it should be. Believing that the consultee *should* or *should not* do or say something and believing that we *must* be treated in a particular way are examples of the WAT distortion. Such a distortion will most likely create a condition in which the consultant becomes angry, since the world experienced is not always going to be the world one prefers.

2. *From one to many (FOTM)*. The FOTM error is exemplified by the consultant who concludes that this or that consultee is "always" doing things wrong, when in fact this was the one time the consultee made a mistake. Similarly, the consultant who failed to get a contract because of budget cuts and who declares to herself, "It's always the same thing—I'll never get a decent contract," is demonstrating an FOTM error in thinking. Believing in concepts like "always" and "never" often leads to feelings of hopelessness and helplessness and may result in a depressed consultant.

3. *Jumping to conclusions*. As experts in the field of human behavior, quite often we find ourselves "reading" our consultees' minds ("She'll think I'm weird if I make this suggestion" or "I know he's angry with me for suggesting he try it this way"). Similarly, consultants are vulnerable to what Burns (1980) calls the "fortuneteller error—that is, treating our predictions as fact ("What's the use of submitting this proposal, it will only get rejected").

4. *Large I*. All too often we, the consultant, identify all too closely with what we do (namely, consult), and thus we fail to remember that rather than being one large I (that is, the me—the consultant), we really are a constellation of a lot of little i's. Failing to remember that "I" am really "i" the parent, tennis player, joke teller, lover, student, and so on creates a condition in which, when faced with failure or incompetence in one area, or one little "i," we may falsely conclude that we are completely incompetent. For example, in a consult, the consultant with a large-I tendency may equate the failure of i the consultant with the failure of I the person and thus begin to view himself as a failure, a waste, a worthless individual. Saying, "I'm no damned good, a real loser," rather than "I really messed up that presentation," is clearly irrational, since a person's self cannot be equated with any one thing the person does.

5. *Personal prism*. Each of us has a philosophical view of self and the world. All too often we use this set, or bias, as a filter through which we perceive events. For example, if on any one day we are angry, or if we expect that the consultee will resist our suggestions, we might select one signal of such resistance and dwell on it exclusively, thus perceiving the entire interaction as negative and resistant. Or a consultant who messed up a presentation might find herself "hearing" the feedback from her friends as completely negative rather than as the constructive mixture of positive and negative commentary that it is. This personal prism is a form of selective attention, in which only that which fits our set, or expectation, is allowed in, while all else is filtered out. Such filtering leads to the false conclusion that the entire world is so colored.

There are many more forms of such dysfunctional thinking, but the point to be made is that dysfunctional beliefs lead to dysfunctional reactions. The consultant therefore needs to begin to identify his or her own forms of cognitive distortions as a second step toward becoming more functional. Identifying one's distortions is facilitated by considering the characteristics of rational thinking as presented by Maultsby (1975): (1) Rational thinking is based mainly on objective fact, as opposed to subjective opinion. (2) If acted on, it most likely will result in the preservation of one's life and limb, rather than premature death or injury. (3) If acted on, it produces one's personally defined life goals most quickly. (4) If acted on, it prevents undesirable personal and emotional environmental conflict.

Insight 3: Challenging and Reeducating. After identifying one's belief patterns (Insight 1) and evaluating their rationality/ functionality (Insight 2), one needs to reformulate the belief so that it conforms to truth, or the evidence of the situation. When convinced that the consultee "has no right" to treat the consultant this way, the consultant might reexamine the facts of the situation and conclude: "I don't like it (fact), but the consultee really can do anything he wants (truth). If I don't like it, it is up to me to do something about it." Exercise 5-4 suggests that the consultant literally rewrite his or her dysfunctional beliefs in a more rational mode. This may seem an unproductive, academic exercise. With time and practice, however, this sort of cognitive retraining will be assimilated and employed automatically.

Exercise 5-4
Challenging Cognitive Distortions

Using the A-B-C log created in Exercise 5-3 as your base, go back to Step 3, identification of your belief, and begin to attack and remove the cognitive distortions. Take each of the irrational or dysfunctional beliefs and ask yourself, "On what evidence do I base this? How would I prove this belief to be true? What makes it so? What is the fact here—and what is the opinion?" Use your answers as the basis for rewriting the belief about the event. After the rewrite, check the new belief against the questions above to make sure it is rational.

Example: John A. is a consultant for a private agency who provides "human relations and communications training" to a number of the major industries on the East Coast. John is currently contracted with Company W to provide a series of ten full-day assertiveness workshops for all B-level managers. The request for this particular consult came from the central office— from Henry L., marketing vice-president.

Over the last two weeks, John has traveled to the central office six times to discuss the whats and whys of this consult.

Exercise 5-4
Challenging Cognitive Distortions, Cont'd.

One of his major concerns has been that Mr. L. was not very clear about why he felt such training was needed. After much discussion, John persuaded Mr. L. to have an open discussion with the regional managers and get back to John with their observations. The fact that Mr. L. delayed in contacting his regional officers didn't concern John until two days before the first of the work sessions. Mr. L. called John and said, "I really appreciate all your ideas over the last couple of weeks, but I decided to talk with the regional people, and, you know—I think we'll just forget it for now. It doesn't seem like a good idea."

John had clearly extended himself, perceived possible problems, and even warned the vice-president of their possibility. His anger (consequence) about the VP's decision to cancel the program (antecedent condition) can be attributed to his belief: "That dirty creep—I can't believe it, after all I've done, all the work down the tubes. That creep is not going to get away with this—no way in hell will he walk all over me!" This belief that (1) the VP is a dirty S.O.B. (and should be punished), (2) all the work (past, present, and future) is down the tubes, and (3) I've been walked on (and it's horrible) needs to be questioned for supportive evidence. If John debates this belief, he may find it unsupported by the evidence. He may conclude: (1) "There is no evidence that the VP is a creep, even though what he did is disappointing to me. In fact, on other occasions he really has supported me." Further: "What tubes? Even though I am not going to use the material for this group, it can still be used as a foundation for a future program. Besides, I sure did learn something about collaborative relationships." And finally, "Walked on? Where's the evidence I was walked on, abused? I wasn't anything; my consulting plan was rejected, not me."

Although the particular events experienced in consulting will vary, and the particular form of one's interpretation may change, the essence of the dysfunctional belief will remain constant unless actively challenged and redesigned. For example, the consultant who finds herself angry about many consulting situations might try to pin the blame on the consultee's lateness, the administrator's ineptness, or some other such particular. Nevertheless, the underlying distorted cognition is that someone or something in the world is not the way it "should" or "must" be. The consultee "has to" or "must" be on time, the administrator "should" be competent, and so on. Similarly, the consultant who is characteristically anxious about consultation may pinpoint the fear as due to driving into the city, meeting the "boss," or losing the contract. Consistent across all such particulars of anxiety is the belief that something horrible and catastrophic is about to occur. It is this cognitively distorted monster—the horrible catastrophe—that needs to be revised, not the particulars. Practicing Exercise 5-4 an hour, a day, or a week after experiencing a dysfunctional attitude and the resulting emotional response, though not undoing the immediate past situation, will be a positive step toward removing the generic distortion. With such practice the consultant will eliminate the attitude, which will otherwise continue to hinder maintenance of a collaborative consultation relationship.

❧ CHAPTER SIX ❧

Consultation Stages and Dynamics

The consultation process moves through a series of clearly defined stages (see Meyers, Parsons, and Martin, 1979). This chapter presents those stages and begins to delineate the skills required for successful movement through them. As previously noted here and elsewhere (Meyers, Parsons, and Martin, 1979), although the stages are presented as discrete, in practice they often fail to occur in sequence or as separate entities. Instead, a consultant may operate at multiple stages simultaneously or may move back and forth between stages before moving on. In this sense, consultation is a dynamic, active process. Despite this caution, it is useful to distinguish the various stages of consultation. They are (1) entry into the system, (2) goal identification, (3) goal definition, (4) intervention planning and implementation, (5) assessment of the impact of consultation, and (6) concluding, or terminating, the relationship.

Stage 1: Entry

Entry is both a socioenvironmental and a psychoemotional issue. Entry entails much more than gaining access to a building, establishing an office, or presenting a formal job description and contract. These are important components of the entry process and cannot be overlooked, but they are only part of the process and will prove insufficient to provide entry into a working relationship.

The consultant, whether from "within" or "outside" the system, will be initially perceived as an intrusive alien. Even though the consultant is invited into the organization, many will regard him with suspicion, as an intruder whose role and allegiances are unknown. Furthermore, defensiveness is likely because the introduction of the consultant into the system indicates that something is not working, that something or someone needs to be "fixed," and that change is about to occur. Under such conditions the consultant's first concern must be to gain entry (that is, acceptance) into the system.

Organizational Level. As an agent responsible to both the organization and the individual with whom he or she contracts, the consultant needs to be familiar with the profile and history of the client and/or the consultee as well as the institution in which they exist.

Organizations can be viewed as either proactive or reactive. Baker and Northman (1981) describe proactive systems as those that anticipate environmental conditions and respond to task demands generated internally, as distinct from those externally imposed. Conditions that press for growth, increased facilities, cost-effectiveness, and the anticipation and forestalling of future difficulties are all part of the operating norm for a proactive system.

Because the proactive system is operating from a state of equilibrium and rational problem solving, the consultant's ease of entering this system depends not so much on the ability to reduce needs as on the ability to generate a need for services. Under these circumstances, because no real, immediate need is apparent, the consultant might find the preventive value of consultation easier to sell. Most proactive systems, however, rely on internal resources in meeting the demands of anticipated future changes. The external consultant will therefore need to explain that consultation will use existing resources, structures, and processes and that the consultant's efforts will be short-term and educative in nature.

Most organizations that consultants are asked to serve are reactive. These systems are generally not motivated to seek consultation by ideas and desires for growth and prevention. They seek consultation only when external forces demand adaptation —for example, when legislation directs a school to desegregate or to mainstream handicapped students or when a labor dispute threatens the continued operation of a business.

Entry into reactive systems appears to be facilitated by such conditions of conflict or crisis. Under such disruption of personnel or organizational equilibrium, boundaries become more permeable, and influence can occur more easily. Nevertheless, the consultant entering in a crisis may encounter concern and suspicion from those who sense a loss of autonomy and power. The consultant must find ways to inhibit this potential resistance. In fact, whether the system is proactive or reactive, the consultant must analyze and reduce all potential sources of resistance. Several general categories of resistance can be identified, and it is valuable to consider how each may be manifest in a particular consultation setting.

Sources of Organizational Resistance. Four types of organizational resistance will be reviewed here: (1) resistance based on a desire for system maintenance, (2) resistance to the consultant as an outsider, (3) resistance resulting from rejecting the new as nonnormative, and (4) resistance to protect one's turf.

The first form of resistance is based on a *desire for system maintenance*. The organization can be thought of as a dynamic system with a variety of inputs, internal processes, and outputs. As an open system, an organization employs a natural flow, or exchange, between the system and its environment. In such a system, a number of subsystems, or components, are interdependently working toward the same general goals. The entrance of the consultant has a reverberating impact on these subsystems, which have an established pattern of working together. Each new input that requires the system to adapt drains energy and threatens the stability of the system. Passage of the consultant through the system's boundaries signals the inclusion of a new input indicating that change is imminent. Viewing entry as a procedure for change enables us to appreciate the added demands placed on the host organization by the very nature of including a consultant within its boundaries. Further change requires system energy expenditure and entails changes in personnel and procedures to help the system adapt. The request for consultation indicates that the system is having difficulty adapting.

Thus, a primary goal of the organization is to move back to a state of equilibrium and stability. The consultant's attempts to reduce the amount and degree of change demanded of a system will facilitate acceptance into the organization. The consultant should look for ways to reduce the financial and psychic costs of including a consultant. Simple things like using an existing office, personnel, and materials may provide cost reductions that will make the consultant more desirable. Similarly, using existing systems, procedures, forms, language, communication channels, and so forth, thus reducing the required expenditure of psychic energy for adaptation, will facilitate entry.

A consultant must seek ways to increase the psychic comfort of those within the organization. The consultant should be careful not to threaten existing roles or challenge others' jobs or role definitions. Instead, he or she must try to maintain the professional integrity of key individuals (administrators or professionals in the system), emphasizing their essential value to the consultant and the organization as a whole. Increasing the administrator's sense of self-worth establishes the psychological foundation that enables the consultant to be hired without a sense of threat or a need to undermine. Under these conditions, the administrator can view the consultant's involvement as a reflection of his or her own competence, rather than a sign of incompetence and failure.

Another way to reduce resistance based on a desire for system maintenance is by trying to fit or be absorbed into the existing system. The simpler the consultant's entry and the less change in structure, tone, process, or product it entails, the easier it will be, and the more easily the consultant can develop a role definition that can be communicated within the organization and will be readily accepted. In this context, it is better, initially, to forgo grand plans of innovation and accept the institution where it is, with plans to shape it slowly toward the ideal. This shaping process becomes much more feasible as the consultant's value and visibility are evidenced.

The second type of resistance is to *the consultant as an outsider.* The consultant is often viewed as an alien in the organization and is treated with suspicion, resistance, and tentative inclusion, at best. The consultant must therefore try to reduce the visible manifestations of "outsider" status. One of the authors (Meyers) experienced an instance in which being an outsider was signaled by the consultant's manner of dress. In this case a consultant was working with an alternative inner-city secondary school program. The teaching staff consisted largely of talented adults from the community who were not trained as teachers. Distrust of professional educators was high. One way "outsiders" were identified was by their dress. The teaching staff dressed informally, in jeans, for example. When outside professionals entered the building in suits and ties, they were immediately rejected as knowing nothing about the particular population of children. Accordingly, when the consultant went to this school wearing a jacket and tie, he was perceived as an outsider and could not achieve entry. When a second consultant was used who dressed and acted informally, the perception of "outsider" dissipated and entry was accomplished.

It is suggested that the consultant become familiar with the institution's history, mission, philosophy, and procedures before seeking entry. This familiarization provides the consultant with a data base for developing a common orientation and language, and the knowledge about the organization will raise the credibility of the consultant's recommendations.

In addition, outsider status can be reduced and acceptance as a member of the organization facilitated by increasing the consultant's availability to and contact with the staff. Failing to attend open meetings or hiding in one's office or failing to participate in common duties found in the organization (such as fire drills or safety training sessions) only highlights one's "outsider" status. Another way to reduce the perception of the consultant as an outsider is to do things that increase referent power —for example, attending coffee breaks, participating in after-work activities such as the managers' baseball team or the faculty basketball league, and mingling and sharing common experiences and background.

A crucial element in becoming perceived as an insider is one's relationship with the individuals serving as the institution's "gatekeepers"—the persons who oversee the consultant's entry. Some have been assigned this role formally, whereas others are in the role informally. Relationships with members of the organization are important, and we concur with Glidewell (1959) that this "politicking" is best directed to those members of the organization who are viewed as status leaders. The status leader need not be the formal-titled leader. In fact, sustained contact with only administrative personnel may signal an alignment or coalition that might later prove alienating when trying to work at the staff level.

Finally, resistance to the consultant as an outsider can be reduced by providing evidence of institutional sanction for the consultant's entry and by providing for some type of reward to consultees who participate in consultation.

The third form of resistance is that which originates in a *desire to reject the new as nonnormative.* Often resistance stems from the simple desire for the status quo, or what Watson (1966) called "conforming to norms." Yet, conforming to existing norms is essentially contraindicated once a consultant has been requested. The very presence of the consultant indicates that the existing normative behaviors are insufficient in dealing with the confronting work problem. However, one must be aware that renorming is a difficult and energy-depleting process. One might experience resistance stemming from the "old guard's" concern that one will tamper with time-honored programs, processes, and procedures that may have taken on a sacrosanct quality. Consultants' attempts to modify such procedures or programs will often be viewed as direct attempts to destroy the very foundation of the organization, resulting in intense resistance. The consultant needs to become sensitive to possible areas of venerability through familiarization with the history and overall functioning of the institution. Further, where possible, any such time-honored practices should be left intact while the consultant is seeking entry and acceptance.

A slightly different twist on this form of resistance occurs when a norm exists suggesting consultation is never needed. Under this condition, the consultant must work closely with the organizational leaders to achieve formal sanction for entry. The consultant must also work to identify the norm setters or opinion leaders and to receive their informal sanctions. Under such circumstances entry can often be achieved with members who are described as institutional innovators (Haveluck, 1973). Such innovators can sometimes provide the needed base of influence. Haveluck (1973) noted that the innovators in an institution are less normative and therefore more open to risk. As the consultant's procedures become more successful and the risk associated with them is reduced, acceptance of the procedures, the consultant, and the norm of consultation assistance will increase.

The fourth and last type of resistance is resistance *to protect one's turf or vested interest.* Often, organization members view the consultant and his or her procedures as an intrusion on their particular areas of interest or professional responsibility. Resistance can emerge in an attempt to protect one's vested interest and to maintain the security of existing roles and functions. While attempting to reduce the negative impact of turf intrusion, the consultant must recognize that a number of areas will be affected. The consultant must work carefully with the personnel in these areas to give them opportunities for involvement in the consultation process. Such involvement will lessen resistance associated with feelings about turf when changes occur.

Now consider Exercise 6-1, which demonstrates the skills necessary to identify and reduce organizational resistance to consultation.

Consultee Level. Once the consultant has gained access to the organization and has achieved formal and informal sanction, requests for service will begin. At this point entry must be accomplished with the consultee. Each consultee will require that a new contract be developed, with new demands for entry and

Exercise 6-1
Identifying Sources of Organizational Resistance

The text has described four bases of resistance to the consultant's entry into any organization. This exercise will reinforce an understanding of these sources of resistance as well as provide a checklist/worksheet that is helpful when attempting to enter an organization with a new consultation contract.

Using the form provided, write a brief anecdotal description of a recent consultation contract in which you had some difficulty entering and being accepted into the system. In Step 1 detail all the principles involved, as well as the people, policies, groups, and so on, and provide quotations or specific examples of how the resistance was manifested. Step 2 asks you to hypothesize the reason for the resistance. In Step 3 identify which of the four forms of resistance listed occurred. In Step 4 consider the diagnostic cues—that is, the individual and organizational behaviors that were harbingers of the eventual resistance—to the existence of such resistance that might prove helpful, as warnings, for the future. Finally, Step 5 asks you to mentally replay the entry process and describe modifications in the initial interview, contract discussions, or contacts that might have reduced this source of resistance.

The data developed in this checklist can be shared with a trainer, supervisor, or peer in order to receive additional corrective feedback.

Step 1: Anecdotal report of an experience of organizational resistance (system maintenance, outsider, rejecting the new, or protecting turf).

Step 2: Hypothesized explanation.

Step 3: Labeled form of resistance.

Step 4: Possible diagnostic cues for this form of resistance and this particular experience.

Step 5: Specific modifications of consultant style and procedures to reduce the resistance in the case reported.

acceptance to be met while establishing the consultative relationship.

To achieve entry with the consultee, it is important to understand the consultee's motivation(s) in seeking consultation. For example, one motivation for the consultee is to reduce the psychic cost of a particular job-related task. Removing Johnny, the problem fifth-grade boy, is not always best for Johnny but is often a prime motive for both the teacher, who feels, "I can't take him anymore!," and the institution, which fears, "If we don't do something, he'll have the whole class in an uproar!" In this type of situation, the idealized motive of optimizing Johnny's growth gives way to the expediency of removing the tensions and stress he creates. This sort of motive often forms the basis for a consultee's decision to contact a consultant. In other instances, the consultee seeks consultation because of an underlying desire to avoid the responsibility of handling a sticky situation, or to have the consultant serve as a scapegoat, or even to justify the consultee's feelings of incompetence—"The problem was so overwhelming that a specialist had to be called."

The consultant's first task in seeking entry is to identify the consultee's motivations and to enter the relationship at a level that will satisfy at least one of these motivational states. In addition to identifying the underlying need and presenting oneself as a possible resource for need satisfaction, one must give evidence of being the most attractive resource available, with the highest possible payoff-to-cost ratio. The importance of this comparative level of satisfaction, discussed under "Exchange Theory" in Chapter Three, is highlighted here because consultants, in their haste to gain entry, often focus on getting to the heart of the problem, while dismissing the potential costs of such a process for the consultee. Entry requires that the consultant not only increase every aspect of reward, or payoff, value to the relationship, including service as a problem solver (expert value), comrade (referent value), and source of ego support, but also take active steps to reduce the costs of participating in the consultation relationship. As might be expected, what constitutes a cost is idiosyncratic to each consultee. However, a number of generic forms of costs can be identified.

1. *Time and energy expenditure—a tangible cost.* It is important to consider the limited time and energy the consultee has to share with the consultant. Even though the goal is significant and the consultation might prove helpful, one must remember that this goal or this consultation is not the consultee's reason for being. The consultee is involved with other work tasks and demands as well. One must schedule meetings at times and places convenient for the consultee. Further, one should use procedures (such as data collection techniques) that are familiar to the consultee and will not require the learning of new procedures. Finally, one needs to take every step possible to reduce the need for the consultee to do the "busy work" that often accompanies problem solving, such as organizing files and keeping minutes of meetings.

2. *Fear of the unknown—a psychic cost.* Because consultation may be a new experience, consultees might feel anxious about the unknown requirements or demands to be made of them or the impact the consultation relationship might have on them personally or professionally. Questions such as "Will it be difficult?," "time-consuming?," "too personal?," "embarrassing?" may all be present, reflecting the anxiety the consultee must "pay" in order to enter a consultation relationship. Many of these costs can be reduced by a skillfully prepared initial interview.

Strong and Schmidt (1970), studying the interview in psychotherapy, noted that a good initial interview could serve as a place where roles and requirements are defined; processes and events likely to be experienced are outlined; and, in general, an overview of what is about to happen is provided. Strong and Schmidt found that such an interview significantly allayed clients' fear and anxiety and increased the therapist's power base.

An initial interview with the consultee not only can allay fear of this unknown but also can go a long way toward assuring the consultee that the consultant knows what is going to happen, resulting in increased expert power for the consultant. During the initial interview, the consultant can outline (1) the responsibilities of each party, detailing what each party is expected to give and receive in terms of number and length of visits, limits of service, and the like, (2) the expected course of problem resolution and consultation, and (3) the nature of the consultant's role in the institution. Because of the suspicion and identity problems often surrounding a consultant, questions arise such as "Whom does the consultant report to?" "What will the consultant say or do?" "What power does the consultant have?" These questions need to be addressed. The consultant needs to assure the consultee that the relationship and exchange are highly confidential and that the consultant is a professional, ethical helper. The issue of confidentiality is extremely important, especially if the consultant has expended much time and energy with the institution's administration, since this is often interpreted as a sign of the consultant's coalition with administration.

The initial interview may consider the alternative consequences that might result from consultation and the steps that can be taken to terminate the relationship. In addition, the consultee needs to be apprised of the possible drawbacks of working with the consultant (work involved, extended hours, and so forth). The consultee also needs to be informed that responsibility for accepting, rejecting, or modifying the recommendations rests with the consultee and that either party can renegotiate the contract at any time.

The initial interview is an opportune time to present the consultee with a rationale for using consultation. Presenting this conceptual model helps the consultee to view consultation within a framework broader than the one specific presenting problem and thus to begin to conceptualize other areas where consultation may seem appropriate.

3. *Fear of being evaluated—personal and professional costs.* Quite often the consultee is unclear about the nature of consultation or the role and function of the consultant and hence may be concerned about a possible stigma or institutional reprisals for involving or "needing" a consultant. In many organizations, seeking consultative help is a sign of weakness that causes the consultation process to be viewed as ominous and the

consultant as threatening. The consultant can reduce this fear by using the relationship-building skills referred to in Chapters Two through Five to create an atmosphere of mutual problem solving between two professionals. The consultant must convey the message that they are fellow professionals, with different skills, orientations, and talents, who are in a process of noneval-uative, mutual, caring, and friendly helpgiving and therefore are, in essence, coworkers in this situation.

4. *Perceiving consultation as a cost without return—a vacuum cost.* The consultee often seeks a consultant only as the last resort, following a long series of attempts to resolve the problem. Most often consultees feel they have tried everything and everyone to little or no avail and consequently expect (and perhaps, given all their effort, even hope) that the consultant will similarly prove unsuccessful. Thus any demands placed on the consultee will be viewed as an expenditure in a vacuum, a cost without return.

To combat this expectation, the consultant must be alert to demonstrating his or her value as a resource for need satisfaction, right from the initial interview. One of the most important maxims given informally to a novice consultant is that, regardless of what one does, one must *do something!*

Doing something is essential for achieving acceptance (entry) with the worker on the front line. One may be able to sell the administration on the future hopes of cost reduction and preventive practices, but the consultee is the worker on the front line who needs relief now rather than theory and promises. When suggesting that the consultant do something, we are not implying a bag full of ready-made solutions. To the contrary, ready-made solutions may prove counterproductive because they signal to the consultee that the consultant may think, "The problem was so easy, how dare the consultee waste my valuable time?," or "How could the consultee be so stupid as not to resolve this simple problem?"

The consultant can also reduce the perceived costs by "doing something" that may appear irrelevant or tangential to the "real" problem and thus may be overlooked or resisted by many consultants. Offering to distribute a memo, carry out a simple errand, or assist in preparing for a meeting may help to remove one of the minor irritants or costs to the consultee and thus demonstrate the "value" of the consultant. It is our belief that the consultant should view "doing something" as a directive focused on a process, rather than a particular product or goal. The consultant does something not in order to finish but to be able to do again. Exercise 6-2 provides the reader with a model for assessing the "generic" costs often experienced by a consultee entering consultation.

Exercise 6-2
Identifying "Costs" of the Consultee's Involvement in Consultation

The text outlines a number of "generic" costs often experienced by consultees when contracting for consultation. The following activity will increase sensitivity to these costs and provide the opportunity to develop strategies for ameliorating them.

Step 1: Using your current or most recent consultation experience, provide two specific examples of each of the following forms of consultee cost.

Time and energy expenditure

a.
b.

Fear of the unknown

a.
b.

Fear of evaluation

a.
b.

Consultation without payoff (vacuum cost)

a.
b.

Exercise 6-2
Identifying "Costs" of the Consultee's Involvement
in Consultation, Cont'd.

Step 2: Provide concrete examples of the steps you took
to reduce these possible costs to the consultee.

Step 3: List at least three additional steps you might have
taken or could still take to further reduce each of these costs.

Step 4: Confer with your consultee in order to validate
your observations. Ask your consultee:

a.   To what degree (0–100 percent) were these costs operative?
b.   What additional costs existed that were not listed?
c.   What was the consultee's perception of the ameliorating ef-
      fects of the efforts you listed in Step 2?
d.   To what degree does the consultee concur that the activi-
      ties listed in Step 3 might have further reduced these costs?

Step 5: Repeat this process following the initial interview
on your next consult.

Stage 2: Goal Identification

As previously noted, the initial interview with the consultee has significant value in that it sets the stage and defines
the norms of consultative behavior. In addition, the first interview is focused on data gathering, rather than rapid diagnosis
and remediation, and marks the beginning of the goal identification stage.

In this stage the consultant surveys the consultee's perceived needs and interests so as to jointly begin to determine
the general concerns to address. Although the focus at this stage
is on the work to be done and the goal to be achieved, it is not
wise, initially, to burden the consultee with extensive survey,
questionnaire, or data collection procedures. Rather, the consultee should have the opportunity to freely discuss his or her
concerns in a relaxed general discussion of perceived personal
and institutional needs. Since the chief goal is to gather data,

the consultant should use "open" questions, as defined in Chapter Two.

The purpose of the initial interview is to develop a picture of the goal. This process not only examines the immediate behaviors but seeks to unearth causal implications regarding the consultee or the institution. This interview helps the consultant determine the level at which he or she will work in responding to the consultee's request for help. By "level," we refer to the four levels of consultation given by the consultation model described in Chapter One—direct service to the client, indirect service to the client, service to the consultee, and service to the system.

In view of the preventive goals of consultation and the focus on reaching the largest number of clients possible with relatively long-term effect, it is our bias that the consultant should first consider the most indirect levels of functioning— that is, first service to the organization, then service to the consultee, then indirect service to the client. This makes sense because organizational factors can influence one's attempts to work with the consultee, and consultee factors can influence one's attempts to work with a client. Nevertheless, practical demands require that the consultant implement this model within the constraints of the contract and the perceived needs of the consultee. Therefore, one major component of the goal identification stage is that the consultant identify the highest possible level of entry that will be acceptable to the consultee, even when this level appears to be less than ideal.

The decision about the level of focus is important because consultation techniques and roles required of the consultant and consultee will vary from level to level. Further, even though the consultant may operate at more than one level at any one time, by focusing on a particular level of service, the consultant and consultee can easily develop a clear joint perception of services to be provided.

Once the level of consultation is identified, the consultant may need to begin narrowing both the population queried and the information received. We have found that the critical incident technique (Flanagan, 1954) is extremely valuable in interviewing individual consultees to get a clearer picture of the parameters of the situation.

The critical incident interview requires the consultee to remember and describe in detail the last time the problem arose. The questions asked are explicit and aim at gathering as much information as possible about the problem; the conditions under which it appears to occur, not occur, and increase in intensity or frequency; the procedures the consultee has tried; and their effectiveness. The consultee is encouraged to provide the data in narrative form, with as much detail as possible, while the consultant records everything that is said. This technique gives the consultant a data base from which to begin to generate hypotheses about the goal and the etiology of the situation, and it gives the consultee the opportunity to become a valuable, contributing member to the problem-solving team.

Stage 3: Goal Definition

Having identified a consultee's goal and the most feasible and desirable level of consultation, the consultant and consultee will use a variety of techniques to refine the goal into a concrete definition. Like goal identification, the goal definition stage is mainly a data-gathering process, the primary difference being that the focus is on increasingly narrow, specific, detailed data, in contrast with the more vague, general descriptions accepted at the goal identification stage.

The goal and level of entry chosen will help to determine the types of diagnostic tools used or questions posed, as discussed in detail in Chapters Seven through Ten. The one consistent overriding principle is that problematic behavior is a function of both the person and the environment. All attempts at behavior definition will therefore incorporate a focus on the environmental conditions under which a behavior emerges as well as on personal manifestations and characteristics related to the behavior. For example, stating that a worker, client, or student is "hostile" may lead one to consider the various dynamics or internal conflicts possibly operative, and this could result in the general conclusion that the person is simply a negative, oppositional type. However, knowing that such hostility increases before lunch, sales meetings, or physical therapy time or perhaps appears only on Fridays might foster a broader and more accurate appreciation for the possible influence of these environmental (spatial/temporal) factors and might lead to an economical intervention strategy.

In developing a coordinate relationship with the consultee, the consultant should clarify the theoretical conceptual framework used to diagnose behavior. By understanding this framework, the consultee will be in a better position to contribute to the definition of the problem and to understand the rationale for many ideas presented by the consultant. The particular theoretical orientation, be it psychodynamic, behavioral, organizational development, or something else, is less important here than is the fact that the framework is conveyed so that the consultant and consultee can begin to speak a common language.

In addition, the consultant needs to help the consultee develop the capacity to define problems in specific terms and to communicate precisely on the relevant problems. To this end, the consultant needs to be prepared to provide the consultee with structured checklists, observational charts, and so on or with detailed instruction on the behavioral observations necessary in this stage of consultation. Chapter Eight offers examples of these techniques. Although there are perhaps as many scales, psychometric instruments, and recording devices as there are situations to define, we have used a number of simple guidelines, such as those in Exercise 6-3, in introducing the consultee to the idea of goal definition. These guidelines are effective in providing clear definitions with minimal cost (psychic or physical) to the consultee.

Stage 4: Intervention

The fourth stage is designated as the period when specific intervention strategies will be developed and implemented. Although intervention planning and implementation is considered a separate stage, it must be noted that interventions often occur at all phases of the consultation. Even during the initial inter-

Exercise 6-3
Developing Clear Goal Definitions

Consider the goal definition phase of a recent consultation and match the goal definition attained against the checklist provided. Use the criteria listed as guides for this stage of your next consult.

- Is the goal defined in observable terms?
- Is the goal defined so that the behavior is countable?
- Is the direction of desired change specified?
- Is the definition descriptive rather than evaluative, judgmental, or interpretive?
- Have the environmental conditions surrounding/accompanying the appearance of the behavior been described?
- Has the impact of the behavior on the environment (including the people in it) been described?
- Have the attempts at intervention used been specified, along with their impact?

view, when goals are more clearly identified, consultees often feel a sense of relief or even direction, and this interview can thus have the effects of an intervention. Even though a number of subtle interventions will be occurring through the helping quality of the consultative relationship, there is generally a need for a specific time in which the two professionals turn their attention to articulating a specific intervention procedure to be attempted.

The consultant needs to have specific knowledge and expertise in a vast number of areas of intervention (see Chapters Seven through Ten). However, all intervention strategies are developed in a cooperative manner (see Chapters Two through Five). Even though the consultee is seeking advice and expects the consultant to provide expert answers, the consultative interventions that have the greatest chance of being effective and educative are those developed jointly by the consultant and consultee. Accordingly, the consultant needs to possess the interpersonal skills that will encourage consultees to suggest the best way to implement the ideas in their particular setting or feel free to reject the consultant's suggestions altogether. It is important that consultees feel they are valuable contributors to "their" intervention plan.

Another task of the consultant is to foster the attitude that there are alternative approaches to a goal. Rather than simply accepting the first recommendation, the consultee should be encouraged to seek alternative approaches to goal attainment. This will increase the consultee's goal attainment skills and support the preventive/educative goals of consultation. Teaching the consultee how to use divergent thinking techniques, such as brainstorming or divergent Delphi, not only broadens the spectrum of possible interventions but again clearly involves the consultee as an active member. Exercise 6-4 presents the brainstorming and divergent Delphi techniques that we use to generate intervention plans along with the consultee. These techniques are an integral part of the work that consultants do at each of the four levels of consultation.

Exercise 6-4
Generating Intervention Plans

Two particularly useful techniques for consultation are brainstorming and the divergent Delphi. With two coworkers, use each of the procedures to develop intervention strategies for a condition of increasing worker absenteeism and low morale.

Part I: Brainstorming

Brainstorming is often considered to mean any free-flowing, loosely structured group discussion. To the contrary, brainstorming is a very specific procedure and requires a degree of structure and foreplanning. These are the steps involved:

1. First, clarify and agree on the general focus or area in which you will generate ideas. For example, the process can be focused by a stimulus sentence such as "We will generate different ideas about how worker/management communication can be increased in frequency and accuracy."

Exercise 6-4
Generating Intervention Plans, Cont'd.

2. Next, a time limit for the process needs to be established. It has been our experience that five minutes is usually sufficient for the first round and that beyond five minutes often proves quite exhausting.

3. Because of the tendency of professionals to resist appearing foolish by offering less-than-adequate suggestions, we have found that using a warm-up exercise in order to demonstrate the process, as well as set the tone for being "creative," helps. In the warm-up it is suggested that an irrelevant topic be chosen or the directive given to create ridiculous responses.

4. The fourth step is for the consultant to act as the recorder. The focus here is on speed and accuracy, with all ideas recorded. The recorder therefore needs to be a person who can write rapidly and think and contribute at the same time.

5. Begin the process by having participants just begin listing ideas. Rules of politeness, of who goes first or next, and so forth are placed on the sidelines, and the norm is to jump in and create. It has been our experience that the creativity emerges after the first few responses, in which standard ideas are stated, and the members begin responding to one another's ideas. The one rule applicable during this stage is that all evaluation of ideas is suspended. Critical evaluation and judgment will occur at the next step.

6. After the designated time has elapsed (that is, five minutes), the process is stopped, and the ideas generated are now evaluated, modified, clarified, developed, and so on. If additional ideas are required, the process can be resumed after a brief rest.

Part II: Divergent Delphi

Divergent Delphi is a procedure that encourages creativity and attempts to generate participation from everyone. A limitation of brainstorming is that the most creative or the most assertive people dominate the process. Dominance by one member

Exercise 6-4
Generating Intervention Plans, Cont'd.

limits the potential contributions by others, which may prove quite valuable. Under these conditions we have found that using the divergent Delphi often produces better results.

As in brainstorming, the process begins by clarifying the area of focus, using a stimulus word or sentence. Then the actual procedure begins. One member at a time offers his or her ideas, followed by the next member. Members are limited to one idea per round. The process becomes more creative after the initial rounds, as the members deplete the standard responses and now struggle to produce a response. The rule at this point is that each member must respond without repeating what was previously said but is free to build on the previous ideas, modify them, or move to the absurd. It is at this point that the innovative, irrelevant, and quite interesting ideas are created.

Throughout the process, all evaluation of ideas is suspended, and picking ideas "out of the blue" is encouraged. With the proper supportive setting, divergent Delphi can work effectively in fifteen minutes. After the generation of ideas, the members again turn their attention to modifying, developing, or in some way beginning to evaluate their product and move the ideas to a more practical form. One technique that facilitates this process is force-field analysis, described in Chapter Ten.

Stage 5: Assessment

The next stage is assessing the impact of consultation. It is unfortunate that evaluation, or assessment of applied programs, is generally implemented only by the "researcher" and that evaluation skills are not viewed as essential for the "practitioner." Assessment of consultation is essential for a number of practical reasons and must be done to ensure long-term effectiveness. Not only do applied research techniques provide a method of judging the degree of effectiveness of the intervention in reaching its goals, but they may also afford an opportunity to make comparisons to identify the most effective proce-

dures, providing a data base for future justification of consultative services and for decisions about which consultation technique to use under which circumstances.

With heavy caseloads and a multitude of responsibilities,
many consultants view research and evaluation as a luxury for
which they rarely have time. However, evaluation is a *necessity*
that improves practice and helps to justify consultation; this
"luxury" is one we cannot afford to omit. The authors' commitment to the importance of program evaluation is reflected
in our having devoted an entire chapter to this topic. Thus, in
the current chapter we are only highlighting the importance of
this stage; Chapter Eleven will describe in detail program evaluation techniques that are practical for the consultant's use.

Stage 6: Concluding the Relationship

The last stage in the consultation process is to conclude
the relationship. Often the consultee's relief at receiving support
and intervention ideas during consultation results in dependency
on the consultant. Dependency can be a particular problem because the consultant may support it out of his or her own need
to be needed. However, dependency interferes with the educa-
tive/preventive goals of consultation, which require the consultee
to function independently as a problem solver in the future.
One countermeasure is for the consultant to plan deliberately
for and establish a clearly defined point of termination. To accomplish this, the consultant must identify his or her needs and
the personal losses that may result from termination of consultation, to be sure that self-serving desires are not operative in
the decision to maintain the relationship. Stage 5, assessing the
impact, may provide a check against such self-serving intentions
should the evaluation reveal an effective resolution of the problem while the consultant shows a strong tendency to hold onto
the relationship.

As emphasized elsewhere in this book, the consultation
relationship is always voluntary, and consultees have the right
to terminate the relationship at any point. Even with this in
mind, many consultees find it very difficult to let go of the con-

sultation relationship, for fear that termination will offend the consultant or those within the institution who have sanctioned the consultation. Further, consultees often resist concluding the relationship because of their apprehension that termination of this contract may impede further requests for assistance. The consultant needs to demonstrate, verbally and nonverbally, his or her availability to negotiate future contracts with the consultee while encouraging independent achievement of goals that clearly lie within the consultee's previous or newly acquired intervention skills. One step in conveying the consultant's ongoing availability has already been established during the problem identification phase, when the consultant discussed the flow chart of the consultation stages (see Chapter One). It may again prove helpful to discuss the process of termination and reentry as a way of easing consultee anxiety about abandonment.

In addition to discussing the flow chart or directly informing the consultee of one's availability, it is helpful to demonstrate this availability by way of follow-up visits, calls, or notes. Nevertheless, while encouraging such contact, the consultant needs to foster independence and self-reliance. When one is asked to assist on a goal that appears similar to the goal of a previous consultation, it may prove more productive and helpful to delay one's entry into the situation, while directing the consultee to apply some of the goal identification and definition skills used before. Often, through such simple directions, the consultee becomes aware of the similarity and develops intervention strategies in a similar manner without additional consultation. This independence should be reinforced, since it will facilitate the preventive/educative goals of consultation.

Termination of any one contract is important: It not only prevents dependency and encourages independent application of learned principles and strategies but also provides the consultee with a sense of closure and achievement in an area that, until this point, has been confusing and time-consuming. Termination, if done with an eye to closing, summarizing, highlighting, and encouraging, can be a renewing experience for the tired professional.

CHAPTER SEVEN

Direct Assessment of Problems: Level One

The consultation model outlined in Chapter One presents four categories of consultation, which vary in the degree to which the consultant provides direct or indirect service to the client. The next four chapters discuss each of these categories, starting with Level I, direct service to the client.

Direct service to the client (Level I) and indirect service to the client (Level II) are similar in that the chief goal of each is to modify the client's behavior, attitudes, and/or feelings. They differ, however, in some of their data-gathering techniques. In Level I consulting, data gathering is based in part on techniques the consultant uses directly with the client. The data in Level II consultation are gathered by persons other than the consultant (for example, the consultee), since there is no direct contact between the consultant and the client. Despite this difference, the resulting interventions might often be the same, because the interventions are focused on the client and because the consultee retains responsibility for implementing the intervention plans. This chapter will discuss those aspects of data gathering, or *assessment*, unique to Level I consultation. Intervention strategies useful in both Level I and Level II consultation will be presented in the next chapter.

Consultation is one of the most complicated and demanding professional roles, and it requires thorough training in diverse areas associated with assessment, intervention, and the consultation process. It is probably impossible for any beginning consultant to be trained adequately in all these areas. However, because we assume that potential consultants have a wide range of assessment strategies available to them, this brief overview will present a number of assessment techniques, cutting across professional (for example, social work, psychiatry, special education) and philosophical (for example, behavioral, psychodynamic) perspectives. The reader is encouraged to pursue further reading and training in the particular approaches and techniques that are most appealing.

Rationale for Alternative Assessment Procedures

The major influence on assessment has been psychometric theory, along with the variety of norm-referenced tests. Although traditional norm-referenced tests have an important place in assessment, they have been overemphasized to the point that development of useful alternatives has been inhibited.

Effective assessment focused directly on the client must incorporate a variety of important principles, some of which may be antagonistic to traditional views of assessment. Without presenting a detailed and comprehensive review of all the issues, we shall highlight the important points in this section. The reader seeking an in-depth analysis of this issue of assessment and alternative approaches is referred to a number of works: Bersoff (1971, 1973), Bijou and Peterson (1971), Brooks (1979), Brown and French (1979), Budoff (1975), Carroll and Horn (1981), Ellett and Bersoff (1976), Feuerstein (1970), Garcia (1981), Haywood and others (1974), Mercer (1979),

Reschly (1981), Scarr (1981), Sewell (1981), and Vygotsky (1978).

One of the most important goals of Level I consultation is to develop intervention plans designed to provide help to the client in a particular environment. Yet most standardized norm-referenced tests do not answer questions about specific interventions. Assessment techniques must emphasize the *link between assessment and intervention*. There is general agreement that an individual's behavior is determined by an interaction of the environment with characteristics of the individual, but diagnosticians continue to emphasize intrapsychic and other intrapersonal factors. A quick perusal of a list of the most-used norm-referenced tests of intelligence, personality, vocational interests, and achievement will demonstrate the dominance of this intrapersonal orientation in testing. The position presented here is that measures of the work environment, social milieu, and interpersonal factors operating are equally important to understanding the individual client's behavior pattern.

In recent years many writers have challenged the validity of standardized norm-referenced tests, and this debate has been particularly heated with reference to intelligence tests. An important part of the debate has been the criticism that these tests are biased against particular groups in our culture. This criticism must be considered carefully, particularly in consultation settings where a portion of the client population is from minority backgrounds. It is important that consultants use assessment techniques that account for differences in backgrounds and experiences which might have bearing on the client's test-taking ability or motivation. Finally, it is essential that the assessment devices be used *in a descriptive manner*. If consultation is to achieve its preventive goals, then assessment devices must be used to do more than pinpoint deficits and diagnose problems. They must also be used to pinpoint and describe the characteristics and style of the client. Describing behavioral styles as well as specific strengths and weaknesses will help the consultant formulate client-specific recommendations with the consultee.

An Assessment Model

Direct service to the client is an approach to consultation that uses an assessment model based on the assumption that behavior is a function of the *client,* the *task,* and the *environment.* Assessment therefore seeks to determine how these factors interact to influence the behavior currently under study. The assessment techniques used must focus on each of the three areas, as well as their interaction. Unique to this model is the shift from sole attention on the client and his or her intrapsychic dynamics to consideration of extrapersonal factors (task and work environment) that come into play in creating and maintaining the current problem. The broad-based assessment provides a basis from which to generate interventions that have a preventive value. The assessment provides the means for establishing a better blend between the client's style and the task and environment presented and thus reducing the likelihood of future problems for that client. Further, such assessment gives the client a number of early warning signals (for example, a particular task or setting) that will allow the client to make early modifications in his or her own style in order to reduce the negative impact (that is, secondary prevention) or avoid the problem altogether (that is, primary prevention).

Such an assessment consists of three phases: global assessment, focused assessment, and testing interactive hypotheses. *Global assessment* uses interview and informal observation techniques and provides the basis for determining some of the more specific questions addressed during the focused assessment phase. *Focused assessment* uses formal behavior observation systems, some structured interview techniques and other self-report measures, some standardized norm-referenced tests, criterion-referenced tests, and task analysis procedures. Using data from these instruments, hypotheses are generated about appropriate intervention approaches for the client. These hypotheses are tested during the last phase of assessment, *testing interactive hypotheses.*

Client, task, and setting are each assessed through a variety of techniques during both the global and focused assessment phases. It is important to note that assessment includes data from a wide variety of sources. Only when our hunches are confirmed from a variety of perspectives can we feel confident in our conclusions. Furthermore, the last phase of assessment directly integrates assessment with intervention by means of such approaches as "trial interventions" (Meyers, Pfeffer, and Erlbaum, 1982). By providing initial demonstrations of the efficacy of various interventions, we can have even greater confidence in the conclusions we derive from assessment.

Assessing the Client. A client is assessed using a variety of approaches—for example, interview, norm-referenced test, observations. The one factor that cuts across all these approaches is that the consultant must have well-developed and sophisticated *observation skills*. Such skills are obviously required for "systematic observation" techniques and are similarly valuable during interview or formal testing sessions.

The following factors can facilitate effective observation during assessment: (1) a framework to help select the relevant behaviors to observe, (2) a clear and descriptive definition of the behavior to be observed, (3) sensitive use of oneself as an observation instrument, and (4) obtaining feedback to validate the accuracy and significance of the observation.

1. *Framework.* An operational framework is necessary in order to help the consultant decide which behaviors to focus on. A wide variety of frameworks are useful in determining which behaviors are most relevant. Some consultants prefer to use one discrete viewpoint (behavioral, psychodynamic, or interactional, for example); others are more eclectic. It is not crucial, from our perspective, which model one uses, as long as a consultant does identify and maintain a consistent frame of reference that can be applied to help focus observations during assessment.

2. *Definitions.* One important contribution by behaviorists in recent years has been their emphasis on the use of operational definitions. It has become accepted that using operational definitions is important when implementing a systematic observation scheme. We feel that it is at least as important when in-

formally observing the client and that it should be included in a narrative report of assessment. It is crucial for the consultant to know what to be looking for in order to observe the client's behaviors effectively and to describe them in such a way as to receive the needed corrective, validating feedback (Step 4).

3. *Self as instrument.* One significant observation skill that often receives little or no notice is use of the self as an assessment tool. Frequently, the consultant's personal reactions to a situation can provide cues about what is salient to observe. For example, when the consultant feels irritated by a client, often the client has engaged in behaviors that similarly affect others in his or her environment and hence are worth noting. However, this is not an easy skill to develop. First, one must be highly aware of one's usual reactions to a variety of situations. This self-awareness can provide a frame of reference from which to evaluate one's reaction to the client during assessment so as to determine which of the behaviors reflect unique and significant characteristics of the client.

4. *Obtaining Validating Feedback.* Once the consultant has made behavioral observations, it is important to obtain feedback to confirm the significance of the behavior. This feedback is generally obtained by gathering a variety of types of data (systematic observation, standardized tests, criterion-referenced tests, and so on). When multiple assessment approaches lead to the same conclusion, the consultant can be confident in it. In addition to obtaining feedback on informal observations through a variety of assessment devices, useful feedback can sometimes be obtained by asking the client about the observations at the moment when they occur. For example, a client's apparent inability to look the interviewer in the eye might be misinterpreted were it not for the client's explanation that the sun was shining in from behind the interviewer.

Exercise 7-1 illustrates the generic observation skills that are so important during assessment. This exercise can also be used to facilitate development of these observation skills.

Assessing the Task. As the assessment model implies, the consultant may also need to assess the task and the setting. The task, be it coordinating a sales meeting, running a training pro-

Exercise 7-1
Developing Generic Observation Skills

Although observation skills are important for all types of assessment situations, they are most difficult to use in situations in which they are an informal adjunct to another technique. For example, during an interview, the consultant's assessment is at two levels. First, the consultant listens to the content of the client's responses and may ask additional questions to further clarify the content of the responses. Second, the consultant observes the client's behavioral reactions and sequence of verbal responses to get additional clues. It is under such circumstances that behavior observation is most difficult to implement, and that is the focus of this exercise.

For this exercise, spend ten minutes interviewing a friend or colleague. You can interview the person about his or her position on abortion, capital punishment, the Equal Rights Amendment, or any other suitable topic. Ask the person to state his position and explain how he arrived at that position. Also ask what he feels are the strongest arguments in support of his position and what he believes are the weakest arguments. Throughout the interview, observe the person's behavior. After the interview, answer the following questions.

1. What framework did you use to guide your observation? Is this the framework you tend to use in other observational situations?
2. What are the operational definitions of the behaviors you observed? Did you develop these operational definitions while conducting the interview? If not, conduct another interview and develop operational definitions for observation during the interview.
3. Did the interviewee concur with the observations and the definitions you used? If not, why, and how might the discrepancy reduce the validity of your observations?

gram, or providing feedback on a consultee's job performance, can be assessed using criterion-referenced techniques. Criterion-referenced procedures assess an individual's performance on a particular task against some fixed standard (for example, completed or not completed), rather than assessing the individual in terms of a group standard or norm (for example, 50th percentile). Thus, if the client's aggressive behavior is the focus of consultation, then rather than using norm-referenced tests, such as the TAT or Rorschach, which focus on underlying constructs, the consultant will observe the occurrence of aggressive behavior directly in a variety of relevant environmental settings.

The interaction between the client and the task can be assessed further using task analysis techniques. Task analysis breaks the task down into its simplest components in order to show which aspects of the task have been mastered and which have caused difficulty for the client. Task analysis may also delineate some of the specific task requirements. For example, to what extent does the task require short-term or long-term memory, abstract or concrete reasoning, receptive or expressive use of language, and verbal or nonverbal performance? This approach has special value because it has direct implications for intervention plans.

Exercise 7-2 provides the reader with an example of task analysis applied to an item from an IQ test, along with suggestions for further use of such a procedure.

Exercise 7-2
Developing Task Analysis Skills

Task analysis can be used with any task and can be a useful adjunct to criterion-referenced or norm-referenced assessment techniques. The best way to develop task analysis skills is to apply the approach. This exercise, for example, applies task analysis to an item from a widely used IQ test, the revised Wechsler Intelligence Scale for Children (WISC-R).

Exercise 7-2
Developing Task Analysis Skills, Cont'd.

First, consider the following item from the Similarities subtest of the WISC-R: "In what way are an apple and a banana alike?" Next, complete each of the following steps.

Step 1: Break the task into its discrete components. That is, what are the distinct elements of the question?

Step 2: Describe how you would use this analysis of the task to develop intervention plans.

Step 3: Read the following section and compare it with your analysis of the item.

Task Demands of the Similarities Item

Since the item is presented orally by the examiner, there are no reading demands for this task. However:

a. The client must hear the item and accurately perceive the words presented.
b. There is a short-term memory requirement, since the item is stated orally and is not available to the client in writing. However, since the item can be repeated on request, this short-term memory requirement is minimal.
c. Fundamental familiarity with the cultural items "apple" and "banana" is required.
d. There is a long-term memory requirement, since the client must recognize the words *apple* and *banana* and remember their meanings.
e. The task requires comparison skills. That is, the client must be able to compare the two items and determine the ways they are similar.
f. Abstract skills are required to perform optimally on this task. Rather than finding concrete, physical elements common to apples and bananas, the best responses require finding commonalities in the two concepts. For example, rather than indicating that apples and bananas are similar because they both have stems or skins, a more adequate response points to the fact that they are both fruit, food.

Exercise 7-2
Developing Task Analysis Skills, Cont'd.

g. After reception and processing of the question, the client must convey his or her response. Such conveyance generally demands minimal expressive language ability.
h. Further, such verbal responding demands a favorable social/ emotional state. An overly anxious client, for example, might be too fearful to be expressive, whereas a client who is completely unmotivated might fail to generate the answer because of his or her negative response set.

Step 4: This analysis demonstrates the many levels and possible foci for an intervention plan based on this task (receptive language, anxiety, cultural knowledge, expressive language, and so forth). Generate as many interventions as possible for the above example.

Step 5: Repeat this exercise with the next client you assess. Use your task analysis to develop intervention plans for that client.

Assessing the Setting. The environment, or setting, can be assessed using a variety of techniques. Observation systems have been derived from a variety of theoretical perspectives, but those that have received the most attention derive from the behavioral perspective (for example, Hall and Hall, 1981; Hall, Hawkins, and Axelrod, 1975; O'Leary, 1975). In addition, ecological theory has been used as a basis for assessing environments using observations and/or questionnaires to gather data (for example, Barker, 1968; Gump, 1975; Moos, 1974a). Many of these data-gathering approaches can be implemented by persons other than the consultant, such as the consultee. Some examples will be described in Chapter Eight. However, some observation systems are best used by the consultant.

These systems can generate data about the interaction between the environment and the client. Consider, for example, the observation system illustrated in Table 5. In this instance it was used to assess the behavior of a residential retarded adult

Table 5. Observations of and Consultee's Responses to Disruptive Behavior.

Person	Minutes																			
	1	2	3	4	5	6	7	8	9	10	11	12	13	14	15	16	17	18	19	20
Client	D	D	N	D	D	D	N	N	D	D	D	D	D	D	N	N	D	D	D	D
Consultee's response	V	V	I	I	V	V	I	I	I	I	V	V	V	V	I	I	V	V	V	V
Comparison subject	N	N	N	N	N	N	N	N	N	N	N	N	D	D	N	D	D	N	N	D

D, disruptive behavior by client or comparison subject; N, nondisruptive behavior by client or comparison subject; I, ignore; V, verbal punishment; R, reinforcement; TO, time out.

who had been exhibiting aggressive behavior in a sheltered workshop setting. However, the system can be adapted for assessing the client/environment interaction in any consultation situation. In the example shown, the consultee was a master's-level social worker who was in charge of the workshop. The observation system represents a twenty-minute observation period during which the consultant observed the client, the consultee, and a comparison client for one-minute intervals. The following factors became clear from looking at these data. First, the client was disruptive during fifteen of the twenty intervals. On first glance, that appears high, and this interpretation is confirmed when comparing this client with the comparison subject, who was disruptive during five of the twenty intervals. The second factor apparent from these data is that the consultee contributes to the client's disruptive behavior by ignoring nondisruptive behavior rather than reinforcing it and by responding to disruptive behavior with verbal punishment (which may be providing negative attention that is actually reinforcing the behavior). Third, although the comparison subject was markedly less disruptive, disruptive behavior increased notably toward the end of the observation period. This helped to confirm the suspicion that the client's disruptive behavior and the attention it was drawing from the consultee were negatively affecting the rest of the workshop environment.

The interventions developed modified not only the client's behavior but also the particular tasks and work environment in which the client performed. As such, these interventions were both remedial and preventive. They were remedial in that the client's disruptive behavior was reduced. They had preventive value for two reasons. Identifying and modifying the extrapersonal variables involved in the problem situation would prevent future similar problems for this client. Further, modifying the client's behavior and the specific consultee reaction to it would reduce disruptive behavior by others in the environment and lessen the likelihood of the consultee's increasing such disruptive behavior in the future through attending to disruptions while ignoring compliance.

Assessing Task/Client/Setting Interactions. The ultimate goal of assessment in consultation is to help determine what intervention to implement. Although it is useful to have separate information about the client, the setting, and the task, the most important information for this goal is obtained by considering the interactions among the three factors. We have already presented one technique to assess task/client interactions (task analysis) and one to assess environment/client interactions (the behavioral observation system in Table 5). Many additional techniques can be used to assess these types of interactions. In order to assess adequately the interactions among task, client, and environmental setting, the examiner must test out the hypotheses developed about the client's behavior during the assessment process. By incorporating coaching, teaching, and interventions, assessment is expanded conceptually to emphasize the linkage between assessment and intervention. The result is that assessment is more likely to lead to interventions that will provide meaningful help to the client. The basic concept is that the consultant modifies some aspect of the task and/or environment during assessment to determine whether this will affect the client in a meaningful way, working from hypotheses developed during earlier components of the assessment. When these modifications affect the client in the predicted manner, there is evidence that the client's characteristics do interact with the task and/or environment as hypothesized. This represents a marked change in assessment, since the process must now do more than develop hypotheses about the most effective recommendations: Assessment must also determine the potential efficacy of these interventions. Consider the following three approaches to testing interactive hypotheses during assessment.

1. *Learning potential assessment* is an approach to assessing intellectual performance that is consistent with the notion of assessing interactive hypotheses (see Feuerstein, 1979; Budoff, 1975). An intelligence test such as Raven's Progressive Matrices is administered. Then the examiner, using task analysis, determines what aspects of the task may have interfered with the client's performance. This information is used as a basis for coaching the client. A posttest is given to determine the impact of the coaching. Such a test-analysis-coach-retest

paradigm need not be restricted to intelligence testing or to the school setting. The model can be used, for example, by business personnel in identifying leadership potential or by mental health workers in assessing their clients' aptitudes or problem-solving abilities.

2. *Diagnostic teaching* is another way to implement the concept of trial interventions. This approach has also been called precision teaching, diagnostic-prescriptive teaching, trial teaching, and clinical teaching. It is implemented for a client in an educational setting who is having difficulty with the curriculum. The emphasis in diagnostic teaching is to determine the client's strengths and weaknesses in learning the curricular material and to use this information to develop teaching strategies and assess their impact. Diagnostic teaching is a continuous assessment and remediation process that uses criterion-referenced measures, task analysis, and trial teaching in a test-teach-test format.

The consultant uses hypotheses formulated during the early part of assessment that consider the client's strengths and weaknesses relevant to the curricular tasks, as well as the client's unique perceptual, motivational, behavioral, and learning styles. Having considered these characteristics of the client in the context of the learning task and the setting, the consultant seeks to modify the environment, the task, or motivational variables or to teach missing skills in ways that capitalize on the client's strengths. This will provide clear instructional plans for the consultee to implement as intervention.

3. *Trial intervention* is conceptually similar to diagnostic teaching, but its focus is behavior in nonacademic settings. A test-teach-test methodology is used, and the assessment focuses directly on the behavior of concern—for example, interpersonal cooperative behavior with other clients in a community home for mildly retarded adults, increased social behavior for a patient on a hospital psychiatric ward, or assertiveness in an unsuccessful middle-line manager. Using information on task, client, and setting variables, the consultant formulates hypotheses about the interrelationship of the client, task, and environment by attempting environmental modification. These hypoth-

eses are tested by determining whether the effects that they predict occur. These trial interventions can be attempted in the consultant's testing room or in the natural environment.

As an example, one goal for a severely retarded adolescent was to increase the frequency with which the client made his bed adequately. The client was referred after one month of efforts to accomplish the behavior change, which had been followed by an increase in tantrums, resulting in injury to persons and damage to property. Baseline observations were gathered for a week, and it was found that the client had completed the task of making his bed twice, and even these performances were not to criterion (blanket not tucked in). Further, there were severe tantrums lasting from fifteen to forty-five minutes each day.

Assessment was continued after the baseline observations as the houseparent implemented a series of intervention plans until the data showed a decrease in tantrum behavior and an increase in bed-making behavior. An overcorrection procedure was used in which the client replaced any objects misplaced during the tantrum, filled out a lengthy damage report, and apologized repeatedly. This procedure was coupled with immediate reinforcement for approximation of the bed-making behavior. Once the data showed an indication that these recommendations had the potential to help, the assessment was complete.

Exercise 7-3 suggests a learning activity aimed at assisting the reader in developing experience with the trial interventions procedure.

Exercise 7-3
Trial Interventions

Trial interventions can be implemented and assessed during any assessment. In fact, consultants sometimes implement trial interventions during assessment just to facilitate the completion of testing. But often these procedures are not viewed as part of assessment and, as a result, are not used in a systematic way.

Exercise 7-3
Trial Interventions, Cont'd.

Consider the next client-centered case you receive as a consultant or consultant-in-training. During assessment, generate a list of the trial interventions you may wish to implement. Choose at least one of the interventions and implement it. Consider how doing so leads to a more complete assessment and the development of clear recommendations for the consultee. If there are problems implementing the trial intervention, discuss them with a colleague, supervisor, or trainer.

CHAPTER EIGHT

Indirect Assessment and Interventions: Level Two

The second level of consultation presented in our model is indirect service to the client. Just as with Level I, the primary goal is to effect a change in the behaviors, attitudes, and/or feelings of the client. This person becomes the focus of consultation once the consultee requests help. Although the types of interventions implemented in Level II consultation are the same as in Level I, Level II service is more indirect in that the consultant does not gather any of the assessment data directly. Instead, someone else, such as the consultee, accomplishes this task. In addition to describing the consultant's role, this chapter will consider the special issues involved in training the consultee to conduct some of the assessment. Finally, the chapter will discuss the approaches to intervention used in Level I or Level II consultation to effect a change in the client.

The Consultant's Role

Indirect service to the client is more economical of the consultant's time, as the consultant is not required to gather data directly from the client. Rather, the consultant's role is to help the consultee develop a careful definition of the problem and together identify the types of data that need to be gathered to plan the intervention. In addition, the consultant may help the consultee (or other persons, such as an aide or secretary) develop the materials needed to facilitate the observation. Finally, once the data are available, the consultant and consultee consider these data in an effort to develop intervention plans. The collaborative model suggests that the consultant seek input from the consultee in developing intervention plans. Some such plans are reviewed later in this chapter.

Once the intervention strategy is in place, data collection will continue in order to determine the efficacy of the intervention. The consultee will again use the same data collection procedures previously used to define the problem.

A major difficulty in implementing this component of the model is that consultees (as well as other personnel in most institutions) resist active involvement in the data-gathering process. They do not feel trained to gather such data and generally view this role as falling in the consultant's domain. Accordingly, they often resent the time demands they believe data collection would place on them.

The consultant therefore needs to give special attention to training the consultee in the rationale for and procedures of assessment. Such training helps change consultees' perception about assessment as a role unique to the consultant and helps consultees develop confidence in their ability to carry out this task. Perhaps most important, training can provide techniques that make minimal time demands on the consultee and thus serve to reduce this real concern and possible source of consultee resistance.

Training the Consultee in Assessment

Chapter Seven discussed approaches to assessing the task (criterion-referenced assessment and task analysis) and the environment (behavioral and ecological observation systems). These approaches can often be administered by the consultee, rather than the consultant. Here we present a model that can be used to train consultees in assessment. This model will include some additional examples of assessment techniques that lend themselves readily to use by the consultee.

This model for consultee training in assessment has four steps: (1) present a model of assessment with its underlying rationale, (2) present at least one or two assessment techniques in sufficient detail to be readily implemented by the consultee, (3) present examples of how the assessment techniques have been used by consultees in other situations, and (4) provide an opportunity for the consultee to implement the assessment procedure in the work setting.

Presenting a Model of Assessment. The model of assessment presented to the consultee should be a modified version of the approach delineated in Chapter Seven. The consultant/trainer can point out that traditional approaches to assessment have emphasized standardized norm-referenced procedures, administered by a consultant. Although these techniques have been good for predicting future behavior in an unmodified environment, they have not helped to intervene effectively with clients. An alternative approach to assessment relies on techniques that do lead to meaningful interventions. Some of the crucial assumptions underlying these alternative approaches to assessment are that (1) there must be a clear link between assessment and intervention, (2) there must be a clear link between assessment and environment, (3) assessment must include continual observation of the target behavior over time, and (4) assessment is viewed as a process of generating and testing hypotheses about the client.

These assumptions lead to techniques for assessing the client, the task, and their environmental concomitants, rather than seeking to determine only underlying causes. Criterion-referenced assessment, direct behavior observation, task analysis, and trial intervention are examples of the kinds of assessment techniques emphasized.

Presenting Assessment Techniques. The consultant should

present specific assessment techniques in enough detail that the consultee will be able to implement them. There are many possible techniques the consultant may wish to use in addition to those mentioned in Chapter Seven. The extent of their use may vary with the setting. A number of general approaches to behavioral and ecological assessment, however, can be useful across settings. Since Chapters Nine and Ten consider application of ecological assessment, behavioral observation will be discussed here in some detail. Note, however, that these are presented only as examples of techniques that might be used in training consultees. Any number of alternatives could be used instead.

Several excellent descriptions of behavior observation systems applicable to consultees exist (for example, Deno, 1979; Deno and Mirkin, 1977; Neisworth, Deno, and Jenkins, 1969; Piper, 1974; Axelrod, 1977). The description provided in this example is derived largely from a detailed approach to training consultees developed by Hall and Hall (1981).

1. *Definitions of behaviors.* The first step in training consultees in observational systems is to facilitate their development of a good, clear working definition of the behavior under study. It is crucial that behavior observation be based on a clear operational definition of the behavior. Vague terms such as *anxiety, hostility, intelligence,* or *aggression* do not translate directly into interventions and therefore should be replaced by descriptors that define *who, what, when,* and *where.*

For example, Frank, aged twenty-three, lived in a group home for retarded adults. He worked as a busboy in a local restaurant, occasionally went to the movies, ate meals at the home with the other residents, and spent most of his time alone looking at magazines or watching television. Although Frank managed to hold down his job, the houseparent, who was the consultee in this case, was concerned that Frank was "shy." Further, the houseparent concluded that Frank's "shyness" was a result of his "anxiety" about being with people. When asked for more details about these problems, the consultee reported that Frank rarely interacted with people. Therefore, the consultee's goal was to increase this behavior.

Using the basic descriptors of *who, what, when,* and

where, we find that the *who* is Frank, a twenty-three-year-old male, who is mildly retarded and works as a busboy while living in a group home. The houseparent was able to provide the *what* by focusing the discussion on Frank's level of interaction with other people. Interacting was defined as any verbal interchange between Frank and another person. Often a consideration of *where* the behavior occurs is crucial to developing an adequate behavioral definition. In this instance, it was reported that Frank never spoke to anyone during lunch, with the exception of the houseparent, and these interactions were limited to one-word responses to the houseparent's questions. Although there was a living room, Frank spent time only in the television area and, when there, did not speak to others. The lack of interaction was so consistent that he would not even speak when someone changed the channel while he was watching TV. Instead of complaining, he would either stay and watch the new show or just leave. Frank also spent a great deal of time alone in his room.

In Frank's case the answer to the question *when* was "All the time." The one notable exception occurred at meals, when Frank would provide one-word responses to statements or questions from the houseparent.

During training it is a good idea to ask the consultee to use these four elements to develop an operational definition for a behavior of the client. Or, as an alternative, we have found that having the consultee use a similar technique in defining one of his or her own behaviors (smoking, reading, eating sweets) is an effective way to help the consultee become comfortable with this procedure. After application of the procedure to self or a client, the consultee should share the definition with the consultant, who can provide corrective feedback.

2. *Measuring the targeted behavior.* After the target behavior is defined successfully, the consultee will need to be instructed in methods of measurement. The following six approaches are particularly suitable for use by a consultee.

The *anecdotal record* is a useful measurement tool, particularly when the consultee is uncertain which behavior to focus on. The anecdotal record is collected by writing a brief description of everything that occurs during a particular time span. This is difficult for most consultees, since it is hard to write down everything that is happening if you have other things to do. This problem can be addressed if the consultee picks one or two short time intervals in which to observe and record events. The advantage of this time-interval approach is that it provides an overview of everything that occurs and thus provides data from which to begin to draw tentative hypotheses about the who, what, when, and where. A disadvantage is that the data may lack precision because it is rarely possible to write down everything that occurs. If the consultee repeats the observation by anecdotal record a number of times (for example, on three separate occasions), potential trends or consistent relationships are more easily and accurately identified.

Direct measurement of products is another approach to data gathering. When a behavior in a particular setting leaves behind a permanent product—a test score, cigarette butt, sales slip, time punch card—that is tied to the operationally defined behavior, then it is easy to use this artifact (or "trace") as a means of assessing the client's behavior. This procedure not only reduces the time demanded of the consultee (just collate existing records) but is generally an easy procedure in which to establish reliability of measurement. Frequently it will be helpful for the consultant to provide a system to ease the task of collating the records.

Frequency recording is a simple way to measure behaviors directly. In the example of Frank, it would be feasible for the houseparent to do a frequency count of the times Frank speaks throughout the evening. This technique is practical in this instance because the unit of observation (speaking) is easily identified as a single word, and it occurs with low frequency. It might not be practical if applied to a highly verbal and friendly college student living in a dormitory.

For frequency counting one can use mechanical counters (golf counters, pocket calculators) or simple checklists. Frequency counts are practical for most consultees, especially if the behavior under study is fairly discrete—that is, has a clear beginning and ending.

Duration measurement is most suitable when the consultee is concerned about the length of time that a behavior is exhibited, rather than simply its frequency. For example, returning to our client Frank, we note that he is late for breakfast each day and often misses it completely. On closer analysis we find that he spends thirty minutes each morning making his bed. Even though he does eventually accomplish this task, the inordinate length of time required is one of the reasons for his inability to get to breakfast on time. Although the frequency of his bed making is not an issue (that is, he makes his bed each day), the time he spends performing the task is, and so a duration recording would appear applicable to this situation.

In *time-interval recording* a recording period is determined—for example, twenty minutes—and is then segmented into equal time intervals (for example, twenty one-minute intervals). The client is then observed to determine whether the behavior occurs at any time during each subinterval. This approach is generally better suited to the consultant's application, since it requires a lot of time and attention and thus is often not practical for the consultee, who simultaneously must attend to other responsibilities.

Time sampling is similar to time-interval recording but is sometimes more practical for use by the consultee. Suppose that the consultee divides the twenty minutes into one-minute intervals, as before. Rather than observe the client throughout the entire minute, however, the consultee records the client's behavior only at the end of each one-minute interval. This requires several brief observations, spaced throughout the recording period.

3. *Establishing reliability.* One problem that can occur with alternative assessment measures is that the reliability of the instrument has not been established. This is important because we need to know that measurement is accurate. With behavioral observation systems, reliability can be checked by determining the degree to which different observers agree on what they have observed. Reliability is calculated by identifying the percentage of agreement between two observers. For example, one observer might record ten tantrums by a preschool child, while a second

observer might record eight during the same period of observation. Dividing the smaller number (8) by the larger number (10) establishes that the reliability, or agreement, was 80 percent in this instance.

When using a time-sampling or interval-recording procedure, reliability is calculated slightly differently. The numbers of agreements and disagreements are both considered. The two time-sampling charts below provide an example. Each chart represents the six observations by an individual at the end of ten-minute intervals throughout a one-hour period.

	1	2	3	4	5	6
Observer 1	X	X	X	X	X	X
Observer 2	X	O	X	X	X	X

Observers 1 and 2 agreed on whether the behavior occurred in five of the six intervals. The observers disagreed about the second interval only. Reliability is calculated by dividing the number of agreements by the total number of intervals. In this example the agreement between the two observers is 5/6, or $83\frac{1}{3}$ percent.

For behaviors that occur infrequently, it is easy to get artificially high reliability scores when using a time-sampling or interval-recording method. In such cases agreement and disagreement should be calculated only for those intervals when at least one of the observers records that the behavior did occur.

4. *Data interpretation.* After data are recorded, they can be presented graphically, for ease of understanding and to show trends over time. Generally, baseline data are collected before intervention to provide a basis for assessing its impact.

Often it is useful to compare observations of the client and others from the client's population. This type of comparison reveals the extent to which the client's behavior is so unusual that it requires special attention and the extent to which the intervention affected the client in comparison with other clients. The same observational procedures are used to record the comparison client's behavior as the client's. The consultant can assist in data collection by giving the consultee observation sheets that provide places for recording the behavior of the client and the comparison client. Similarly, the consultee will be most likely to present the observation results graphically if the consultant demonstrates an easy way to do so and provides the appropriate forms or graph paper.

Presenting Examples of Consultee Use. Once the specific observation techniques have been presented, detailed examples are needed to demonstrate to consultees how it can be practical for them to help gather the necessary data. This clarifies the techniques recommended as well as addressing some of the realistic concerns of consultees about the feasibility of these procedures for their situation. Chapter Seven included an example of a consultant's use of an interval-recording system to observe the behavior of the client and consultee. This example or the one to follow, which demonstrates a consultee's use of a frequency-recording technique, can be used to illustrate these techniques and their feasibility.

A nurse on a cancer ward sought consultation about a patient whose family were having difficulty coping with the client's condition. The patient, a man of forty-four, wanted to return home, since there was nothing else the hospital could do. However, his wife and mother did not want him to return home and were unable to carry on an effective conversation with him. They constantly talked unrealistically about his cure, which would occur "soon," and were unwilling to listen when he tried to discuss the realities of his situation. Generally, they appeared depressed. Although the nurse agreed that the patient would be better off returning home, she was concerned that the depressive home environment would accelerate the decline in his health. The nurse was frustrated in her attempts to work with the family, even though she had abundant experience counseling families in similar situations. Together, the consultant and the nurse/consultee developed a plan to observe the family interacting and use the resulting data as a basis for developing consensus among the family that a change in their pattern of interaction really was necessary.

Two behaviors were defined for observation by the nurse. She was to note, first, the number of times that the wife and/or mother interrupted a conversation the patient had started, resulting in a topic change, and, second, the number of depressive statements made by the wife. Depressive statements were operationally defined as those which focused on activities that could not be initiated or completed and which were made while frowning.

The consultee agreed to observe for a twenty-minute period each day during family visits. After one week of observation the consultant and consultee met to discuss the observations, which are shown in Figures 3 and 4. These results were dramatic. It was evident that the patient was unable to interact

Figure 3. Percentage of Interruptions Observed on
Six Successive Days.

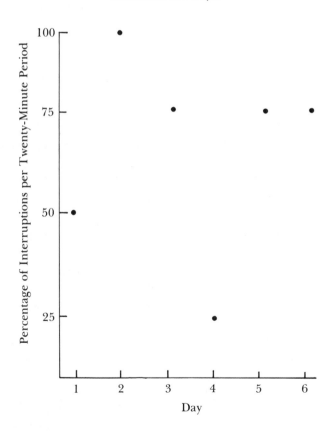

Figure 4. Number of Depressive Statements Observed
on Six Successive Days.

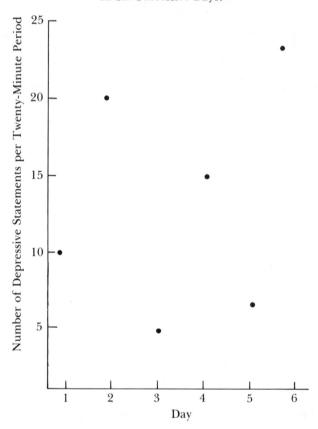

effectively, being interrupted approximately 67 percent of the
time. Similarly, the negative, depressed attitude conveyed by
the wife was evident from the average of fourteen depressive
statements per twenty-minute period.

The nurse/consultee was able to use these data as a basis
for stimulating the first productive discussion among the patient,
his wife, and his mother. As a result of this and some follow-up
discussion, the patient was able to return home, to a supportive
environment.

Providing an Intervention Opportunity for the Consultee.
There are a limitless number of intervention approaches that the
consultee might implement when the goal is to change the cli-

ent's behavior and/or attitude. These will vary dramatically with the setting and the client. The choice of techniques will also be influenced by the goal of consultation and the theoretical perspective used in developing the interventions.

It is beyond the scope of this book to detail the various theoretical models (psychodynamic, behavioral, group process, and so on) and to indicate how each might lead to a different set of interventions (see, for example, Bergan, 1977; Caplan, 1970; Schmuck and Schmuck, 1974). This chapter provides an eclectic perspective on intervention strategies.

Two important sets of skills are generic to all client-centered interventions: those necessary for selecting an intervention and those required for designing interventions that build competence in the client population.

1. *Determining the intervention.* The model of assessment presented in this book has the unique advantage of leading directly to intervention. Behavior is viewed as an interaction among the task, the setting, and the client, and interventions are developed from this perspective. Many traditional models (for example, psychodynamic models) develop interventions from the basis of a focus on the client. Although this approach is often quite helpful, and certainly some interventions need to focus on intrapsychic factors, it is important to develop interventions that address environmental factors. This goal is facilitated by assessment that considers interactions among task, client, and setting. Exercise 8-1 illustrates some of the ways in which

Exercise 8-1
Developing Interventions

Consider the following client-centered consultation case and develop the interventions you would be likely to recommend. Jot these plans down and then read the discussion of our interventions to compare the extent to which your recommendations address the same breadth of attack.

The client presented to the consultant was a twelve-year-old seventh-grader having learning and adjustment problems in school. James's family had

Exercise 8-1
Developing Interventions, Cont'd.

a long history of disruption in which the father had been physically abusive of the mother, even, on one occasion, stabbing her. Divorce had resulted. Growing up in this environment, the son began using withdrawal as a coping style, did poorly in school, and developed an unusually close relationship with his mother. The child was referred by one of his teachers, who complained that although James seemed to have average ability, he was failing academically, particularly in reading.

Achievement tests revealed that James performed inconsistently in reading comprehension, fluctuating between the third- and sixth-grade levels. Further, projective testing, interviews, and observations of his interaction with his mother suggested that he was highly anxious and that he felt a good deal of hostility toward his mother, blaming her for the divorce. It was hypothesized that hostility toward the father was repressed because of his fear of losing the father and that instead the mother became the focus of any hostility.

Interventions often recommended in cases like this include the following:

1. Individual psychotherapy to help James work out his feelings of hostility toward his mother, as well as his hostility/fear orientation toward his father.
2. Family therapy, with both James and his mother, to reduce their overly dependent relationship.
3. A resource room to provide special academic assistance, particularly in reading.
4. Positive reinforcement from the teacher so that James can develop a better feeling about himself and become less withdrawn in the school situation.

Exercise 8-1
Developing Interventions, Cont'd.

These recommendations and many others like them might be effective with James. However, other recommendations, based on the interaction among the task, the child, and the setting, could probably provide more specific help. The following recommendations exemplify those that might follow from an interactive hypothesis.

1. One hypothesis is that anxiety often distracts James from his work. This may help to explain his inconsistent performance in reading. This hypothesis might yield a variety of interventions to increase his attention or reduce the anxiety-based interference—for example, suggesting that he read the entire story carefully so he will be able to answer questions about it; read each word and each line of the story slowly so that he gets the whole message; determine what the story is about from the topic sentence and then read the remaining sentences in search of support for his prediction; review the story silently after completing it so that he reinforces his memory (overlearning); read stories that are illustrated and use the illustrations before and after reading to reinforce his memory of what the story intended; or develop his own "pictures" of the story as a means of remembering its essence.

In each of these recommendations we have taken our understanding of the client's characteristics (his inconsistency in attending to detail) and considered this in relation to various task characteristics (lack of pictures, presence of topic sentences, availability of review time). Each of the recommendations is based on a hypothesis that would have to be tested.

2. James's tendency toward withdrawal can be considered in relation to environmental characteristics. Although he tends to be passive and withdrawn in school, his behavior seems to vary considerably once out of school. Sometimes with his mother or with one of his neighborhood friends, his social behavior is controlling, aggressive, or even friendly. The consultee could seek to draw out these behaviors from James by using nonacademic activities (for example, playing a video game with him)

Exercise 8-1
Developing Interventions, Cont'd.

and/or altering the style of interaction so that the consultee de-emphasizes the authority role and emphasizes James's special skills. This relationship could be used later to draw in other children and to include more academic activities. This recommendation is based, in part, on the interaction between the characteristics of the client (withdrawn under certain academic situations) and the characteristics of the environment (some tasks deemphasize the academic nature of the environment, and the consultee's manner can alter the setting by making it more or less of an authority situation).

3. James's shy behavior can be considered in relation to the interaction with the environment by examining the physical structure of his classroom. Since seats are assigned to students in this school, the teachers could facilitate James's interaction with others by seating him next to the children most likely to interact with him. Similarly, in small-group activities James could be given active roles (such as recording secretary) that he would be comfortable taking on. His increased interpersonal comfort in the classroom should facilitate his attention to academic activities.

4. Given that his highest skills in reading are one grade level behind his grade placement, James needs special help in reading to complete his work adequately. One step, which should actually have been part of the diagnostic work-up, is for the resource-room teacher to have him read samples of the readings from his different subject areas, to estimate the percentage of words he does not know. Lists of these words could then be used in teaching him reading. In this way, the supplemental instruction in the resource room would bear directly on his other seventh-grade work. Since James has particular problems with reading recognition, these words should be taught by creating (or having James create) stories that include these words as well as others that he does know. The percentage of unknown words should be small so that he experiences a high degree of success and so that the learning demands are not too great on a given

Exercise 8-1
Developing Interventions, Cont'd.

task. This approach involves an interaction between the task demands and James's characteristics, which are evaluated through
criterion-referenced assessment. As a result, the intervention involves modifying the tasks given James by developing stories
based on his current material at his instructional level in reading.
    5. The evaluation revealed two characteristics about
James that tasks must take into account if he is to perform at
his maximum potential. First, James's withdrawn approach to
school reduces his motivation for academic tasks. He has an "I
don't care" attitude. Second, he has unresolved angry feelings
that are consciously directed toward his mother and are uncon-
scious in relation to his father. Academic tasks could be ad-
justed to increase James's motivation (characteristic one) by taking advantage of his unresolved anger (characteristic two). For
example, the class could be assigned to read and discuss stories,
plays, or historical incidents that involve families of divorce or
families in which the child has strong feelings of hostility
toward one or both parents. Having children make up stories or
dramatizations based on these themes would also be productive.
Considering the interaction of these motivational factors with
task structure can aid in development of intervention plans that
draw more active and productive involvement from James.
    Contrast your recommendations with those just outlined.
Identify your primary focus—the client, the task, the setting,
and/or the interaction. Choose the two areas given the least attention in your recommendations and generate two more recommendations from each of those orientations.

consideration of task/client/setting interactions can lead to interventions that are tied more specifically to the client's needs
and thus maximize the probability of meaningful change. Exercise 8-1 makes this point in general terms. However, it is equally
important for the consultant to determine how this approach
can be applied in his or her own unique setting. With this goal in
mind, consider Exercise 8-2.

Exercise 8-2
Recommendations Based on Interactional Hypotheses

Pick the most recent referral you have received at your work setting where the focus is on a single client. Develop a list of recommendations based on the interactions of task, client, and setting. Compare this list with your original recommendations. How do these recommendations differ from those based solely on client characteristics? What additional assessment is necessary to have an adequate data base for these recommendations? How might their impact differ from the impact of recommendations with only a client orientation?

2. *Designing interventions that build competence.* Interventions that build competence have particular implications for the preventive goal of consultation.

Interventions that provide the client with the fundamental means for assessing reality, identifying and resolving real problems, establishing personal goals and the means for achieving them, and, in general, helping the client develop and maintain a sense of well-being and self-worth can be effective in preventing future mental health problems as well as remediating the immediate problem. Examples include Parent Effectiveness Training, which provides parents with knowledge about child development and skills for achieving effective communication and child management; "marriage encounter" programs, aimed at making good marriages better through communications training; and stress management programs, which provide executives with the skills to identify potential stressors and symptoms of excess stress and to modify their life-styles in order to reduce the occurrence and impact of stress.

One focus of competence building that has received much attention of late is social competence. The literature (Curran and Wessberg, 1981) is replete with research pointing to the importance of social inadequacy as a contributing factor in major forms of psychopathology. This same literature points to the association of social inadequacy with dysfunctional behaviors such as sexual problems, alcohol and drug abuse, social anxiety, and work dysfunction. Although a number of psychotherapeutic strategies have been used to remediate social skill deficits, social skills training can be used to increase the skills and competence of those not yet experiencing inadequacy or dysfunction. Such training, be it termed "social competence training," "assertiveness training," or "communications training," focuses on increasing skill and competence and thus preventing future problems.

Cowen (1977) has noted that four core questions must be answered to facilitate the use of competence and adjustment to promote prevention: (1) What are the basic skills that are requisite to positive adjustment? (2) Can these skills be taught to children using a specific curriculum? (3) Can it be shown that acquiring a particular competence will lead to gains in interpersonal adjustment? (4) Does improved adjustment maintain itself over time? These questions have been addressed in some recent research (for example, Spivack and Shure, 1973; Allen and others, 1976; Blank and Covington, 1965; Heber, 1978), and they should guide research in this area for some years to come.

The work of George Spivack and Myrna Shure is particularly impressive in developing techniques to teach children social problem-solving skills. They (Spivack and Shure, 1973; Spivack, Platt, and Shure, 1976) have studied interpersonal cognitive problem-solving skills, which include "sensitivity to interpersonal problems, ability to generate alternative solutions, ability to understand means-ends relationships, and awareness of the effect of one's social acts on another" (Gesten and others, 1979, p. 224). The curricular material they have developed has proved effective with adolescents, adults, and preschool and kindergarten children as well as with emotionally disturbed and mentally retarded populations.

Cowen and his associates (Gesten and others, 1979) have blended the basic principles identified by Spivack and Shure with Meichenbaum's procedures (Meichenbaum and Goodman, 1971) to create an interpersonal problem-solving procedure. The detailed curriculum used involves the following steps.

First, the prerequisite skills for interpersonal problem solving are taught. These include awareness and understanding of others' feelings. During this stage children are taught to look for signs of upset and unhappy feelings. The second step is problem definition. At this stage the child is taught the skills needed to assess exactly what the interpersonal problem is and to define that problem. Step 3 is to decide on a specific goal that derives from the prior problem definition. Step 4 teaches the child to delay expression of impulses. This is done by encouraging the child to stop and think before acting, perhaps talking out loud to oneself to facilitate impulse delay. Step 5 is to generate alternatives; the child is encouraged to think of as many solutions as possible to the interpersonal problem. The sixth step is to encourage the child to consider the consequences of his or her behavior. For each potential solution the child is asked to brainstorm the variety of outcomes that might result. Step 7 is to implement the problem-solving strategy that the child has chosen, and Step 8 is to recycle through the process if the prior solution did not work. Curriculum materials are available for implementing these steps; materials can also be developed specifically for an individual population, following these eight steps as guides.

In attempting to develop intervention plans that not only remediate but build competence, a model that we have found facilitative is Arnold Lazarus's (1976) multimodal therapy. Lazarus's model focuses on seven interactive modalities that, according to Lazarus, make up one's personality. The seven modes are *b*ehavior, *a*ffect, *s*ensation, *i*magery, *c*ognition, *i*nterpersonal relationships, and *d*rugs-*d*iet, yielding the mnemonic acronym BASIC ID. We have found that by using these seven dimensions as a holistic guide to the functioning person, we can decide what types of skills need to be addressed in order to facilitate competence. Exercise 8-3 provides examples of the skills attended to under each of the aforementioned dimensions and offers you the opportunity to develop competence in each of these areas.

Summary of Issues in Level II Consultation

Indirect service to the client is an approach to consultation that will inevitably stimulate resistance, which the consul-

Exercise 8-3
Intervening for Competence

Review the seven modalities listed and the sample foci for skill development. Identify one skill or competency that you would like to develop in yourself and briefly sketch out the appropriate skill development strategy. After using the model on yourself, apply the same procedure to detail intervention strategies for building competence for your current or most recent client.

Modality	Focus	Strategy for Development
Behavior	Too sedentary	Start jogging
Affect	Job-anxious	Relaxation training
Sensation	Music interest	Begin flute
Imagery	Sees oneself as shy	IALAC (Simon, 1973)
Cognition	Must be perfect	Rational-emotive training
Interpersonal	Overly private	Start to disclose
Drugs/Diet	Too much coffee	Vitamins/decaf.

tant must consider carefully. However, this approach has one clear advantage that should facilitate its implementation—the focus is on the client. It is more acceptable to consider problems associated with the client than to focus on the consultee or the system as a whole. Nevertheless, indirect service to the client involves some breaks with tradition, which may also stimulate resistance. In particular, the focus on assessment techniques that are tied closely to the environment, involve continuous rather than one-shot measurement, and focus on the link between assessment and intervention will result in nontraditional, informal techniques that require more active involvement by the consultee. This involvement runs directly counter to the expectations of many consultees that the consultant will solve the problem. Careful work will be required to make clear to consultees why their involvement during both assessment and intervention is so important. This can be done through organized efforts to train them in the skills needed to take advantage of consultation.

A second issue associated with both Level I and Level II consultation is the work required of the consultant to develop and implement very specific interventions. Consultants are accustomed to developing quick, vague recommendations that are not designed specifically for the client. Instead, the consultant must be trained to understand the interactions among client, task, and setting in order to develop interventions tailored to the unique characteristics of the client. This is a difficult challenge, but the consultant can meet it by using the interactive framework based on the notion of generating and testing interactive hypotheses.

Finally, like Level I, Level II consultation is focused on the individual client. It is consistent with the preventive model presented in this book because of its potential for stimulating profound changes in the consultee. The training provided the consultee and the resulting skills can be applied to benefit a variety of clients in the future. In addition, this chapter stresses interventions designed to promote growth and development (competence) in clients, not just those that are provided to remediate a problem or resolve a crisis. Finally, as mentioned in Chapter One, frequently Level I or II consultation is used to enter the system and develop the opportunity to provide the more generalized services found in Levels III and IV.

❧ CHAPTER NINE ❧

Promoting Knowledge and Skill Development: Level Three

Service to the consultee is the third level of consultation presented in our model. Whereas the focus of earlier approaches is on creating change in the client, in this level the consultee is the primary focus of service. The goal is to create change in the consultee's attitudes, behaviors, and/or feelings. Because the consultee is an important part of clients' environment, it is assumed that the changes in the consultee will benefit many of the clients currently under the consultee's care, as well as many clients in the future. This sort of generalized effect is key to the preventive potential of consultation and rests as the main factor in the success of consultation. For these reasons service to the consultee is an important component of the consultation model.

Caplan's (1970) consultee-centered case consultation is similar to Level II consultation. However, Caplan sought to foster growth in the consultee from a deficit orientation that sought to identify what was wrong with the consultee and then tried to remediate this situation. For example, Caplan (1970) describes four possible reasons for consultee-centered case consultation: lack of knowledge, lack of skill, lack of confidence, and lack of objectivity. His deficit orientation is clear from these labels, which identify weaknesses, or deficits, that need to be addressed. In contrast, we use a positive orientation aimed at promoting *growth* in all consultees, rather than being limited to those with "problems." We do not feel that the consultee must experience deficiencies in order to benefit from consultation.

Our model differs from Caplan's in another important way. Caplan places most emphasis on the consultee's lack of objectivity as the basis for consultee-centered case consultation. Although helping a consultee regain professional objectivity can indeed be a powerful intervention (see Meyers, 1975, for an example), we have found that often there are other, more important reasons for consultee-centered case consultation. A study by Gutkin (1981) has confirmed this viewpoint. An approach that promotes the growth of the consultee's knowledge and development of skills proves much more effective for the preventive goal of consultation.

Although our position differs from that of other mental health consultants because of our emphasis on prevention, we do not mean to imply that it discounts the traditional consultation techniques that derive from Caplan's work. Rather, our approach expands traditional methods to include those that promote the development of the consultee's knowledge and skill. The current chapter focuses on these methods for promoting such professional and personal growth, as well as those for increasing professional objectivity.

Development of Consultees' Knowledge and Skills

Roy Martin has developed a system for developing the knowledge and skills of teachers, which can be modified and applied to consultation in a variety of settings (see Martin, 1974; Meyers, Parsons, and Martin, 1979). The basic assumption is that a consultee might seek growth for several reasons. First, the consultee may not be aware of a particular aspect of his or her professional behavior. Second, some aspect of the consultee's professional behavior may not be consistent with the consultee's professional ideals. Third, the consultee may not be aware of the current research or expert opinion in the field on ideal professional practice. Last, the consultee's views of ideal practice regarding a particular issue may differ from the views of experts in the field. Consistent with the collaborative model, this system relies on the consultee's active involvement for developing his or her knowledge and skill. The consultant serves as a mirror and a source of information about current views of professional practice, and the consultee is given the opportunity to decide whether to change his or her behavior. It can be invaluable for the consultee to receive objective, nonevaluative feedback and to make a professional decision about how best to respond to that feedback. This system is diagramed in Figure 5.

The first phase of this system is to provide feedback to the consultee about the systematic observation. The first step is for the consultant to observe the consultee. Since a critical issue for the consultant is to use the observational data as a basis for objective, nonevaluative feedback to the consultee, it is important to use a systematic observation system. The second step is to ask the consultee to estimate the data that were observed. For example, if the consultant observed the number of commands the consultee gave the client during a half-hour period, the consultant will ask the consultee to estimate how many commands were directed toward the client during that period. In the third step, the consultant provides objective feedback to the consultee based on the observations recorded. As part of this step, the consultant and consultee compare the consultant's observations with the consultee's estimates. In Step 4, which concludes this phase of the process, the consultant and consultee determine consultation goals, based on any discrepancies between the observations and estimates.

In the second major phase of this system, the consultant and consultee examine whether the consultant's observations reveal behaviors congruent with the consultee's attitudes and values about ideal professional practice. Where there are discrep-

Figure 5. Developing the Consultee's Knowledge and Skills.

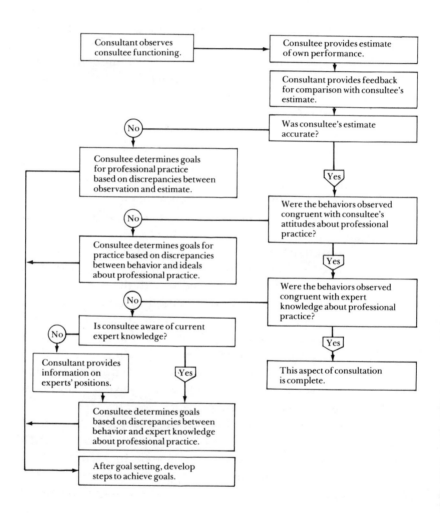

Source: Adapted from Martin (1974).

ancies, Step 5 is required, in which consultant and consultee work together to determine goals designed to resolve those discrepancies.

The third major phase of the process requires the consultant and consultee to consider discrepancies between the observed functioning of the consultee and experts' views on professional practice. If there is no discrepancy, then this aspect of consultation is concluded. However, when there is a discrepancy *and* the consultee is not aware of the current views of experts, then the consultant provides this expert knowledge to the consultee (Step 6). When a discrepancy exists even though the consultee is aware of the current expert opinions, the consultant and consultee determine goals based on the discrepancy (Step 7).

In all instances, once goals are agreed on, the consultant and consultee must work together to develop an action plan that delineates what they will do to achieve these goals. When increasing the consultee's knowledge or information base is the goal of the consultation, the consultant will act as a resource to facilitate knowledge acquisition. When the goal involves increasing the consultee's skill, a series of additional steps is followed. First the consultant and consultee determine how the consultee should implement the new approach. Then the consultee roleplays this skill and receives corrective feedback from the consultant. A modification of this second step when roleplay is not practical is a pencil-and-paper simulation in which the consultee is asked what he or she would do in response to hypothetical situations. This modification is less desirable since it identifies the consultee's ability to understand the skills under discussion but fails to provide evidence of ability to translate knowledge into performance. Once the roleplay (or simulation) is satisfactorily accomplished, the third step occurs—the consultee attempts the new skills in the real situation. The final step is for the consultant to observe the consultee implementing the new skills and provide additional corrective feedback. This process continues until the consultee implements the new skill in a satisfactory manner according to the criterion developed by the consultant and consultee during the planning phase.

Although the consultant is rather directive during the development process, it is implemented in a collaborative manner that maintains the consultee's total active involvement at each phase—observation, planning, and implementation.

The process of knowledge and skill acquisition is often quite difficult to implement with a consultee. Exercise 9-1 provides an opportunity for the reader to implement such a process with a consultee.

Exercise 9-1
Applying the Knowledge and Skill Acquisition Model

Since consultation is so often initiated because of a crisis, it is often difficult to implement knowledge and skill development. One reason is that consultees may resist because they do not recognize the importance of this aspect of consultation. However, careful negotiation with the organization and systematic education about the goals and activities available through consultation can slowly overcome this resistance. The second source of difficulty may be harder to overcome because it involves the consultant. If the consultant has not used this sort of approach and/or is not comfortable with these types of data-gathering techniques, he or she will be less likely to try. This exercise provides an opportunity for the consultant to implement the process of knowledge and skill acquisition with a consultee.

Select a consultee who is interested in skill development and select an observation technique or questionnaire technique for gathering data about the environment in the consultee's work setting. Be sure to complete the entire skill development process, including the seven steps involved in goal development and the four involved in skill development. After the process is complete, use the following checklist to evaluate each component of the process. This evaluation can be used to determine how to implement this process next time.

Checklist: Knowledge and Skill Development Process

For each stage listed, rate your satisfaction with your performance (1, highly satisfied; 3, neutral; 5, highly dissatisfied)

Exercise 9-1
Applying the Knowledge and Skill Acquisition Model, Cont'd.

and comment on the key aspects of the process and changes you wish to consider.

I. *Negotiating contract* for knowledge and skill development in the absence of a crisis to stimulate a request for consultation.

    Rate your satisfaction:

    Key aspects and changes:

II. *Steps in goal development*

    1. Observing the consultee.

        Rate your satisfaction:

        Key aspects and changes:

    2. Asking consultee to estimate observation.

        Rate your satisfaction:

        Key aspects and changes:

Exercise 9-1
Applying the Knowledge and Skill Acquisition Model, Cont'd.

3. Providing feedback to consultee.
    Rate your satisfaction:

    Key aspects and changes:

4. Determining goals based on discrepancies between ob-
    servation and estimate.
    Rate your satisfaction:

    Key aspects and changes:

5. Determining goals based on discrepancies between ob-
    servations and consultee's ideals.
    Rate your satisfaction:

    Key aspects and changes:

6. When necessary, providing knowledge to the consultee
    based on the data currently available.
    Rate your satisfaction:

Exercise 9-1
Applying the Knowledge and Skill Acquisition Model, Cont'd.

Key aspects and changes:

7. Determining goals based on discrepancies between the observations and current expert knowledge.

    Rate your satisfaction:

    Key aspects and changes:

III. *Steps in skill development*

1. Consultant and consultee collaborate on specific plans to achieve the goals identified.

    Rate your satisfaction:

    Key aspects and changes:

2. Consultee roleplays key aspects of implementing the plan and receives feedback from the consultant.

    Rate your satisfaction:

    Key aspects and changes:

Exercise 9-1
Applying the Knowledge and Skill Acquisition Model, Cont'd.

3.   Consultee implements the plan in the work setting.

Rate your satisfaction:

Key aspects and changes:

4.   Consultant observes consultee in Step 3 and provides
corrective feedback.

Rate your satisfaction:

Key aspects and changes:

Development of Consultees' Personal Growth

The preventive goals of consultation can be served by facilitating the consultee's personal growth as well as developing
knowledge and skill. Although this goal is similar to two traditional foci of consultee-centered case consultation—lack of self-
confidence and lack of objectivity (see Caplan, 1970; Meyers,
Parsons, and Martin, 1979)—some important distinctions need
to be made.

The effects of the consultee's lack of self-confidence or objectivity were first considered systematically by Caplan (1970).
One key assumption for Caplan was that reduction of either of
these problems in a particular case will generalize to the con-

sultee's professional functioning in other situations. This approach can be valuable for enhancing the consultee's personal development. However, it is limited by being derived from a deficit model in which personal development is facilitated only for consultees experiencing a crisis related to a problem of lack of objectivity or lack of confidence. A proactive approach requires that consultants develop techniques to provide consultation that facilitates the personal growth of all consultees.

This section presents a framework for achieving this goal of promoting growth and thus serving the preventive aim of consultation. This framework considers two issues: (1) developmental stages of the consultee and (2) consultee stress.

Developmental Stages of the Consultee. Just as individuals, relationships, and groups have a developmental life cycle, one's professional development appears to pass through a series of specified stages, and theorists have begun to identify and describe the cycle of professional development. Katz (1977) has discussed this concept as it applies to the professional development of educators. We have found that the model outlined by Katz can be adapted and applied productively to any consultee, with useful implications for professional development. The following is a brief description of the developmental stages, adapted from Katz (1977).

During Stage 1, the *survival stage,* the consultee is concerned about the basic issues of professional survival in the work setting. During this period consultees are likely to be concerned with learning the ways performance is assessed; developing relationships with other staff members, particularly with key persons such as administrators; establishing clear professional routines that meet the stated demands of the role; and demonstrating to themselves and significant others that their performance is adequate. During this period discrepancies are frequently noted between the consultee's expectation of success and the realities of the job. Such discrepancies can intensify feelings of inadequacy, which interfere with personal/professional growth and may prevent the consultee from moving effectively to the later stages of professional development.

Stage 2, the *consolidation stage,* is approached once the

consultee has demonstrated basic competence at the fundamental requirements of the job. For example, a drug counselor/consultee needs to demonstrate an ability to relate effectively to clients, an adequate conceptual understanding of drug problems and counseling strategies, the capacity to intervene in a crisis, and the organizational skills to manage a schedule of appointments. The consolidation stage occurs as the consultee develops feelings of competence at such aspects of the job and becomes clear about the job skills he or she has developed. At this point, also, the consultee identifies the tasks and skills that need to be mastered next and begins working on these.

Stage 3, the *renewal stage,* is reached after the consultee has mastered the basic tasks and skills associated with the job. After some period of competent performance, the consultee is likely to become tired of doing the same old thing and will seek out something new. This search often takes the form of following recent developments in the field to learn new ideas and approaches.

Stage 4, the *maturity stage,* comes after the consultee has integrated the new ideas sought during Stage 3. As the consultee assimilates these new ideas, a modified approach to professional practice emerges. Once this new approach has been implemented to the degree that the consultee uses it confidently, the maturity stage is reached; the consultee begins to accept the point to which he or she has developed professionally. Although the consultee will continue to grow professionally, it is at this stage that a feeling of self-satisfaction develops about professional accomplishments and one's present professional role.

We believe that this or some similar model can be used to guide the consultant's efforts to facilitate personal growth among consultees. Awareness of these developmental issues enables the consultant to form a unique understanding of the consultee's situation. This understanding can be used to help the consultee develop insight that includes an understanding of one basis for the current work situation and to facilitate productive discussions among consultees about their feelings of competence and purpose in their professional life.

This framework can be used as an adjunct to general consultative contacts with consultees, and it is also promising as the basis for preventive consultation sessions with groups of consultees to promote personal growth. Consultees can fill out the Professional Stages of Development Survey in Exercise 9-2 to generate data for a group discussion of feelings surrounding their current professional functioning. This topic includes a consideration of their current developmental stage, how it compares with where they had hoped to be at this time in their lives, and what goals they can establish for the next year.

Exercise 9-2
Professional Stages of Development Survey

This survey can be used to help consultees grow personally and professionally by considering their current stage of professional development. The best way to learn about the use of this scale is to fill it out oneself. Fill out the survey with reference to your current professional situation; then use the completed survey as a basis for initiating a discussion with a colleague. After the discussion, record process notes pointing to the experienced effects of participating in such a discussion. Such process notes may facilitate your empathic understanding of consultees' experience when this survey is used in your own consultation practice.

The survey asks the respondent to estimate the degree to which each statement accurately describes the issues and concerns currently experienced within his or her profession (1, very much; 2, much; 3, somewhat; 4, little; 5, not at all).

Stage 1: Survival

_____ I am trying to become clear about each of the job responsibilities and duties tied to my current post.

_____ I make a particular effort to perform competently in each area that is used to assess my performance.

_____ I want to demonstrate my competence to others.

_____ I want to develop new relationships with my colleagues.

_____ I am concerned about establishing professional routines that will help me accomplish the demands of my job.

Exercise 9-2
Professional Stages of Development Survey, Cont'd.

Stage 2: Consolidation

_____ I feel competent in each of my job-related tasks.
_____ I feel that I belong among my colleagues.
_____ I am beginning to identify areas for professional growth and skill development.
_____ I participate in continuing education experiences in order to upgrade myself in terms of status and salary.
_____ I participate in the voluntary in-service provided at work.

Stage 3: Renewal

_____ I have mastered all the basic skills and tasks associated with my job.
_____ I have been functioning at this high level of mastery for over a year.
_____ I am feeling tired of doing the same old thing in my job.
_____ I would be interested in taking on new job challenges.
_____ I am interested in learning new ideas that have been developed recently.
_____ I have begun experimenting with new approaches to my job.

Stage 4: Maturity

_____ I have integrated a variety of professional approaches into my work style.
_____ I have developed a successful approach to the performance of my professional duties.
_____ I am satisfied with the extent and quality of my professional accomplishments.
_____ I feel that my contributions will have an impact on my profession and work setting.

Stress Management. A second significant way to promote consultees' personal growth is by increasing their ability to identify and manage stress. It is unnecessary to document that stress is a dominant factor in society today. Demands from our jobs, our families, and the ever-changing and problem-fraught environment are the material of which stress and stress overloads are made. Consultees, by the very nature of their overdemanding, underresourced jobs, are targets for stress overloads and burnout. Consequently, personal and professional growth can be facilitated by (1) minimizing the environmental factors that create stress for the consultee, (2) minimizing the effects of stress on the consultee, and (3) strengthening the consultee's capacity to cope with stress.

There is a vast body of literature describing stress reduction techniques (for example, Jacobson, 1938; Wolpe, 1958; Rachman, 1968; Bernstein and Borkovec, 1973; Goldfried and Davison, 1976; Hartman, 1976). We have found stress reduction an effective preventive goal in work with groups of consultees. Helping consultees identify signs of stress and stress overload (see Exercise 9-3) is often the first step toward providing the

Exercise 9-3
Stress and Its Manifestations

Stress is something that each of us experiences daily. We cannot avoid stress, but our hope is to reduce its negative effects on our psychic and physical systems. Stress can keep us alert and provide a certain amount of energy for daily functioning, but excessive amounts lower our ability to solve problems and to function physically, often resulting in general dissatisfaction. To identify excessive stress build-up or overload, ask yourself whether any of the following items currently describes your own state.

Fatigue. Do you feel excessively tired much of the time? Are you weary for no apparent reason? Do you experience diffuse aches and pains, particularly in your back, neck, and head?

Heart Irregularities. Have you noticed your heart beat fast or loud? Does it appear to flutter or skip a beat?

Respiration. Do you find your breathing to be shallow and short? Do you find yourself breathing rapidly and excessively without having experienced physical exertion?

Digestive Disturbances. Have you experienced diarrhea, pains, nausea, or vomiting without a specific cause such as flu or food poisoning?

Orientation. Have you found yourself having trouble fo-

Exercise 9-3
Stress and Its Manifestations, Cont'd.

cusing? Orienting yourself? Not sure what you are supposed to be doing or where to go next?

Sleep Disturbances. Do you have trouble falling asleep or staying asleep? Do you wake up in the night, unable to fall back to sleep? Are you often too keyed up to sleep?

Mood. Have you been irritable? Moody? Feeling down? Overwhelmed? Uncontrollably angry?

Eating. Have you recently lost or gained weight without trying or dieting? Do you have difficulty swallowing your food? Have you generally lost your appetite? Do you have cravings?

needed direction for personal growth and increased facility for stress management. We have found that the use of a survey such as that in Exercise 9-4 enables the consultee to identify potential sources of stress. These two exercises are then used to stimulate discussion designed to heighten awareness about stress and its impact.

Exercise 9-4
Identifying Sources of Stress

As with a number of the previous exercises, one of the most effective ways to become familiar with this scale is to use it on oneself.

Complete the following survey with reference to your own job functioning. Then review your responses and develop a plan of action for reducing the stress related to your own job situation.

Consultee Stress Survey

For each statement, indicate the extent to which you experience stress in your professional role (1, not stressful; 2, mildly stressful; 3, stressful; 4, very stressful).

1.   Generally work is a stressful experience   1 2 3 4

Exercise 9-4
Identifying Sources of Stress, Cont'd.

2.	Clerical work and paperwork are too great	1 2 3 4
3.	My professional work suffers because of the number of interruptions	1 2 3 4
4.	Managing the behavior of the clients is a stressful part of my job	1 2 3 4
5.	It is difficult to obtain equipment that is necessary for my work	1 2 3 4
6.	I do not have sufficient input into decision making	1 2 3 4
7.	The specific steps for performing my role are prescribed too rigidly	1 2 3 4
8.	There is considerable destruction of property at this organization	1 2 3 4
9.	There is too much conflict with the administration	1 2 3 4
10.	The relatives of the client population often interfere with my professional functioning	1 2 3 4
11.	I am responsible for too many clients to perform at the best of my ability	1 2 3 4
12.	Too little time is available for me to plan ahead	1 2 3 4
13.	There are significant outside influences affecting my current stress level	1 2 3 4
14.	Other sources of stress I have identified are	1 2 3 4

One outcome of this type of discussion should be specific plans for steps that the consultees can take to reduce stress and/or its negative impact. It is the consultant's task to serve as a resource for such ideas. Providing consultees with progressive relaxation training (Bernstein and Borkovec, 1973), assertiveness training (Alberti and Emmons, 1974), rational-emotive training (Ellis and Harper, 1975), and quieting response training (Stroebel, 1978) can help reduce the impact of stress. Further, helping consultees develop behavior management programs for improving diet, drinking, smoking, and exercising regimens and helping them establish effective time management procedures can facilitate their own reduction of significant sources of stress in their personal and professional lives.

Increasing Consultees' Professional Objectivity

As noted earlier in this chapter, the literature on consultee-centered consultation has devoted most of its attention to techniques for increasing consultees' professional objectivity. Although this approach is not usually relevant, it sometimes is. In such instances techniques for increasing professional objectivity can be a powerful approach to intervention.

Our earlier work (Meyers, Parsons, and Martin, 1979) criticized Caplan's approach to lack of objectivity for addressing a narrow range of problems and for promoting the use of indirect, rather than direct, confrontation techniques. At that time we argued that a broader range of consultee conflict areas that can be operationally defined is needed and that carefully used approaches to direct confrontation are preferable to the indirect techniques Caplan suggests.

We believe that a consultant attempting to increase a consultee's objectivity needs two sets of skills: The consultant must know, first, how to assess the consultee to determine whether lack of objectivity is a problem and, second, how to discuss this issue so that defensiveness is not generated and the confrontation is productive.

Assessing Lack of Objectivity. The consultant can determine whether lack of objectivity is a factor by assessing the *process of interaction* shown by the consultee and the *content of the statements* the consultee makes. When either of these factors suggests that lack of objectivity, or professional distance, affects the consultee, the consultant may choose to discuss this with the consultee. This decision should be based on the nature of the consulting relationship, its stage of development, the nature of the presenting problem, and the consultee's emotional state.

The process of interaction exhibited by the consultee is assessed by carefully observing the consultee's interaction style during the consultation interview. Significant changes in verbal or nonverbal style suggest the possibility of lack of objectivity about the issue being discussed. The consultant can look at such nonverbal factors as eye contact, body posture and positioning, nervous movements or muscular tension in some part of the body (hands, jaw, and so forth). Verbal factors that can be observed include rate of speech, stuttering or hesitation, sudden changes in topic, stereotyped or rigid thinking, and statements by the consultee that are extremely vague or only tangentially related to the consultant's previous statement. To confirm that lack of objectivity is an issue, the consultant could systematically change the topic of conversation so as to stimulate the recurrence of the behaviors identified as symptomatic of lack of objectivity.

Direct Confrontation. As noted earlier, confrontation is not synonymous with attack but, rather, should be viewed as an invitation to look at a point of concern between two persons in communication. In Chapter Four we offered guidelines for promoting facilitative confrontation. When faced with a consultee showing lack of objectivity, the consultant must be all the more ready to use appropriate confrontation skills.

Caplan (1970) suggested that indirect confrontation techniques be used because he believed that direct confrontation would break down the consultee's defenses, making the consultee vulnerable and resentful of the consultant. Our position, as noted in Chapter Four, is that when confrontation damages a relationship, it was used inappropriately. When introduced skillfully, confrontation is a constructive and even supportive technique that does not break down defenses or destroy relationships. For confrontation to achieve the desired benefits, the consultant must have the skills (1) to determine whether the relationship is sufficiently well established to withstand direct confrontation, (2) to present key issues in a tentative, descriptive manner that invites the consultee to disagree with, agree with, or modify the statement, and (3) to point out contradictions in the consultee's verbal or nonverbal behaviors.

To assess the strength of the relationship, the consultant needs to consider several factors: To what extent has the con-

sultee responded freely to the consultant's questions? To what
extent has the consultee presented his or her own ideas, even
when these differed from the consultant's? Has the consultee
felt free enough to explore a variety of issues concerning his or
her professional role? How frequently has the consultant been
accurate when making summary, empathic statements? Finally,
to what extent does the consultee express resistance during consultation? The resistance scale in Exercise 9-5 assesses this last
factor.

Exercise 9-5
Assessing Resistance to Consultation

The following scale can be used, in conjunction with
tapes or transcripts of consultation sessions, to assess resistance
to consultation. For purposes of professional growth, consultants should routinely audiotape their consultation sessions. Resistance can then be assessed by using the following scale on
ten-minute samples from the taped session. Direct confrontation
of the consultee's resistance may be counterproductive under
conditions of high resistance. Under these conditions it is suggested that the consultant assume that a mistake was made in
the process of consultation and that he or she needs to move
backward in the relationship. For example, if you are at the intervention stage, you should redefine the problem or renegotiate the contract to ensure reestablishment of a collaborative
relationship focused on the correct problem. When resistance is
low, it is more likely that you can use direct confrontation.

It is important to note that resistance should not be assessed during a segment of the tape in which lack of objectivity
is exhibited, since the signs of lack of objectivity can overlap
with the signs of resistance.

Consultee Resistance Scale

This scale can be used with the audiotape of consultation
that you have been using with the text. It might help to assess a
portion of the tape in which you think resistance was evidenced.

Exercise 9-5
Assessing Resistance to Consultation, Cont'd.

Identify the frequency of each category of resistance noted below by rating each consultee statement in the audiotape.

1. *Withdrawal.* Rejecting the relationship. Openly expressing the desire to terminate the relationship. Questioning the value of the relationship as a whole.

2. *Verbal attack.* An open verbal attack on the consultant, the consultant's manner, or the consultant's technique. Any consultee statement that criticizes the consultant directly.

3. *Disagreement.* Any consultee statement that argues or disagrees with consultant's statements. Overt disagreement about a recommendation, interpretation, or statement made by the consultant. Limited to arguments focused on what the consultant says—not verbal attacks on the consultant as a person.

4. *Qualified agreement.* Statement in which the consultee qualifies the extent to which he or she agrees with the consultant. The statement reflects only partial agreement. The statement begins with "Yes, but . . ." (or this is implied).

5. *Failure to respond.* Failing to respond to a question or lead of the consultant. The response is reflected by comments that either state or imply "I don't know," "I'm not sure," and the like.

6. *Tangential responses.* Responses not clearly related to the consultant's lead or question. The consultee introduces a new and unrelated topic.

7. *Vague responses.* Nonspecific, vague consultee statements. The statements may be either wordy or short and non-elaborated. The key factor is that the response cannot be understood clearly.

In theory it is easy to present observations or ideas in a tentative manner, but it is sometimes less easy in practice, given the consultant's belief in the validity of his or her ideas. Tentative confrontations can be made by phrasing the confrontation as a question: "Do you think this suggests that your anger influences your professional decisions with this client?" Similarly, starting a confrontation with a mild disclaimer, such as "I'm not certain, but . . . ," may signal the tentative nature of the observation so that it will be received more productively.

The last important skill necessary for successful, productive confrontation is to be able to point out contradictions in the consultee's verbal and nonverbal statements. When this is done in a tentative manner, describing the contradiction rather than judging or blaming, the consultee will most likely perceive the confrontation as an invitation for self-exploration. It must be reiterated, however, that the most wonderful intentions will not make confrontations productive or facilitative if the consultant fails to possess the essential relationship-building and communication skills already described (see Chapters Two through Five).

✧ CHAPTER TEN ✧

Working to Prevent Problems Systemwide: Level Four

Judged by preventive potential, service to the system offers the most promise as an approach to consultation. In fact, because of its capacity to have broad effects on the system and thus reach all current and future clients, Level IV consultation is our first choice for intervention.

Elsewhere we have reviewed the theoretical influences that form the historical roots of this approach (Meyers, Parsons, and Martin, 1979). These influences include Lewin's field theory, McGregor's Theory X and Theory Y, and the work begun by the National Training Laboratories. Our bias is that people at all levels of the organization should participate in decision making, planning, and problem solving. Too often we have seen hierarchal, authoritarian organizations, with one-way communication from the administration *down* to the staff and with no opportunity for staff input into decision making. The unfortunate result is what Argyris (1970) calls "adaptive antagonistic activities," such as absenteeism, staff turnover, union militance, apathy, alienation, and goals that are solely monetary.

Service to the system has several purposes: to increase awareness of the current nature and status of the system (for example, "X" or "Y"); to identify factors maintaining the current status; to identify alternative natures/statuses for the system and the means of achieving these; and finally, to facilitate the system's capacity to pursue the first three of these goals on a continuing basis.

This chapter will present the skills necessary to provide service to the system, including some sample techniques we have found useful. There is an extensive body of literature in the area of organizational consultation, and space will not permit us to delineate all the techniques that have been described. The interested reader is encouraged to pursue a variety of sources describing additional theories and techniques that can be useful for the systems-oriented consultant (for example, Beckhard, 1969; Bennis, 1969; French and Bell, 1973; Gallessich, 1982; Huse, 1975; Meyers, Parsons, and Martin, 1979; Schein, 1969; Schmuck and Miles, 1971; Schmuck and others, 1972).

A Framework for Understanding Organizations

To assess organizations and intervene effectively, the consultant needs an operational framework to conceptualize how organizations function. Several frameworks have been discussed in the literature (for example, Alderfer, 1980; Friedlander, 1980; Moos, 1974a). We present here an eclectic model that culls key issues from the literature and has proved useful to us in practice. The entire framework is not necessarily used each time we wish to determine the appropriate assessment or intervention techniques for Level IV consultation. Instead, one or more aspects of the framework are usually emphasized in a given case. According to this framework, systems can be viewed as entities composed of units which are actively interrelated and interdependent and which have a characteristic effect. Analysis of an organization entails identifying its characteristic elements, the structures and processes governing their interaction, and the forces affecting the system.

Elements of the System. One needs to consider all three components of the system: the *people* involved, the *physical* environment, and the *product* elements. From this perspective the people are identified as *individuals*. They can be either clients or staff, and each person brings unique values, skills, and orientations that contribute to the current functioning and climate of the organization. In considering the people element, it is important to recognize that these individuals are combined in a variety of *groups*. These groups, again, can include both clients and staff, and they flavor the climate of the system and its ability to be effective, through the unique characteristics of the individuals making up the group.

Among physical elements that need to be considered, the physical plant, arrangement of materials, and use of space can have a profound impact on the system. As Edward Hall (1966) noted, space is often the "hidden dimension" affecting human interpersonal relations. Such factors as office space, availability of telephones, proximity to various elements in the system, and the type of equipment available can have major effects on staff functioning. Similarly, physical space, available resources, and degree of crowding can affect clients' behavior and attitudes.

The third important dimension of the system is product elements. The nature of the "product" of a system—for example, education, human services, tangibles—colors the system and affects its other elements. The demands on a system whose product is suicide prevention will necessarily differ from those on one whose product is the microchip. The nature of the product has obvious effects on who will use the system, how often it will be used, and what procedures and resources it needs to function effectively.

Structure and Processes. Systems differ in structure and operational characteristics. For example, whereas Christmas Toys, Inc., would be structured according to the market cycle of seasonal buying, a community mental health agency is organized in accordance with the values of the profession and the particular needs of the community. The structures and processes that emerge have far-reaching effects on the organization's climate and efficiency.

The structure of an organization consists of roles, norms, and channels for communication and decision making. Formal roles include status in the hierarchy of the system—for example, client, staff member, administrator. Often the range of formal staff roles is broad, including professional, paraprofessional, and nonprofessional roles. Each of these roles carries different expectations, responsibilities, and behaviors for the individual filling the role. What roles exist in the system, how they are structured in relation to one another, and how clearly they are defined can have a profound effect on morale and on productivity of the system.

Often informal roles are just as influential as formal roles. For example, frequently the real power in decision making rests with a professional staff member who has been in the system for a long time. Most of us have experienced an organization that really seems to be run by the secretary, rather than the administrator or professional staff.

The norms and values of the system can also have profound effects. For example, a system whose primary value is productivity, as measured by financial gain, number of products completed, or number of clients seen, will certainly influence its members' attitudes, behavior, and general functioning differently than will one in which the values include humanistic interpersonal relations. An organization's values are often reflected in its reward structure. What behaviors of staff members result in rewards, and what sorts of rewards are administered—money, professional recognition, freedom in the use of time?

The decision-making process and patterns of communication also have profound effects on the organization. For example, the authoritarian organization in which decisions are made by the upper administration with no input from staff is very different from the organization that is run more democratically. Similarly, morale and productivity can differ substantially depending on whether an organization has open, two-way communication between staff and administration. One-way communi-

cation flowing down from administration to staff can worsen
the climate of the organization.

Forces Affecting the System. A number of internal and
external forces may prove significant to the assessment of a system. Gallessich (1974) has differentiated among these "internal" and "external" forces and the "trajectory" of the system.
Internal forces include the factors discussed under "Structure
and Processes." This section will consider external forces and
the trajectory of the organization.

External forces are the factors external to the organization that have a significant impact on its functioning. One
example is the community advisory board, associated with
many organizations, which approves decisions about personnel,
budget, and professional philosophy. Neighborhood and community groups can have a significant impact, as can churches,
local and state politics, consumer groups, and government agen-
cies. These forces can influence the goals and philosophy of the
organization, as well as its structure and processes. For example, if the school board imposes a shift in educational philosophy from humanistic education to a "back to basics" approach, profound changes in the way a school functions will
follow. Similarly, a community advisory board can have profound effects on a community mental health center's policies
for reintegration of its clients into the community.

The trajectory of the organization is the third force that
must be considered. This factor concerns the history of the organization. Past trends in, for example, social issues, professional philosophy, staff morale, and the organization's source of
identity in the community, observed through a historical framework, are projected to the future in an effort to predict how
these factors will affect the organization.

The organizational trajectory can influence the consultant's approach. In one example, the consultant initially was
trying to help a community mental health center improve the
effectiveness of a satellite center. However, an examination of
the trajectory revealed a steady decrease in clientele over a five-
year period that had occurred because the neighborhood was
becoming industrialized. A careful assessment based on this in-

formation suggested that the most appropriate course of action was to help close down this satellite center, rather than trying to save it.

Data Collection Techniques

Consistent with the model of consultation presented throughout this book, the collaborative model of process is viewed as an essential component of success when assessing an organization. To gather valid, useful objective data about the system in a collaborative manner, the consultant must ensure that the consultee system has free choice in assessment and intervention and must develop and maintain internal commitment to change by the organization and its members.

A general rule for data gathering is to proceed from less structured to more structured methods (see, for example, Alderfer, 1968; Alderfer and Brown, 1972). This minimizes threat in the system and allows for increasingly specific assessment designed to answer hypotheses raised in earlier stages of assessment. Thus, the consultant can move from unstructured observation to individual interviews to focused observation strategies and finally to survey/questionnaire procedures. This guideline, however, does not mean a rigid sequence must be followed invariably. The consultant will not always use each of these assessment approaches, and sometimes there will be a good reason to change their order.

Unstructured Observation. To gather information about the climate, the feel, the daily working of the system, it is essential that the consultant become a participating member of that system. Consequently, the first forms of data collection are intended to produce minimal reactivity among system members. At the beginning, the goal of such unstructured observations is to develop a sense of the client in this system, with its unique structure and dynamics. The hope is that, having developed this sense, the consultant will begin to formulate hypotheses, which, in turn, will help to determine the next type of data required. Careful and prudent use of observational strategies, even at this informal level, can extend the knowledge base used to assess the system. Valid approaches for this level of analysis include naturalistic and participant-observation strategies, along with content analysis of existing system documents.

Because of the perceptual difficulties of becoming a good observer and trying to attend to everything, plus beginning to focus and hypothesize about relationships, some guidelines are needed. In a classic presentation on observation, William Stern (1930) presented guidelines for the inexperienced observer. By blending his ideas with some of our own, we have developed the following guidelines for observation.

- Make a clear distinction between what you actually see or hear and the conclusions you draw from it. Distinguishing fact and opinion is essential, yet often difficult.
- Be empathic in your conclusions; that is, try to interpret what you observe from the viewpoint of those involved rather than imposing your own standards and professional biases. Such empathic interpreting requires that you become assimilated into the system and feel its pressures, trajectory, and unique profile, while remaining a neutral, objective observer.
- Draw no conclusions that cannot be verified by the data you gathered. It is certainly acceptable to speculate and hypothesize about what the data may mean, but it is important to keep these hypotheses distinct from the observational conclusions, which can be verified empirically.
- Take prodigious notes. What might appear insignificant may later appear to be the missing link. So record everything and in as much detail as you can.
- When notetaking, try to separate out what you observe from what you think and feel, by listing separately your own reactions to the events or situations.
- Where possible, gather examples, quotations, and products that will clarify and support your conclusions.
- Treat the information as confidential and respect the right of privacy of those you observe.
- Familiarize yourself with the ethical standards of your professional organizations, particularly those pertaining to research with human subjects.

Exercise 10-1 provides a structured learning activity that will enable you to practice these guidelines.

Exercise 10-1
Unstructured Observation

Select a local fast-food restaurant and, after placing your order, sit and unobtrusively observe the events of the workers involved with the counter and customers. For fifteen minutes keep careful notes of what goes on, including the interactions, conversations, "system climate," and anything else that you feel would help a second party to picture the workings of the system.

To check for the influence of subjectivity, ask a coworker to lunch (perhaps you'll have to pick up the bill!) and ask your coworker to observe the same section or work unit at the same time as you do. After the observation period, compare your observations. Consider such questions as "How did we differ?," "What did one of us miss?," "How was the same recorded event presented—similarly, differently?," and "How would a third party's impressions of this sytem differ should the person read my data or my coworker's?"

Survey Techniques. Surveys are among the most efficient ways to gather a great deal of data for organizational diagnosis. They permit the consultant to gather data from many more members of the system than would be practical with observation or interview, and the anonymity they offer gives respondents more freedom to provide valid information about sensitive topics than direct observation or interview. Consequently, we use survey techniques as part of the assessment almost every time we do Level IV consultation.

Generally survey techniques are used as the second step in assessment, after informal, anecdotal observations have been used to raise hypotheses about the organization. The survey is formulated on the basis of these hypotheses to gather more specific information from the entire organization. The results provide a broad data base for some tentative conclusions, which can be followed by more intensive data gathering (interview) as well as more specific approaches to assessment (focused observation techniques).

Numerous survey techniques are available, and the interested reader is encouraged to examine the sources cited earlier. One measure we like to use is the Community Oriented Programs Environment Scale (Moos, 1974a). This scale, designed for use with human systems organizations, is valuable because it provides data on ten separate factors shown to relate to the success of various organizations: involvement, support, spontaneity, autonomy, practical orientation, personal problem orientation, anger and aggression, order and organization, program clarity, and staff control. Moos (1974a, p. 231) has defined these subscales as follows.

1. *Involvement.* How active members are in the day-to-day functioning of their program.
2. *Support.* The extent to which members are encouraged to be helpful and supportive toward other members and how supportive staff are toward members.
3. *Spontaneity.* The extent to which the program encourages members to act openly and to express their feelings openly.
4. *Autonomy.* How self-sufficient and independent members are encouraged to be in making decisions about their personal affairs (what they wear, where they go) and in their relations with staff.
5. *Practical orientation.* The extent to which members' environment orients them toward preparing for release from the program. Such things as training for new jobs, looking to the future, and setting and working toward goals are considered.
6. *Personal problem orientation.* The extent to which members are encouraged to be concerned with their personal problems and feelings and to seek to understand them.
7. *Anger and aggression.* The extent to which a member is al-

lowed and encouraged to argue with members and staff, to become openly angry, and to display other aggressive behavior.

8. *Order and organization.* The importance of order and organization in the program in terms of members (how they look), staff (what they do to encourage order), and the physical facilities (how well they are kept).

9. *Program clarity.* The extent to which members know what to expect in the day-to-day routine of their program and the explicitness of the program rules and procedures.

10. *Staff control.* The extent to which the staff uses measures to keep members under necessary control (for example, in the formulation of rules, the scheduling of activities, and the relationship between members and staff).

An additional reason we like this scale is that there is a growing research base for its interpretation. Nevertheless, we sometimes modify it. One reason is that the full form consists of 100 items—a little too long to ensure staff cooperation in some settings, so that the 40-item short form is often a desirable alternative. Moreover, there are times when the specific consultation needs of the organization are best served by modifying the scale. For example, the modified version that follows was designed to assess the organizational functioning of a group-home program run by a neighborhood community association. The scale was designed to be administered only to the staff. Discussion with the administration revealed an interest in certain questions not covered explicitly by the original scale. Consequently, the scale was revised with these considerations in mind. Seven of the original ten subscales were omitted (Spontaneity, Autonomy, Personal Problems, Practical Orientation, Program Clarity, Staff Control, and Anger/Aggression), and four new ones were added (Staff Time and the Program, Rules, Conflict among Staff, and Communication and Problem-Solving Patterns of Staff). In addition, descriptive questions were included that asked for strengths and weaknesses of the existing management system. Item numbers are presented so the reader can reconstruct the sequence of items.

Item #	Scoring Direction	

Staff Time and the Program

1	F	Too often residents are left alone.
8	T	The staff makes optimum use of its time with residents.
15	T	There are clear and meaningful goals for each resident.
22	F	Instructional goals are rarely attained.
29	T	Staff and administration agree on goals for the residents.

Order and Organization

2	T	Activities are carefully planned.
9	T	This is a very well-organized program.
16	T	The staff makes sure that this place is always neat.
23	F	Things are sometimes very disorganized around here.

Rules

3	T	If the residents break a rule, they know what the consequences will be.
10	T	The program rules are clearly understood by the residents.
17	T	Everyone knows who's in charge here.
24	F	Too often consequences are not administered consistently.
30	F	People are always changing their minds here.
32	F	There are often changes in the rules here.
34	T	It is important to carefully follow the program rules here.
36	T	The staff makes and enforces all the rules here.
38	F	Too often punishment is administered too strongly.

Item #	Scoring Direction	

Conflict Among Staff

4	F	Some of the staff often criticize or joke about other staff.
11	F	Staff sometimes argue openly with each other.
18	F	Staff members often gripe.
25	T	Staff members and aides work together with optimum productivity.

Communication/Problem-Solving Patterns of Staff

5	T	The staff is expected to take leadership here.
12	F	The administration tends to discourage criticism and/or questions from the staff.
26	T	The administration almost always acts on staff suggestions.
31	T	The staff here is strongly encouraged to be independent.
33	T	Administration changes as a result of input from the staff.
35	T	Organizational problems are usually solved by the administration based on input from the staff.
37	F	The administration is not open to input from the staff.
39	T	During staff meetings the staff members feel free to express their viewpoints.

Involvement

6	T	The staff puts a lot of energy into what they do.
13	T	This is a lively place.
20	T	The staff is proud of this program.
27	F	There is very little group spirit in this program.

Item #	Scoring Direction	
		Support
7	F	Staff has relatively little time to encourage residents.
14	F	The staff seldom helps each other.
21	T	Staff is very interested in following up.
28	T	Staff always compliments a resident who does something well.
40		Describe briefly the significant strengths of the behavior management system employed.
41		Describe briefly the significant weaknesses of the current behavior management system.

Interviews. The interview is used at all phases of consultation. For example, it is used at the beginning to develop clear goals for the organizational assessment. It is particularly useful as an intensive follow-up to other approaches, and we generally include it as the third stage of assessment, providing follow-up to survey data. Used in this capacity, the interview provides feedback on the data gathered from the organization as a whole and provides a basis for formulating specific hypotheses.

We have developed a checklist as a guide to structure the interviews we do and to ensure that significant issues are covered. The checklist appears in Exercise 10-2.

Exercise 10-2
The Systems-Oriented Interview

Recall the last time you met with an administrator to discuss organizational factors. Remember the interview in as much detail as you can. (If you have not done such an interview recently enough, initiate one as a part of your job or with an administrator you know nonprofessionally.) Once you have recalled the interview in detail, read through the following checklist. Note which aspects of the checklist you covered and which you failed to cover. Then consider whether there are any changes

Exercise 10-2
The Systems-Oriented Interview, Cont'd.

you would make if you were to conduct the interview again. One final part of the exercise, though difficult to achieve, can be quite educative: Return to the administrator interviewed and reintroduce the topics missed in the first interview. Should this last part be possible, consider how these new factors add to your insight about the system.

Checklist for a Systems-Oriented Interview

1. If it has not been achieved, negotiate a clear contract regarding the focus of organizational consultation. Define the consultation request below.
2. Focus interview on the various *elements* of the system.
    a. People (unique values, skills, orientations, roles, groupings).
    b. Physical elements (space analysis, arrangement of materials and personnel, unique physical characteristics).
    c. Product (what is the product, what special requirements exist, how are supply and demand balanced, and so on).
3. Focus interview on *structures* and *processes* of the system.
    a. Formal and informal roles enacted (leader, antagonist, maintainer, tension reducer, information processor, gatekeeper, and so on).
    b. Norms (formal and informal rules of behavior and interaction).
    c. Communication pattern (one- or two-way; circular, chained, and so forth).
    d. Decision making (authoritarian, democratic, consensus, abdication, and so forth).
    e. Reward structures.
4. Focus interview on the *forces* affecting the system.
    a. Internal forces (exclude factors covered above; focus on climate, mood, satisfaction, and trust levels).
    b. External forces.
    c. Trajectory.

Focused Observation. Numerous observation techniques that focus on some specific aspect of the system are available to facilitate the last phase of assessment. Not all these specific strategies can be reviewed here; the interested reader is referred to the sources cited on page 182.

The technique illustrated in Exercise 10-3 is particularly useful in assessing organizations with communication problems.

Exercise 10-3
Observing Organizational Communication

The next time you attend a staff meeting, take a passive role so that you can sit back and observe. Use the scale reproduced here as a basis for observing the communication patterns in the staff meeting. The scale is designed to assess such features of communication patterns as the frequency of statements made by individuals. For this tool a statement is defined as a word or series of words uttered by one person which begins after the previous speaker stops talking and which ends when or before the next speaker begins talking.

Communication Observation Scale

Person Speaking	Person Spoken to				
	1	2	3	4	Entire Group
1		x(13)			
2			x		
3	x				
4					x

The numbered rows refer to who makes the statement; the numbered columns refer to who is spoken to. The last column, labeled "Entire Group," is used to record instances when the group is spoken to, rather than an individual.

Whenever a person makes a statement, an x is placed in the space corresponding to the row representing the person speaking and the column representing the person spoken to.

Exercise 10-3
Observing Organizational Communication, Cont'd.

In addition, when someone interrupts another speaker, an I is placed in parentheses next to the mark, with a number to indicate who was interrupted.

In the communication recorded in our sample, four statements were observed. Person two said something to person three; person three said something to person one; then person one interrupted person three while saying something to person two. Finally, person four said something to the entire group. Although the observation scale does not reflect the sequence of communication, it does provide the following kinds of data.

1. Frequency of speaking. In this example, person one = 1, two = 1, three = 1, and four = 1.
2. Frequency spoken to. For the example, speaker one = 0; two = 2; three = 1; four = 0; and the group = 1.
3. Interruptions (total = 1 for sample).
4. Frequency of interruptions by each person. For this example, speaker one = 1, the rest = 0.
5. Frequency each person was interrupted. Speaker three = 1, the rest = 0.

It is a useful follow-up to interviews and survey data because it provides objective data about the nature of communications within the organization. It is used to observe a subgroup of the organization in an activity such as a staff meeting. The system is fairly easy to use and to adapt to the particular situation under study. Its purpose is to determine (1) the frequency of statements made by each person, (2) who is spoken to most frequently, (3) the frequency of interruptions (both for the total group and for each individual in the group), and (4) who is interrupted most frequently.

Intervention Skills

Many intervention techniques have been cited in the literature. Rather than describe all of them, at the end of this chapter we will present, in detail, one intervention plan (force-field analysis) that we have found particularly useful in a variety of settings and with a variety of presenting problems. First we describe the steps in developing and implementing an intervention plan.

Steps in Developing Intervention Plans. The first step in this intervention model is to give the system and its members feedback about the data that have been gathered, providing them with increased understanding of their system. One well-known model for providing feedback is that built around the notion of the system as a family group (Bowers and Franklin, 1974). This model views the organization as made up of inter-related "family groups" that include supervisors and immediate subordinates. It prescribes that feedback occur in separate small-group meetings of peers in which hierarchal distinctions are omitted. The feedback sessions have three main objectives: to make the data public knowledge within the system, to develop consensus about the accuracy of the data, and to develop intervention strategies.

The next phase of intervention begins with elaboration and development of plans generated during the feedback session. These intervention plans are formulated collaboratively; both the consultant and the staff members attending the meeting should feel free to contribute ideas and reach consensus about the intervention plans. This is a crucial stage of consultation, since the consultant wants to be sure the members of the consultee system are actively involved in the process of developing plans so that they will feel "ownership" of these plans. Consistent with our emphasis on the preventive nature of consultation, the collaborative development of such intervention plans serves as a staff development procedure, moving the staff toward greater competence at developing plans on their own in the future. Therefore, although the consultant may need to contribute ideas, it is important that this be done tentatively, so that the consultant will not inhibit the staff from contributing actively during this stage.

The interventions developed can vary a great deal. They are dependent on the participants' active involvement, their creativity, the resources available within the group, and the facilitative nature of the group process. During this process the consultant needs to serve not only as an expert resource but also as a group facilitator, maximizing the productivity of the group by facilitating effective interaction (for example, reducing dominance by one member, withdrawal, or noninvolvement). The consultant acts as a checks-and-balances system to ensure that the interventions developed are tied directly to the diagnostic data gathered during the assessment phase. The Checklist for a Systems-Oriented Interview (see Exercise 10-2) provides an overview of factors that might be targets of interventions (elements of the system, structure and processes of the system, and forces affecting the system).

Three types of plans might be generated at this time: (1) gathering objective data in order to provide focused feedback for a particular unit of the organization (for example, gathering information on retirement plans or benefits packages for the personnel department), (2) intervention plans that can be implemented by existing personnel within the existing structure (for example, modifying meeting times or communication media), and (3) creating structural changes needed to promote the goals identified during assessment (for example, formally structuring a weekly discussion among key staff members or establishing a new staff position with responsibility for planning and development of new approaches).

1. *Gathering objective data* is sometimes a necessary part of intervention strategies. One of the most significant problems for many professional organizations is the lack of objective, nonevaluative data on the staff's functioning. Such data, when made available on a regular basis and in a nonevaluative manner, can facilitate optimum professional development and performance by the staff. One simple example is the increased accountability and efficiency that can result when individual units get quarterly feedback on the status of their budgets. Simple content analysis of expenditures often increases cost-effectiveness for a unit and the system as a whole.

Although survey techniques, interviews, and content analysis may be used to generate these data, direct observation is often needed for providing the kinds of data that can facilitate continued change—observation of communications at staff meetings, activity in sections of the library or lunchroom or time spent during breaks, for example.

2. *Interventions that can be implemented within the existing structure* are important because they can be implemented fairly readily. For example, leadership and communication issues can be dealt with by changing the conduct of staff meetings to provide for more staff involvement. Similarly, when confusion and ambiguity regarding role definitions exist, role clarification procedures, such as simply reviewing job definitions, can be implemented. For example, the relevant members of the organization can form a group in which the first step is for each group member to write notes to all the others about his or her role in the organization. The notes include statements about (1) one aspect of the person's role that is currently satisfactory and should stay the same, (2) one aspect of the person's role that is good but needs to be implemented to a greater extent, and (3) one aspect of the person's role which the person does not like and which should be reduced or eliminated. These notes are exchanged and read. A group discussion follows to answer any questions about the notes and to clarify the roles of members.

3. *Structural changes* in the organization may be among the most important interventions possible, because the structural change will facilitate continued implementation after consultation is complete. Inherent resistance to change by the organization makes structural changes difficult to accomplish. Consequently, they are generally not developed in their entirety at the initial plan-development meetings. Instead, a group of staff members can be made responsible for developing detailed plans for needed structural changes, along with recommendations for implementing them. The composition of this ad hoc work group is crucial to its success. The group should be selected carefully, with input from all relevant levels of the organization.

Once a series of intervention plans has been established, the consultant should begin to withdraw, leaving the responsibility for implementation with the consultee staff. The consultant must be sure *at least one person in the organization takes responsibility for implementing each intervention plan,* and that person must be identified as such. Then, when the consultant comes back for a follow-up, it is clear who should have overseen the implementation of each plan. Thus the system has a means of accountability, which will help to ensure success. It is not expected that each intervention will be working smoothly at the time of follow-up. However, with a built-in accountability system, the process of revising and improving the plans that have not worked will be more efficient.

Force-Field Analysis. Force-field analysis, a procedure derived from Kurt Lewin's field theory (Lewin, 1951; Lewin and others, 1941), is a good example of the type of intervention we do with organizations. It can be used with a large group, and we have found it helpful for the group to be composed of staff members from all hierarchal levels and organizational units. Generally we use force-field analysis after assessment data have been gathered and analyzed. Using it at this point maximizes the potential for effectiveness of the interventions developed.

The first step in the process is for the group to identify the problem they wish to work on. This step should involve a good deal of discussion in the group, because consensus about the significance of the problem to be addressed is important. To arrive at a problem definition, the consultant encourages the group members to offer ideas and jots these down where all can see them. When consensus on a problem statement is reached, the other ideas are disposed of, and the statement is displayed prominently.

The second step is to restate the problem as a goal for change. For example, the stated problem "Not enough communication among the staff" can be restated by indicating that the goal is to increase communication among the staff.

The connection of force-field analysis to Lewin's field theory is seen most clearly in its emphasis on identifying restraining forces and moving forces. Moving forces are forces in the environment that create pressure to accomplish the goal for change; restraining forces are aspects of the environment that inhibit achievement of this goal. According to this framework, a balance between these forces maintains the current status, and the goal for change can be achieved by upsetting this balance and increasing the power of the moving forces while decreasing the power of the restraining forces.

The third step in force-field analysis is to generate a list of moving forces. This is done through a brainstorming process in which the consultant has the members of the group suggest any possible moving forces. Members are encouraged to produce a variety of creative ideas. At this point there is no evaluation of the ideas; they are simply listed. When the group's ideas have been exhausted, an evaluation process is initiated. The entire list is reviewed, and the key moving forces are underlined after seeking consensus about the importance of each and the degree to which it can be manipulated by the organization. Depending on the problem, a single moving force may stand out, or there may be two or three that seem to have potential.

The fourth step is to generate a list of restraining forces. Again brainstorming is used to facilitate production of ideas without evaluation. The evaluation process will generally result in consensus that one to three of the restraining forces should be underlined.

The fifth step is to generate action plans for each moving force that was underlined. Creativity is needed in developing the list of action plans, so again brainstorming is used. For each moving force, the group generates as many action plans as possible. The same process is pursued in the sixth step, which is to generate action plans for each restraining force.

The seventh step is to evaluate the action plans and select those that will be implemented, by group consensus. Then, in the eighth step, these action plans are listed, along with the resources needed and the staff member who will be responsible for implementing each plan.

The ninth step is to determine how to evaluate the effectiveness of these action plans. It is important to try to develop a comprehensive evaluation while keeping in mind the practical limitations often found in attempting to implement such an evaluation strategy. This sets the stage for the tenth step, in which the consultant returns to provide follow-up. At this point the consultant helps to determine how successfully each plan was implemented by considering the evaluation criteria and talking with the staff member who was responsible for implementing the plan. At this time modifications are made in the action plan as needed.

Force-field analysis is learned best by seeing it in action. Exercise 10-4 will help to develop the reader's skills with the approach.

Exercise 10-4
Implementing Force-Field Analysis

Force-field analysis can be used to help a group solve an organizational problem. For this exercise, choose a group of which you are currently a member—a family group, work group, social group, or study group, for example—and practice using force-field analysis. The group chosen must have at least three members who are willing to allow you to practice with the technique.

The exercise should take between 60 and 90 minutes. It will prove most helpful if the group can consider a real problem, but it need not. The primary goal of this exercise is to help you develop the skills needed for using force-field analysis, rather than to resolve your group's work-related problem. Use the following checklist as a guide to the process.

Force-Field Analysis Checklist

1. Identify the problem.
2. State the problem as a goal for change.
3. Generate a list of moving forces, using a brainstorming or divergent Delphi process, and place checkmarks next to the key forces.
4. Generate a list of restraining forces and place checkmarks next to the key forces (again use one of the creative techniques, and remember to refrain from evaluating the suggestions initially).

Exhibit 10-4
Implementing Force-Field Analysis, Cont'd.

5. Generate as many action plans as possible for each of the
    moving forces that you checked.
6. Similarly generate action plans for each of the restraining
    forces that you checked.
7. Review the action plans from Steps 5 and 6 and select
    those that seem most promising.
8. In tabular form, list the action plans you have selected and,
    next to each, the resources needed for that plan and the
    person(s) responsible for implementing it.
9. Determine an evaluation plan.

An Example of Service to the System

An example will illustrate how assessment techniques and
intervention techniques can improve an organization's morale
and productivity. A neighborhood community association hired
a consultant to help its four group homes for retarded adults institute a new behavior management system. In an interview with
the director of the board, the consultant learned that behavior
management was a serious problem in these homes and had resulted in numerous community complaints. An agreement was
reached that consultation would consist of four steps: (1) conduct informal observations supplemented by brief interviews,
(2) working from the early observations, develop and administer
a survey to determine staff perceptions of the existing behavior
management system, (3) provide feedback to the staff about all
the data gathered, and (4) develop and implement a new behavior management system with input from the staff.

Global Assessment Approaches. Consultation began with
informal observations, which revealed a variety of serious problems in the interaction between the staff and the client population. There were no planned activities for the residents, whose
boredom often erupted into acting-out behavior. Often the residents were not treated with respect; they were frequently teased
by staff members. In one incident a retarded woman who also

had emotional problems was laughed at when she made a bizarre comment. Later, this same woman made inappropriate physical advances toward a male staff member. Instead of discouraging this behavior, the staff member responded with an unnecessarily seductive hug. When disruptive behavior occurred, there seemed to be inconsistent use of negative consequences and much yelling; however, there was no systematic use of rewards for positive behavior.

The anecdotal observations were supplemented by brief interviews with staff members, which suggested a set of unexpected additional problems. Staff members seriously disagreed over disciplinary strategies, and there was conflict between staff and administration. The administrator in charge of the group homes operated in an authoritarian manner, apparently seeking no input from the staff. She held staff meetings in which a series of boring directives was read and no staff input was sought. When staff members were late for meetings or work, their behavior was rated. No attention was paid to positive efforts by the staff. Moreover, this administrator made it clear that she sided with one of the two major groups involved in the staff conflict. This situation had recently exploded when an effort was made to fire a staff member from the faction that was not aligned with the administration. The result was that this group of staff members became militant in their opposition to the administration. Whenever they received a directive, they would passively resist or overtly rebel. Several times they had complained to the board of the neighborhood community association, and invariably the board had supported them at the expense of the administrator.

Focused Assessment. A survey was developed to administer to all staff members. It included a variety of questions focused on behavior management and on the system already in use at the group homes. Other questions (those in the adaptation of Moos's scale reproduced earlier in this chapter) concerned the overall program, morale, communication between staff members, and relations between staff and administration.

At least 80 percent of the staff perceived serious problems in communication patterns with administration and in conflict between staff members. At least 70 percent indicated substantial problems associated with low staff involvement—that is, poor morale. In addition, over 50 percent indicated substantial problems with use of staff time, order and organization, and implementation of rules. The descriptions of the behavior management system indicated that agreement among staff about important operational definitions was lacking and that these differences effectively resulted in enforcement of different sets of rules by different staff members.

Just before the survey was officially distributed, the consultant observed a staff meeting. The administrator did over 90 percent of the talking. When the staff raised questions, they were not answered, and the staff was never asked to give input.

Data Feedback and Intervention Plans. The data from the survey, as well as a summary of the earlier observations and interview data, were fed back to the entire staff. Throughout this process (which lasted for three one-and-one-half-hour sessions) the staff was asked to comment on the results presented so that consensus about the organization's problems could be reached. Several intervention plans resulted, which were implemented during the next year.

1. The administrator agreed to change the format of staff meetings, to reduce the boring paperwork, and to increase staff input into important decisions.

2. The staff agreed to hold several staff parties during the next year. These parties were to be held outside the group homes, with everyone invited.

3. The staff agreed to take complaints directly to the administrator rather than the board, and the director of the board agreed to turn any complaints over to the administrator so as not to undercut her authority.

4. The staff formed a committee to study rules and discipline and to develop a proposal for revising the behavior management system. The entire staff was freed for six half-days during a three-month period to work with the committee on this project.

5. The administrator retired. Although it was never confirmed that this occurred because of the staff conflicts, it did

occur two months after the data feedback sessions had been completed. The staff asked to have three representatives on the search committee looking for a replacement. This request was granted.

Summary of Effects. Several concrete results occurred. The staff did hold two parties over the next six months, and communication among staff members improved. Staff/administration relations also improved on several counts. The board no longer undermined the administrator's authority, and direct contact between the administrator and staff increased. The conduct of staff meetings also improved markedly. Not only did staff members have more active input, but they were happier about the meetings. Moreover, the six half-days, the input into hiring an administrator, and the presence of the organizational consultant were all viewed as strong signs of support from the administration and the board of the community association.

It was felt that the most important interventions had to do with the active role given to the staff in developing a behavior management system and in hiring a new administrator. These were both positive activities that forced the staff to work together on concrete projects with clear goals.

Evaluating the Process and Impact of Consultation

Evaluation of the consultation process and its impact is very often viewed by consultants and consultees as superfluous or as only tangential to the primary function of consultation. Further, evaluation is often perceived as requiring skills and knowledge usually reserved to the professional evaluator and thus outside the realm of the practicing consultant.

Evaluating the impact and process of one's consultation is presented here as not only an essential ingredient of all consultation but an unavoidable one. Evaluation can provide useful information for both the consultant and the consultee. The consultee can find out how the implementation of the procedures derived through consultation went and how well they worked. The consultant can check on the efficacy of the consultation intervention and his or her own consulting technique or process. The data collected can provide pragmatic justification for continuation of consultation as a service delivery model.

Despite the apparent benefits to be derived from evaluating the consultation process and outcomes, most consultants still resist including evaluation in their consultation practices. One reason is that evaluation often arouses concerns of judgment or evaluation of worth, as well as worries over "What did I do?," "Is it good?," and "What will happen to me as a result of this evaluation?" In this context evaluation is inevitably unpleasant to some degree. This discomfort can be reduced significantly if evaluation is thought of as constructive and is geared toward the needs of *both* those performing consultation and those being served by it.

A second source of resistance is the view that the scientific "rigor" required for valid evaluation belongs to the researcher, not the practitioner. Although evaluation does share many characteristics with research, a distinction should be made. The goal of research is to generate and confirm or disconfirm hypotheses about particular phenomena. This goal requires research to be highly focused and controlled in order to permit generalization to circumstances and events beyond those immediately studied. Although an evaluation program similarly hopes to gather data that will help to confirm the hypothesized intervention effect, the main concern is to gain insight into the workings of a consultation program and to determine the factors that seem to increase its positive impact. Unlike the researcher, the evaluator is concerned mostly with practical decisions about one particular program, occurring at one time and in one place. This focus deemphasizes the need to provide generalizable answers to basic theoretical questions or heuristic concerns.

Types of Evaluation

All too often those interested in evaluating the process, procedures, and impact of a program give consideration to evaluation only after such procedures have been formulated and implemented. Evaluation should not be limited to the end of the consultation process. Rather, evaluation of the consultant or consultee and the conditions surrounding the work-related situation is, ideally, an integral part of the entry, goal identification, and goal definition stages. Evaluation, as an ongoing consultative concern, often takes two forms: formative and summative evaluation. Both are critically important.

Formative Evaluation. Only recently, through the efforts of such theorists as Michael Scriven (1967), have formative procedures been acknowledged as an approach to evaluation. Formative evaluation is used at strategic points throughout the consultation interaction to assist in the ongoing decisions to continue or modify the presented intervention. Its purpose is to gather data that expedite decision making about the upcoming steps and procedures in the consultation or intervention process. Such evaluation provides the basis on which to better "form" the process for attaining desired outcomes. This formative element enables the consultant and consultee to identify their own assumptions and expectations about the consultation and its prevention procedures, to determine the success of their own individual contributions, and to find ways to improve their performance.

Formative evaluation can often be achieved by setting aside time in the consultative interchange for the consultee and consultant to "process," or discuss, the procedures used up to that point. Often an informal procedure such as asking consultees for their feelings about the plan or the progress of other aspects of consultation sessions will provide invaluable data for guiding the upcoming steps in the consultative relationship. As a tool for the formative improvement of an ongoing program, this type of evaluation should be conducted continually during consultation.

Although formative evaluation will often involve informal procedures such as the one just described, sometimes a more formal, systematic data-gathering process will be required. Because of their reluctance to use research strategies, consultants are often resistant to using formal approaches to formative evaluation. It is one extra step and often there is not time for it. Consultants would be more likely to use these procedures if clear guidelines and assessment techniques were more readily available. Table 6 and Exhibit 2 are designed to meet this need. Table 6 provides a list of guidelines for incorporating formative

Table 6. Formative Evaluation Checklist for Consultants.

Directions: For each stage of the consultation process, feedback and request for corrective feedback from institutional representatives and consultees are both appropriate and desirable. The checklist provides a broad framework from which to conceptualize the specific formative function to be used within your particular consultation relationship.

Name of Institution _____ Name of Consultee _____ Date of Initial Contact _____

Formative Issue	Entry	Consultation Stage			
		Goal Identification	Goal Definition	Intervention	Assessment
1. Record of contacts (record dates, length of sessions)					
2. Special focus of contacts— concerns emerging for later consideration					
3. Provide feedback to highest relevant administrator (acceptable direction, time line, cost tone)					
4. Request feedback from consultee: Expectations met? Specific concerns? New needs? Suggestions for modification of program? Consultant style? Or administrative details (meeting times, rooms, and so on)					
5. Stage-specific concerns	All relevant personnel contacted? Collaborative atmosphere? Relationship skills?	Agreement on level of entry? Optimal entry point? Possible recontact?	Consultee's skill; cooperation; Facility in data gathering/ reporting? Data complete?	Feedback to consultee on joint ownership? Consultee accept? Agree? Understand? Modifications? Joint agreement?	Outcomes? Inputs? Process? Design? Decision options? Assessment as collaborative effort?
6. Consultant's perception of process to date — new paths tried					

Exhibit 2. Consultee Satisfaction Form.

For each statement listed, check the one most appropriate response as it applies to the current consultative interaction. Your response is viewed as extremely important to the ongoing improvement and facilitation of the consultation program and to the consultant's professional growth. Thank you for your assistance.

	1 Strongly Agree	2 Agree	3 Dis- agree	4 Strongly Disagree

I. *Efficacy of Consultation*

The goal definition was accurate, complete, and sufficiently concrete

The data-gathering procedures provided the necessary data

The data-gathering procedures were easy to use

The intervention plan makes sense for my unique situation

The intervention plan has been easy enough to implement

The intervention plan has been effective to this point

II. *Consultant Expertise*

The consultant knows his or her "stuff"

The consultant is apparently versed not only in the subject matter but in the process of helping others

The consultant presents information and directions clearly

III. *Consultant's Administrative Abilities*

The consultant makes efficient use of time

The consultant is prompt in providing feedback

The consultant has efficiently distributed work assignments

IV. *Interpersonal Style*

The consultant is comfortable to talk with

The consultant is a good listener

The consultant is generally pleasant

(continued on next page)

Exhibit 2. Consultee Satisfaction Form, Cont'd.

	1 Strongly Agree	2 Agree	3 Dis- agree	4 Strongly Disagree
The consultant is self-expressive without being overpowering				
The consultant has encouraged me to be an active participant in the consultation process				
V. *General Comments* (regarding your likes, dislikes, recommendations for improving this and future consultations).				

evaluation into the consultation process. These guidelines reflect a number of the formative evaluation questions that can be asked at each stage of consultation. Note that these are meant as *guidelines* indicating the approaches to formative evaluation that the consultant *might* consider, not a rigid set of requirements that must be followed.

Even with the guidelines provided in Table 6, the consultant will not be likely to implement formative evaluation unless he or she has a specific idea of what to do. As noted previously, one straightforward approach is to ask for feedback informally. As a more formal data collection mechanism, one could consider survey tools such as the Consultee Satisfaction Form (Exhibit 2). This form enables the consultee to provide feedback on problem definition, data gathering, interventions, and characteristics of the consultant. The scale is presented in a general format, which the consultant may want to adapt.

Summative Evaluation. The consultant and consultee are typically interested in finding out what impact the consultation procedures have had. Although it is valuable for a consultant and consultee to periodically share their perceptions of the quality or efficacy of the relationship, the bottom line to be assessed is whether the goal has been achieved—sales increased, achievement improved, absenteeism reduced. Addressing this issue of goal attainment falls within the domain of summative evaluation.

The specific intent of a summative evaluation is to show that the program has reached its original objectives. This type of evaluation encourages those involved in the program to gather data that may be used later to demonstrate the value of consultation and the program(s) derived from it. These data are important for those who set policy and make decisions that affect the future of the program.

A summative evaluation generally addresses the following issues: Were the objectives attained? Can goal attainment be attributed to the consultation and the resulting strategies? What factors contributed to goal attainment and what factors inhibited it? What is the value of this intervention in contrast to alternative interventions? What influence has the consultation had on other programs or activities in the institution?

A Model for Evaluation by the Consultant

To perform effective evaluations, a consultant must be knowledgeable about (1) the processes entailed in performing the two types of evaluation (formative and summative), (2) the tools available, and (3) the design and administration of formative and summative evaluations. Because of the complex and dynamic nature of the consultation process and the varied contexts and techniques, adequate evaluation can be difficult to achieve. Here we provide a generalized model for evaluation that is adaptable to each consultant's available resources and conditions and applicable to intervention strategies in all four levels of service delivery discussed in Chapters Seven through Ten. This model can be used to perform either summative or formative evaluation.

Evaluation requires a clear idea of the particular consultation, its goals, and the techniques used to assess goal attainment. Our model facilitates the consultant's development of these ideas. Currently there is a trend among those engaged in evaluation to use competency-based approaches in which the program specifies goals, which are then used as the only basis for evaluating efficacy. Such an evaluation neglects the important ancillary effects that often occur. In reaction to this weakness of goal-based approaches, some evaluators use goal-free orientations, attempting to record and describe everything that occurs before and after the program, without concern for the goals. Noting the strengths and weaknesses of goal-based models, we have chosen an outcome orientation that includes elements of both goal-based and goal-free evaluation. In this model, outcomes are defined broadly to include not only the impact of the intervention on the specific target situation or program goal but also related impacts on the consultee organization and ancillary programs. In addition, this model incorporates formative and summative approaches to evaluation.

Step 1: Specifying Outcomes and Their Measures. The process of specifying the desired outcome of consultation and its intervention strategies is the same whether the focus is the client, the consultee, or the organization. An organizational goal might be "After the staff has participated in the four-week communication training workshop [the intervention strategy], statistically significant gains from pretest measures on the Person Orientation and Leadership Style scales will be noted for each participant [the goal]." A similar goal for a client (in this case a student) might be "Johnny will be able to spell correctly nine out of ten spelling words randomly selected from list A of the Holt spelling series." The process used to develop each of these outcomes has the same four phases: identification, specification, developing criteria and measurement techniques, and ratification.

1. *Identification.* The first step in developing outcomes for a consultation is to identify the possible outcomes of the program. These include the specific goals for which the consultation was contracted, along with possible ancillary effects of the consultation. During the identification process, the consultant must make sure that the identified outcomes reflect the organization's mission *and* the consultee's needs. For example, an objective of reducing the amount of calling out in class might appear appropriate to the mission and philosophy of the school yet be inconsistent with the needs of the teacher who has difficulty stimulating class discussion.

As the first step in the process of specifying outcomes, identification provides the broadest possible perspective on the outcomes. The next two phases (specification and developing criteria) provide increased specificity of outcomes. Thus, identification is a procedure for bringing to one's attention the variety of outcomes that may possibly be relevant to the evaluation. During this stage the consultant and consultee(s) brainstorm all possible impacts of consultation, including those directly or indirectly related to explicit program goals. During this brainstorming, it is important for the consultant/evaluator to make sure goals are identified that reflect all possible levels (client, consultee, and organization) and all possible behavioral domains (motoric, cognitive, affective).

2. *Specification.* Specification moves beyond the broad approach to outcomes taken in the identification phase to a more specific and goal-based approach. In particular, specification requires that outcomes must be measured. Outcomes are presented in behavioral terms, phrased in measurable or countable form, with the conditions under which these outcomes are expected to occur clearly depicted. The process of specification has been discussed under the stage of goal identification in Chapter Six. Specification skills are crucial to successful program evaluation. Exercise 11-1, designed to strengthen the consultant's specification skills, gives examples of both adequate and inadequate specification of program outcomes.

Exercise 11-1
Developing Outcome Statements

Part I lists a series of consultation outcomes. In Part II two of these outcomes have been written in completed form, incorporating behavioral referents, specific conditions of occurrence, and criteria for scoring. Review the sample outcomes listed and then attempt Part III. It is suggested that you discuss the examples and your responses with a peer for corrective feedback.

Part I: Listed Desired Outcomes

The following is a sampling of typical outcomes.

1. Increased worker productivity
2. Better communications

Exercise 11-1
Developing Outcome Statements, Cont'd.

3. Increased program efficiency
4. Higher-quality student achievement
5. Less organizational tension
6. [List your own consultation outcome]
7. [List a second consultation outcome of your own]

Part II: Examples of Inappropriate and Appropriate Outcome Specification

Inappropriate	*Appropriate*
1. After the film viewing, workers will show an increase in productivity. (Limitations: behavior not countable, criterion unclear)	After worker viewing of the film *Your Company, Be Proud,* the per diem production total will increase from 15 per worker to a minimum of 18 and be maintained for at least 10 consecutive days.
2. After participation in a communication workshop, school chairpersons will show better communications with staff. (Limitations: Under what conditions will the improvement be shown? What defines "better"? How must the effect be registered to be considered an occurrence?)	After participation in "Project Open Lines," a two-week interpersonal training laboratory given to the school's five chairpersons, faculty perceptions of chairpersons' willingness to discuss ideas will be increased by at least 10 points on the Faculty Evaluation Scale and will remain at this 10-point or better gain over three consecutive administrations (Feb. 1, Apr. 1, June 1).

Part III: Improving Outcome Statements

Rewrite the following to include the elements required for appropriate outcome statements.

Exercise 11-1
Developing Outcome Statements, Cont'd.

1. Shifting budgetary responsibility to the departmental level will reduce administrative costs for marketing and item production (Focus on criteria for "reduce" and what constitutes an acceptable outcome).
2. Use of a programmed text will increase student reading scores.

3. *Developing criteria and measurement techniques.* After identification and specification of outcomes, the next task is to develop criteria and methods for defining the effectiveness of consultation. What constitutes success or failure is situation-specific and thus cannot be determined by a simple formula. The consultant needs to make decisions about the use of norm-referenced tests, criterion-referenced tests, existing records, simulated activities, and observational approaches as methods for assessing the effectiveness of consultation.

Some outcomes can be assessed with *standardized, norm-referenced tests.* For example, when success in reading is defined as achievement at a particular grade level, clients' reading levels can be compared against national norms by using standardized tests. Many outcomes do not lend themselves to norm-referenced measures, however, and then criterion-referenced procedures should be used.

A *criterion-referenced procedure* assesses the outcome in terms of some fixed standard, rather than in comparison to the performance of others as in norm referencing. The evaluator identifies the minimal acceptable performance level, which serves as the criterion for goal attainment. For example, a supervisor in a sheltered workshop uses a criterion-referenced procedure when he notes whether a client can correctly place a nut on a bolt. Similarly, the salesperson who can demonstrate competence in presenting her rehearsed sales pitch is performing up to a criterion of 100 percent accurate recital.

A second consideration to be addressed is whether new tools for evaluation even need to be developed. Often direct impact on the targeted problem area can be assessed by *analysis of existing agency or organizational records.* The consultant with an inventive mind can translate many of the objectives of the consultation into forms that can be assessed using available records. The advantages of using existing records for evaluation have been fully described by Webb and others (1966) in their chapters on archival records. These authors noted that the primary advantage is that existing records allow "unobtrusive" evaluation and are therefore nonreactive to the evaluation process. Such an approach has been used in evaluating consultation. Stephenson (1973) used information from a variety of records to demonstrate the effects of four years of mental health consultation to a child and family welfare agency. Referral records were examined for a change in percentage of cases referred to an outside psychiatrist. Attendance of the children from the agency at a local emergency department was compared with attendance from another child welfare agency. Requests from the agency for the different types of consultation were tracked, as well as time spent, in order to note whether the number and kind of requests changed.

Another means of outcome assessment, *direct observation,* is especially apt when the outcome involves the consultee's behavior. Although this may be too time-consuming for the consultant/evaluator to do, there are others who can conduct this assessment, and this is particularly feasible when observation is a natural part of the other person's role (for example, supervisor, some peers).

Flaherty (1979) has suggested several steps to maximize the likelihood of gathering valid data. Flaherty recommends that the consultant (1) ensure that the behaviors rated are directly related to the objectives of the program, (2) check that they are defined as concretely as possible, (3) establish a procedure for rating them that will discriminate the degrees to which the behaviors appeared (for example, all the time, most of the time, some of the time), (4) ensure that the raters are unaware of objectives so that the observation will be unbiased, (5) use coraters as a validity check on rater bias, (6) require the raters to rate others not participating as a method of controlling for rater set in rating, and (7) arrange for at least two ratings in a pre-post intervention design.

Direct observation of the consultee's behavior is often inconvenient and too time-consuming, given the demands on both the consultee and consultant. An alternative to direct, *in vivo* assessment is the use of *simulations,* which provide conditions similar to the job-related situation and require the consultee to roleplay his or her response. By observing the consultee's roleplay before and after intervention, the consultant can observe change or lack of change in the behavioral dimensions deemed important to the program's objectives. This method is particularly effective in evaluating interventions to increase consultees' skill or knowledge base, as in hotline or crisis intervention teams, human relations training, and teacher training.

Roleplay may be felt to be inappropriate to the nature of the consultee or the organization, or it may elicit extreme anxiety, thus proving unproductive. In such situations the evaluator might provide simulated experiences through paper-and-pencil techniques. Parsons, Stone, and Feuerstein (1977) used one such approach to assess the effectiveness of an in-service training workshop for teachers aimed at reducing dysfunctional attitudes and beliefs about students. Exhibit 3 shows excerpts from the simulation used.

Exhibit 3. Excerpts from Paper-and-Pencil Simulation Used to Test Impact of In-Service Training on Teachers' Rational Beliefs.

In each of the following cases you are presented with a typical situation you may have experienced in your years of teaching. Read the following scenarios and check *the* response that you feel most closely approximates how you would respond. We are asking that you be honest and respond as you feel you would under those conditions rather than responding the way you feel you *should.*

Pretest Sample Item

Mr. Hawkes, a first-year teacher who teaches the "worst" fourth grade, is anxiously awaiting his first evaluation by his supervisor. Hoping to impress the supervisor, Mr. Hawkes attempts to "control" the class so that they are "good." Once the supervisor enters the room, however, the children respond "typically" by being nonattentive and disruptive and generally pulling Mr. Hawkes away from his well-prepared lesson. As Mr. Hawkes, you would

a. feel very upset and angry with the children and punish them severely once the supervisor left.

(continued on next page)

Exhibit 3. Excerpts from Paper-and-Pencil Simulation Used to Test
Impact of In-Service Training on Teachers' Rational Beliefs, Cont'd.

---

   b. become extremely anxious about your ability to teach and begin to consider another profession.
   c. feel that although things did not go as you had hoped, you did
the best you could under the circumstances.
   d. seek out the supervisor and attempt to offer explanatory ex-
cuses for your poor performance.
   e. feel that nobody could have done any better.
   f. other (explain).

Posttest Sample Item

   Ms. Johnson, the math teacher, had just finished presenting her
elaborate development of an example pointing to a particular math proof
when Johnny, her star pupil, raised his hand to suggest a much simpler,
clearer solution. As Ms. Johnson, you probably would
   a. say, "Pay attention, this is the proper way. We are doing it this
way!"
   b. praise Johnny for his creativity and math insight.
   c. have Johnny present his proof and then discuss the two methods.
   d. ignore him.
   e. (although you had not thought of the solution) say, "I was
about to give that solution after presenting the more elaborate proof."
   f. other (explain).

Source: Adapted from Parsons, Stone, and Feuerstein (1977).

Caplan (1970) reported a similar use of simulated situations to evaluate a three-year consultation program for public
health nurses. A fictitious case record was created, involving
two families presenting a large variety of health problems. The
nurses were asked to respond to two questions about the case:
"What are some of the important problems in this situation?"
and "What, if anything, do you think a nurse could do in this
situation?" (p. 316). After they responded in writing, they were
interviewed about the responses. The interviews, though helpful
in interpreting the responses, could be omitted by the consultant facing time constraints.
   One final example of a paper-and-pencil simulation was
described by Lambert, Sandoval, and Corder (1975). These authors were interested in establishing criteria for goal attainment,
where the goal was consultee satisfaction. They used a "vignette-
based" questionnaire, which presented a brief case history of a

child, followed by a list of school support personnel. The teachers were asked to select which school personnel they would seek out for assistance in dealing with this child. The assumption underlying this method was that teachers will continue to request assistance from those psychologists who have aided them satisfactorily in the past. Though developed for use with teachers, the approach is clearly adaptable to a variety of settings and a variety of consultees.

4. *Ratification.* In line with our emphasis on establishing and maintaining a coordinate relationship with the consultee, we advise that the consultant allow the consultee to ratify the final list of outcomes and their criteria and methods for measurement, in order to ensure both inclusiveness and relevance. The consultee should be asked to consider whether and how the criteria assess the two purposes of consultation—that is, to change the client and to foster the development of skills and knowledge that will enable the consultee to resolve similar situations in the future. The consultant and consultee must agree that the outcomes for evaluation reflect this dual nature of consultation.

Step 2: Specifying and Evaluating Program Inputs. Specification and assessment of outcomes have received much attention, but a productive evaluation will answer more than the question "What happened?" Such an evaluation should also answer "What were the elements that constituted the program (that is, inputs)?" and "To what degree were these elements in operation (that is, process)?" Step 2 of our program evaluation model suggests that an evaluation must clearly identify the various input elements that make up the consultation and the intervention strategies. For example, modifications in consultee style, materials, techniques, or work-space environment may all be active inputs in the intervention plan. Keeping accurate records or minutes from the consultation sessions can provide a valuable source for identifying such input data. Additionally, a checklist such as Exhibit 4 facilitates identification of program inputs.

An input analysis may help to underscore that there are many resources available to support the intervention plans. However, the inputs must be operating properly (that is, process) if outcome attainment is expected to occur. If evaluation

Exhibit 4. Program Input Checklist.

Identify the inputs operating in the current consultation program to be evaluated. The consultant should indicate which of the following classes of inputs were operative and provide examples. There might be many types of examples of each class of inputs in a given program.

Input Types	*Concrete Examples*
Available money	
Facilities	
Client characteristics	
Consultee characteristics	
Administrator characteristics	
Organizational needs	
Personnel needs	
Physical environment	
History of institution	
Consultee's history	
Problem intensity	
Problem duration	
Program (intervention) specifications	
Program materials	
Frequency and length of contacts	
Other: _____	

is to be useful, then, as Georgopoulos (1972) noted, an input/output approach to evaluation will not suffice. Analysis of process is required as well.

Before drawing conclusions about the success or failure of an intervention or consultation program, therefore, the evaluator must determine the level to which the program inputs were implemented. Content analysis of documents, structured interviews with the consultees or system managers, use of questionnaires to staff and consumers to determine their perception of the operation of the identified program elements, and direct observation of program implementation are all useful procedures for evaluating program inputs. A number of very good observational instruments are available for analyzing a wide variety of program inputs, such as teaching style, leadership and management style, organizational climate and communication styles, and interpersonal style. Often, however, the evaluator may find that the particular program inputs under evaluation require creation of a unique instrument. The process checklist in Exercise 11-2 can help the consultant focus on the generic concerns for process evaluation. The reader is cautioned that the questions listed are intended to be generic and may not cover all the process concerns applicable to each consultation program.

Exercise 11-2
Process Determinants

The program factors listed below are intended to stimulate identification of benchmarks for determining the operation of program inputs in the consultation under evaluation. Using a recently completed consultation as your data base, list as many manifestations as possible of the factors listed below. For each manifestation list as many manifestations as possible. For each manifestation, establish a criterion for acceptability and then, in the last column, note whether the manifestation reached criterion.

Program Factor	Manifes- tations	Criterion	Active? (yes/no)
Consultee behavior?			
Desired materials used?			
Desired physical environment established?			
Desired administrative response established?			
Desired client response achieved?			
Desired milieu established?			

Step 3: Identifying an Appropriate Design. The consultant needs to consider what conclusions will be drawn in evaluation and how to be sure they are valid. The consultant seeking to describe what happened, to specify the role the program played in terms of what was experienced, or to ascribe worth or

comparative value to the program will need to use an appropriate evaluation design. Although the issue of design may instill
anxiety in the hearts of some practitioners by conjuring up im-
ages of complicated statistics and alien (to many clinicians)
terms such as *heterogeneity, degrees of freedom,* or *internal
threats to validity,* it need not.

Whether we wish to recognize it or not, evaluation designs are part of our daily functioning. Our simple judgment of
which sandwich in the deli line looks best or a professional decision ranging from diagnostic labeling to selecting an assessment tool to use in a particular situation is an evaluation design
of the simplest sort—that is, comparison with a standard, or criterion. Under such conditions, the evaluator is concerned simply with "What do I expect or hope to obtain, and does this event
reflect that outcome?" For example, the decision to take the egg
salad over the tuna rests on the criterion one holds for a "satisfying sandwich" and one's comparison of the outcomes—tuna or
egg salad—against that criterion. In program evaluation, simple
comparison against the criterion of whether the desired outcome
occurred (for example, communication improved; work production increased; assertiveness increased; in-class disturbances were
eliminated) entails an elementary form of program design: obser-
vation-treatment-observation. Often such an elementary design is
all that is required, especially when performing formative evaluation (for example, asking the consultee, "How are we doing?").

It is our feeling that consultants and consultees need to
go beyond this simple formative evaluation. The specific factors
included in the consultation (such as consultant style, interactional process, intervention strategies, and so on) need to be
identified, isolated, and tested for their contribution to the outcome. Consultation has two goals, remediation and prevention;
and the double layer of questions required to address both these
issues demands sophisticated evaluation designs rather than a
simple comparison with criterion.

The thought of using sophisticated designs may lead readers to ask, "But where do I get the time, money, and cooperation needed for studies with large subject samples, randomized
control groups, and so on?" Although such large-scale research

can give the evaluator control over threats to internal and external validity and thus allow for certainty and generality of consultation effectiveness, the reality (in terms of time, resources, and priorities) faced by most consultants is light-years away from such ideal conditions. Valid designs can still be used, however. The quasi-experimental approaches presented by Campbell and Stanley (1966) offer a useful and often necessary compromise between the evaluator's need for a carefully controlled, experimental design and the program staff's need for maximal flexibility and minimal interference in serving the changing needs of the institution or client.

The time-series design is one such design that is particularly applicable to evaluation in consultation (Meyers and others, 1978). This approach requires that the evaluator(s) take periodic measurements of the expected outcomes so that any changes that occur can be contrasted with the status before intervention. Such changes can be contrasted (1) to the criterion and (2) to the baseline level. Although this design certainly increases one's ability to exclude alternative explanations for the occurrence of the outcomes (compared with the simple contrast-to-criterion design), it is far from ideal. For a detailed discussion of the strengths and weaknesses of this and other designs, see Campbell and Stanley (1966).

A form of the time-series design that adds experimental control is the multiple-baseline approach (Baer, Wolf, and Risley, 1968; Hall and others, 1970). The technical considerations of this design in consultation research have been presented elsewhere (Meyers, Parsons, and Martin, 1979) and will not be repeated here. Exhibit 5 does present simple guidelines for use of this design, and the reader is encouraged to see the thorough discussions of this method in the literature just cited.

Step 4: Implementing Evaluation. The program inputs have been specified and the outcomes and their measurements developed. All that remains is to carry out the evaluation. A number of real managerial issues arise at this point in the evaluation process, such as "When do I find the time or energy?," "How do I keep my calendar clear?," and "What do I do about those 101 unexpected snafus in our well-devised plan?" Particu-

Exhibit 5. Guidelines for Small-*N*, Multiple-Baseline Designs.

The multiple-baseline design, originally conceived to study multiple behaviors treated one at a time in a stepwise manner, can be adapted for use in situations wherein one treatment is administered to more than one subject (client, consultee) in a stepwise manner so as to observe the sequential impact over treatment. The rationale for such a design is that should the outcome (client or consultee behavior or attitude change) occur at the point of program introduction (that is, treatment), and no comparable outcomes occur for those clients or consultees who have yet to receive treatment, a causal relation between consultation program and outcome can be inferred. We list the steps to be followed in developing and using a small-*N*, multiple-baseline design.

Step 1: Defining Outcomes. The first step is to develop a precise definition of the outcome to be derived. The outcome needs to be established in such a way that it includes a description of the behaviors, a prescription of level and rate of responding, and a specified time period in which the expected outcome is to occur.

Step 2: Observation. Through pretreatment observation one collects baseline data to be used for comparison. Baseline collection may occur in at least three ways, the method being a function of the goal of the consultation (Hall, 1971): Data may be collected on the rate of a response within a given period of time (response frequency) or the amount of time on task (response duration) or by time-sampling procedures. Whatever the method, a comparative base of outcome occurrence before treatment needs to be established for all subjects.

Step 3: Developing a Treatment Schedule. Decide which client (or consultee) will be introduced to the program/intervention first and what the order will be for the remaining target-group members. Random assignment to treatment is the procedure of choice, if at all possible.

Step 4: Recording Observations. This step may require development of a coding instrument and should involve the use of coraters to control for rater bias and provide increased rater reliability. Reliability may be assessed by calculating the correlation coefficient between observers' ratings (agreement below 80 percent may be questioned as indicating limited reliability) or simply by determining the number of intervals rated the same, dividing by total intervals observed (that is, agreed and disagreed), and multiplying by 100 (Bijou and others, 1969). The result of this procedure is the percentage of rater agreement. The current convention regarding such agreement in accepted training levels is 80–85 percent.

Step 5: Charting Data. Since one is observing so few elements, traditional descriptive statistics such as mean or standard deviation add little to one's understanding of the events under observation. Visual presentation of the observations on each subject, in chart or graph form (for example, histograms with the vertical axis representing frequency and the horizontal representing time), can be much more valuable.

---

lar issues will be situation- and consultant-specific, but we shall highlight a few of the most generic concerns for this stage of program evaluation.

Implementation of an evaluation requires not only that stages or steps of evaluation be detailed and time lines established for them but also that the evaluator identify the responsibilities of all involved in the evaluation, to ensure that all facets will be covered with minimal overlap and inconvenience.

Although setting time lines and duties is an important part of implementing an evaluation, the main concern at this stage is to ensure that collaboration between consultant and consultee is maintained. It is worthwhile to reflect on the intended purpose of an evaluation: to be helpful and growth-producing for consultant and consultee alike. For this goal to be achieved, the interpersonal processes and the relationship-maintaining skills previously presented need to be highlighted so that the real needs of the consultee and points of concern can be detected and ameliorated, thus ensuring collaboration in this very important aspect of the consultation relationship.

Step 5: Decision Making and Dissemination. Now that the data have been collected and appropriate analyses performed, interpretations are about to be made. The evaluator's concerns at this stage are how valid the assessment was, where there might have been significant weaknesses in the data collected or the design used, and to whom to report the findings and for what purpose.

It is suggested that, before report writing and dissemination, the consultant review some of the technical aspects of the evaluation, such as these: Were all the outcomes defined? measured? Were all the significant program inputs identified? observed? operable? Did the design provide a means for determining the role the intervention program played in the observed outcomes? Were the measures valid? reliable?

After such reevaluation of the form and process of the evaluation itself, the evaluator needs to consider what decision options are available and what criteria for selection can be used. Figure 6 charts the types of determinations to be made in deciding about the evaluation outcomes.

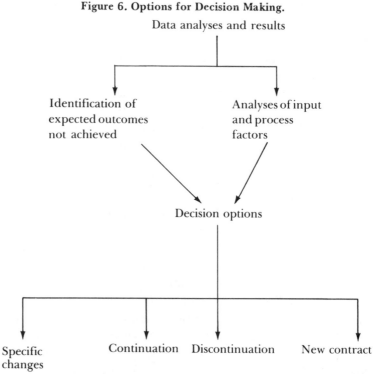

Figure 6. Options for Decision Making.

Finally, after decision making and post mortem analysis of the evaluation process, the consultant needs to provide feedback (written and oral) to all concerned with the program. Such feedback should be written as soon as possible after completion of the evaluation and in clear, understandable language, free of jargon, with opportunities offered to the audience for seeking clarification or putting forward rebuttal. Presentation of the written feedback not only signals to the institution and the consultee the end of one consultation but may also act as a stimulus for renewed contact and establishment of a new consultation contract.

Toward Continuing Professional Development

The focus of the previous chapters has been the development and assessment of consultation relationships, processes, and procedures. Chapters Two through Six considered some of the assessment skills necessary for developing and maintaining a collaborative relationship. Chapters Seven through Ten detailed the assessment skills used in consultation where the focus is the client, the consultee, or the system. Finally, Chapter Eleven presented an approach to assessment applicable to evaluating the consultation outcome and process.

In addition to being sensitive to the need to assess and evaluate one's consultation program, the successful consultant will also be competent in self-assessment. Ongoing assessment and development of one's consulting skills and knowledge lie at the heart of competent consultation.

The authors' experience in conducting in-service training

workshops and coordinating other approaches to professional development has led to some skepticism. Many training programs stimulate a variety of novel ideas and promote excited discussion yet lead to little behavioral change. We have found a number of reasons: Quite often little or no opportunity is provided for the follow-up necessary to facilitate change; the system often has structural characteristics that interfere with change; and quite often consultants become satisfied with their performance and see no need for continued development. It is hoped that the current work will stimulate attitude change and provide techniques that consultants can use to facilitate the needed structural changes in the organization.

As noted in the Preface, this book can be used in two ways—as a traditional text or to facilitate professional development. The second approach will lead to the meaningful behavioral change that is often lacking with in-service training. This approach requires that the book be used in a self-study format, in which the consultant uses the suggested exercises and assessment techniques to evaluate his or her own skill level and the systemic blocks to change. This assessment can then be used to develop detailed plans for one's ongoing professional development. We believe strongly that this sort of self-study format will be used increasingly because of its potential for creating change and stimulating professional development.

For professional growth and competence to be maintained, an ongoing regimen of personal and professional assessment and skill development must be established. Most consultants tend to develop their consulting skills through trial and error or on-the-job training programs, but formalized training and self-study, at both the preprofessional and the postdegree levels, is slowly becoming a reality. Generalized agreement on the minimal entry-level competence for practicing consultants has not yet been identified, nor has a specific formal curriculum of courses or experiences been offered. Although a university-based training program increasingly provides fertile ground for continued skill development, the most untapped and under-developed source of personal and professional growth is you, the consultant.

Professional development can be accomplished most effectively using a system that includes instruction, practice, feedback, support, and *in vivo* application. *Instruction* can be accomplished by reading this book, doing the written exercises provided, and discussing the ideas. *Practice* can be accomplished by using the exercises, which have been developed to provide systematic practice. *Feedback* can be obtained through the assessment devices included in many of the exercises. Consultants can use these techniques to provide feedback to themselves or to obtain feedback from others (peers, supervisors, consultees). *Support and encouragement* can occur if the consultant works with a few colleagues in a "learning group" atmosphere. It is helpful to receive support from colleagues who are also attempting to change. These colleagues can discuss taped work segments as a means of providing corrective feedback and support to the consultant. As a final step in professional development, one must systematically apply the newly acquired skills within the work setting—that is, *in vivo practice* must be used.

Although the entire book presents ideas and techniques that can be used to facilitate professional development, we would like to point to some sections that may be particularly useful for this goal.

Chapter Eleven presents program development skills that can be used to assess the consultant's performance. In particular, the Consultee Satisfaction Form provides a basis for obtaining feedback from the consultee about both the process and outcome of consultation.

Chapter Nine presents skills for promoting growth in the consultee that can be adapted for the consultant. The approach to knowledge and skill development can be used as a basis for the consultant's professional development. The scale for assessing consultee stress can be used to generate intervention plans to reduce the consultant's stress. Finally, the approach to assessing the consultee's stages of professional development can also provide insight into facilitation of change by the consultant.

Chapters Two through Five provide a variety of scales for assessing interpersonal process. The consultant can use these, as well as the resistance scale in Chapter Nine, to assess both the interpersonal relationships established during consultation and the degree to which the consultant uses various process skills.

Finally, the skills related to assessment and intervention with systems offered in Chapter Ten can facilitate professional development. As noted earlier, an institution's structural characteristics often inhibit application of the skills learned as a result of continuing professional development. The skills presented in Chapter Ten enable the consultant to assess the organization in order to develop plans for creating the structural changes necessary for the consultant's continuing professional development.

This book has presented a comprehensive view of a collaborative model of consultation. It has shown how consultation can be used to promote primary prevention, and it has made a significant step in delineating the specific skills necessary for effective consultation. Further, we have shown how this book can be used as a basis for the consultant's professional development.

We look to two particular directions for future work in consultation: (1) increased efforts to define the individual skills and techniques necessary for effective consultation and (2) further research into the impact of particular consultation techniques on specified outcomes. Finally, there is a need for large-scale implementation of consultation programs that support the crucial preventive/educative goals of consultation.

References

Adler, R. B., Rosenfeld, L. B., and Towne, N. *Interplay*. New York: Holt, Rinehart and Winston, 1980.

Albee, G. W. "Social Science and Social Change: The Primary Prevention of Disturbance in Youth." (Third annual Gisela Konopka Lecture, delivered May 21, 1980.) Occasional Paper No. 2, Center for Youth Development, University of Minnesota, 1980.

Albee, G. W. "The Politics of Nature and Nurture." *American Journal of Community Psychology*, 1982, *10*, 1-36.

Alberti, R. E., and Emmons, M. L. *Your Perfect Right: A Guide to Assertive Behavior*. (2nd ed.) New York: Impact Press, 1974.

Alderfer, C. P. "Comparison of Questionnaire Responses With and Without Preceding Interviews." *Journal of Applied Psychology*, 1968, *52*, 335-340.

Alderfer, C. P. "The Methodology of Organizational Diagnosis." *Professional Psychology*, 1980, *11*, 459-468.

Alderfer, C. P., and Brown, L. D. "Designing an Empathic Questionnaire for Organizational Research." *Journal of Applied Behavioral Psychology,* 1972, *56,* 440-456.

Allen, G., and others. *Community Psychology and the Schools: A Behaviorally Oriented Multilevel Preventive Approach.* Hillsdale, N.J.: Erlbaum, 1976.

Alpert, J. L. "Some Guidelines for School Consultation." *Journal of School Psychology,* 1977, *15,* 308-319.

Alpert, J. L., and Meyers, J. (Eds.). *Training in Consultation: Perspectives from Mental Health, Behavioral, and Organizational Consultation.* Springfield, Ill.: Thomas, 1983.

Altrocchi, J. "Mental Health Consultation." In S. E. Gohann and C. Eisdorfer (Eds.), *Handbook of Community Mental Health.* New York: Appleton-Century-Crofts, 1972.

Argyle, M. *The Psychology of Interpersonal Behavior.* Baltimore: Penguin Books, 1967.

Argyris, C. *Intervention Theory and Method.* Reading, Mass.: Addison-Wesley, 1970.

Axelrod, S. *Behavior Modification for the Classroom Teacher.* New York: McGraw-Hill, 1977.

Baer, D. M., Wolf, M. M., and Risley, T. R. "Some Current Dimensions of Applied Behavioral Analysis." *Journal of Applied Behavioral Analysis,* 1968, *1,* 91-97.

Baker, F., and Northman, J. E. *Helping: Human Services for the '80's.* St. Louis, Mo.: Mosby, 1981.

Barker, R. G. *Ecological Psychology.* Stanford, Calif.: Stanford University Press, 1968.

Barker, R. G., and Gump, P. *Big School, Small School.* Stanford, Calif.: Stanford University Press, 1964.

Bateson, G. "Culture Contact and Schizomogenesis." *Man,* 1935, *35,* 178-183.

Bateson, G. *Noven.* (2nd ed.) Stanford, Calif.: Stanford University Press, 1958.

Beckhard, R. *Organization Development: Strategies and Models.* Reading, Mass.: Addison-Wesley, 1969.

Beier, E. G. *The Silent Language of Psychotherapy.* Chicago: Aldine, 1966.

Bennis, W. G. *Organization Development: Its Nature, Origins, and Prospects.* Reading, Mass.: Addison-Wesley, 1969.

Berenson, B. G., and Mitchell, K. M. *Confrontation for Better or Worse!* Amherst, Mass.: Human Resource Development Press, 1974.

Bergan, J. R. *Behavioral Consultation.* Columbus, Ohio: Merrill, 1977.

Bergan, J. R., and Tombari, M. "Consultant Skill and Efficiency and the Implementation and Outcomes of Consultation." *Journal of School Psychology,* 1976, *14,* 3-13.

Berne, E. *Games People Play: The Psychology of Human Relationships.* New York: Grove Press, 1964.

Bernstein, D. A., and Borkovec, T. D. *Progressive Relaxation Training.* Champaign, Ill.: Research Press, 1973.

Bersoff, D. N. "Current Functioning Myth: An Overlooked Fallacy in Psychological Assessment." *Journal of Consulting and Clinical Psychology,* 1971, *37,* 391-393.

Bersoff, D. N. "Silk Purses into Sow's Ears: The Decline of Psychological Testing and a Suggestion for its Redemption." *American Psychologist,* 1973, *28,* 892-899.

Bijou, S. W., and Peterson, R. F. "Functional Analysis in the Assessment of Children." In P. McReynolds (Ed.), *Advances in Psychological Assessment.* Vol. 2. Palo Alto, Calif.: Science and Behavior Books, 1971.

Bijou, S. W., and others. "Methodology for Experimental Studies of Young Children in Natural Settings." *Psychological Record,* 1969, *19,* 177-210.

Blank, S. S., and Covington, M. "Inducing Children to Ask Questions in Solving Problems." *Journal of Educational Research,* 1965, *59,* 1-27.

Bowers, D. G., and Franklin, J. L. "Survey-Guided Development: Using Human Resource Measurement in Organizational Change." *Journal of Contemporary Business,* 1974, *1,* 43-55.

Brooks, R. "Psychoeducational Assessment: A Broader Perspective." *Professional Psychology,* 1979, *10,* 708-722.

Broussard, E. "Neonatal Prediction and Outcome at 10/11 Years." *Child Psychiatry and Human Development,* 1976, *7* (entire issue).

Brown, A. L., and French, L. A. "The Zone of Potential Development: Implications for Intelligence Testing in the Year 2000." *Intelligence,* 1979, *3,* 255-273.

Budoff, M. "Measuring Learning Potential: An Alternative to the Traditional Intelligence Test." In G. Gredler (Ed.), *Ethical and Legal Factors in the Practice of School Psychology.* Harrisburg, Pa.: Department of Education, 1975.

Burns, D. D. *Feeling Good: The New Mood Therapy.* New York: William Morrow, 1980.

Campbell, D. T., and Stanley, J. C. *Experimental and Quasi-Experimental Designs for Research.* Chicago: Rand McNally, 1966.

Caplan, G. *Principles of Preventive Psychiatry.* New York: Basic Books, 1964.

Caplan, G. *The Theory and Practice of Mental Health Consultation.* New York: Basic Books, 1970.

Caplan, G., and Killilea, M. (Eds.). *Support Systems and Mutual Help: Multidisciplinary Exploration.* New York: Grune & Stratton, 1976.

Carkhuff, R. R. *Helping and Human Relations.* (2 vols.) New York: Holt, Rinehart and Winston, 1969.

Carroll, J. B., and Horn, J. L. "On the Scientific Basis of Ability Testing." *American Psychologist,* 1981, *36,* 1012-1020.

Cienki, J. A. "An Exploration of Expert and Referent Power in Consultation with Elementary School Teachers." Unpublished doctoral dissertation, School of Education, University of Pennsylvania, 1982.

Cowen, E. L. "Baby Steps Toward Primary Prevention." *American Journal of Community Psychology,* 1977, *5,* 1-22.

Curran, J. P., and Wessberg, H. W. "Assessment of Social Inadequacy." In D. H. Barlow (Ed.), *Behavioral Assessment of Adult Disorders.* New York: Guilford Press, 1981.

Curtis, M. J., and Anderson, T. "Consultant Observational Assessment Form." Department of Educational Leadership, University of Cincinnati, 1975.

Curtis, M. J., and Watson, K. "Changes in Consultee Problem Clarification Skills Following Consultation." *Journal of School Psychology,* 1980, *18,* 210-221.

Curtis, M. J., and Zins, J. E. "Consultative Effectiveness as Perceived by Experts in Consultation and Classroom Teachers."

In M. J. Curtis and J. E. Zins (Eds.), *The Theory and Practice of School Consultation.* Springfield, Ill.: Thomas, 1981.

Deno, S. L. *A Direct Observation Approach to Measuring Classroom Behavior: Procedures and Application.* Research Report No. 6. Institute for Research on Learning Disabilities, University of Minnesota, April 1979.

Deno, S. L., and Mirkin, P. K. *Data-Based Program Modification: A Manual.* Reston, Va.: Council for Exceptional Children, 1977.

Deutsch, M. *The Resolution of Conflict.* New Haven, Conn.: Yale University Press, 1973.

Egan, G. *Face to Face.* Monterey, Calif.: Brooks/Cole, 1973.

Egan, G. *You and Me.* Monterey, Calif.: Brooks/Cole, 1977.

Ellett, C. D., and Bersoff, D. N. "An Integrated Approach to the Psychosituational Assessment of Behavior." *Professional Psychology,* 1976, 7, 485-493.

Ellis, A. *Reason and Emotion in Psychotherapy.* New York: Lyle Stuart, 1962.

Ellis, A., and Harper, R. A. *A New Guide to Rational Living.* North Hollywood, Calif.: Wilshire, 1975.

Erchul, W. P. "A Relational Communication Analysis of Control in the Consultant Consultee Dyad: A Proposed Study." Research proposal submitted to the Educational Psychology graduate faculty, University of Texas at Austin, 1981.

Erchul, W. P., and Gallessich, J. "Decision Making in Consultation." Paper presented at annual convention of the National Association of School Psychologists, Houston, 1981.

Ericson, P. M., and Rogers, L. E. "New Procedures for Analyzing Relational Communication." *Family Process,* 1973, 12, 245-267.

Feuerstein, R. "A Dynamic Approach to the Causation, Prevention, and Alleviation of Retarded Performance." In H. C. Haywood (Ed.), *Social-Cultural Aspects of Mental Retardation.* New York: Appleton-Century-Crofts, 1970.

Feuerstein, R. *The Dynamic Assessment of Retarded Performers: The Learning Potential Assessment Device, Theory, Instruments, and Techniques.* Baltimore: University Park Press, 1979.

Fine, M., Nesbitt, J., and Tyler, M. M. "Analysis of a Failing Attempt at Behavior Modification." *Journal of Learning Disabilities,* 1974, *7,* 12-17.

Flaherty, E. W. "Evaluation of Consultation." In J. J. Platt and R. J. Wicks (Eds.), *The Psychological Consultant.* New York: Grune & Stratton, 1979.

Flanagan, J. C. "The Critical Incident Technique." *Psychological Bulletin,* 1954, *51,* 327-328.

French, J. R., Jr., and Raven, B. "The Basis of Social Power." In D. Cartwright (Ed.), *Studies in Social Power.* Ann Arbor: Institute for Social Research, University of Michigan, 1959.

French, W. L., and Bell, C. H., Jr. *Organization Development.* Englewood Cliffs, N.J.: Prentice-Hall, 1973.

Friedlander, F. "The Facilitation of Change in Organizations." *Professional Psychology,* 1980, *3,* 520-530.

Gallessich, J. "Training the School Psychologist for Consultation." *Journal of School Psychology,* 1974, *12,* 138-149.

Gallessich, J. *The Profession and Practice of Consultation: A Handbook for Consultants, Trainers of Consultants, and Consumers of Consultation Services.* San Francisco: Jossey-Bass, 1982.

Garcia, J. "The Logic and Limits of Mental Aptitude Testing." *American Psychologist,* 1981, *36,* 1172-1180.

Georgopoulos, B. S. *Organizational Research on Health Institutions.* Ann Arbor: Institute for Social Research, University of Michigan, 1972.

Gesten, E. L., and others. "Promoting Peer Related Social Competence in Schools." In M. W. Kent and J. E. Rolf (Eds.), *Primary Prevention of Psychopathology.* Vol. 3: *Social Competence in Children.* Hanover, N.H.: University Press of New England, 1979.

Glidewell, J. C. "The Entry Problem in Consultation." *Journal of Social Issues,* 1959, *15,* 51-59.

Goldfried, M. R., and Davison, G. C. "Relaxation Training." In M. R. Goldfried and G. C. Davison (Eds.), *Clinical Behavior Therapy.* New York: Holt, Rinehart and Winston, 1976.

Gump, P. V. "Education as an Environmental Enterprise." In R. A. Weinberg and F. H. Woods (Eds.), *Observation of Pupils and Teachers in Mainstream and Special Education Set-*

tings: Alternative Strategies. Reston, Va.: Council for Exceptional Children, 1975.

Gutkin, T. B. "Relative Frequency of Consultee Lack of Knowledge, Skill, Confidence, and Objectivity in School Settings." *Journal of School Psychology,* 1981, *19,* 57-61.

Gutkin, T. B., and Curtis, M. J. "School Based Consultation: Theory and Techniques." In C. R. Reynolds and T. B. Gutkin (Eds.), *The Handbook of Social Psychology.* New York: Wiley, 1982.

Hall, E. T. *The Hidden Dimension.* Garden City, N.Y.: Doubleday, 1966.

Hall, L. "Comments." *Journal of School Psychology,* 1971, *9,* 269-270.

Hall, R. V., and Hall, M. "Observation Based Assessment." In J. Tucker (Ed.), *NonTest-Based Assessment.* National School Psychology Inservice Training Network, University of Minnesota, 1981.

Hall, R. V., Hawkins, R. P., and Axelrod, S. "Measuring and Recording Student Behavior: A Behavior Analysis Approach." In R. A. Weinberg and F. H. Woods (Eds.), *Observation of Pupils and Teachers in Mainstream and Special Education Settings: Alternative Strategies.* Reston, Va.: Council of Exceptional Children, 1975.

Hall, R. V., and others. "Teachers and Parents as Researchers Using Multiple-Baseline Designs." *Journal of Applied Behavioral Analysis,* 1970, *4,* 141-149.

Hartman, C. H. *Mixed Scanning Relaxation Training.* New York: BioMonitoring Applications, 1976.

Haveluck, R. G. *The Change Agent's Guide to Innovation in Education.* Englewood Cliffs, N.J.: Educational Technology Publications, 1973.

Haywood, H. C., and others. "Behavioral Assessment in Mental Retardation." In P. McReynolds (Ed.), *Advances in Psychological Assessment III.* San Francisco: Jossey-Bass, 1974.

Heber, R. "Socio-Cultural Mental Retardation: A Longitudinal Study." In D. G. Forgays (Ed.), *Primary Prevention of Psychopathology.* Vol. 2: *Environmental Influences.* Hanover, N.H.: University Press of New England, 1978.

Hinkle, A., Silverstein, B., and Walton, D. M. "A Method for the Evaluation of Mental Health Consultation to the Public Schools." *Journal of Community Psychology,* 1977, *5,* 263-265.

Huse, E. F. *Organization Development and Change.* St. Paul, Minn.: West, 1975.

Ivey, A. E. *Microcounseling: Innovation in Interviewing Training.* Springfield, Ill.: Thomas, 1971.

Ivey, A. E., and Gluckstern, N. B. *Basic Attending Skills: Participant Manual.* North Amherst, Mass.: Microtraining Associates, 1974.

Jacobson, E. *Progressive Relaxation.* Chicago: University of Chicago Press, 1938.

Katz, L. G. *Talks with Teachers: Reflection on Early Childhood Education.* Washington, D.C.: National Association for the Education of Young Children, 1977.

Kelly, J. G. "Towards an Ecological Conception of Preventive Interventions." In J. W. Carter (Ed.), *Research Contributions from Psychology to Community Mental Health.* New York: Behavioral Publications, 1968.

Klaus, M. H., and Kennell, J. H. *Maternal Infant Bonding.* St. Louis, Mo.: Mosby, 1976.

Krumboltz, J. D. "An Accountability Model for Counselors." *Personnel and Guidance Journal,* 1974, *56,* 321-323.

Kuhn, T. S. *The Structure of Scientific Revolutions.* (2nd ed.) Chicago: University of Chicago Press, 1970.

Lambert, N. M. "Perspectives on Training School-Based Consultants." In J. L. Alpert and J. Meyers (Eds.), *Training in Consultation.* Springfield, Ill.: Thomas, in press.

Lambert, N. M., Sandoval, J., and Corder, R. "Teacher Perceptions of School-Based Consultants." *Professional Psychology,* 1975, *6,* 204-216.

Lazarus, A. A. (Ed.). *Multimodal Behavior Therapy.* New York: Springer, 1976.

Lewin, K. *Field Theory in Social Science.* New York: Harper & Row, 1951.

Lewin, K., and others. "Level of Aspiration." In J. McV. Hunt (Ed.), *Personality and the Behavior Disorders.* New York: Ronald Press, 1941.

McGuire, W. J. "The Nature of Attitudes and Attitude Change." In G. Lindzey and E. Aronson (Eds.), *The Handbook of Social Psychology*. Vol. 3: *The Individual in a Social Context.* (2nd ed.) Reading, Mass.: Addison-Wesley, 1969.

Mark, R. "Coding Communication at the Relationship Level." *Journal of Communications,* 1971, *21,* 221-232.

Martin, R. "Increasing Teacher Awareness Through Systematic Classroom Observation: A Neglected Model of Psychological Consultation." Unpublished paper, Temple University, 1974.

Martin, R. "A Critique of Two Major Assumptions of Caplan's Approach to Mental Health Consultation." Unpublished paper, Temple University, 1977.

Martin, R. "Expert and Referent Power: A Framework for Understanding and Maximizing Consultation Effectiveness." *Journal of School Psychology,* 1978, *16,* 49-55.

Maslow, A. H. *Motivation and Personality.* (2nd ed.) New York: Harper & Row, 1970.

Maultsby, M. C., Jr. *Help Yourself to Happiness.* New York: Institute of Rational Living, 1975.

Mehrabian, A. "Orientation Behaviors and Nonverbal Attitude Communication." *Journal of Communication,* 1967, *17,* 324-332.

Meichenbaum, D., and Goodman, J. "Training Impulsive Children to Talk to Themselves." *Journal of Abnormal Psychology,* 1971, *77,* 115-126.

Mercer, J. R. "In Defense of Racially and Culturally Non-discriminatory Assessment." *School Psychology Digest,* 1979, *8,* 89-115.

Meyers, J. "Consultee-Centered Consultation as a Technique for Classroom Management." *American Journal of Community Psychology,* 1975, *3,* 111-121.

Meyers, J. "Resistance in Teacher Consultation: A Relationship Model." Paper presented at annual meetings of the National Association of School Psychologists, Houston, 1978.

Meyers, J. "Mental Health Consultation." In T. R. Kratochwill (Ed.), *Advances in School Psychology.* Vol. 1. Hillsdale, N.J.: Erlbaum, 1981.

Meyers, J., Parsons, R. D., and Martin, R. *Mental Health Consultation in the Schools: A Comprehensive Guide for Psycholo-*

gists, Social Workers, Psychiatrists, Counselors, Educators, and Other Human Services Professionals. San Francisco: Jossey-Bass, 1979.

Meyers, J., Pfeffer, J., and Erlbaum, V. "Process Assessment: A Model for Broadening the School Psychologist's Assessment Role." Paper presented at annual meetings of the National Association of School Psychologists, Toronto, 1982.

Meyers, J., and others. "A Research Model for Consultation with Teachers." *Journal of School Psychology,* 1978, *16*(2), 137-145.

Moos, R. H. "Conceptualization of Human Environments." *American Psychologist,* 1973, *28,* 652-665.

Moos, R. H. *The Social Climate Scales: An Overview.* Palo Alto, Calif.: Consulting Psychologists Press, 1974a.

Moos, R. H. *Evaluating Treatment Environments: A Social Ecological Approach.* New York: Wiley, 1974b.

Neisworth, J. T., Deno, S. L., and Jenkins, J. R. *Student Motivation and Classroom Management.* Lemont, Pa.: Behavior Technics, 1969.

Newman, R. G. *Psychological Consultation in the Schools.* New York: Basic Books, 1967.

O'Leary, K. D. "Behavioral Assessment: An Observational Slant." In R. A. Weinberg and F. H. Wood (Eds.), *Observation of Pupils and Teachers in Mainstream and Special Education Settings: Alternative Strategies.* Reston, Va.: Council for Exceptional Children, 1975.

Parsons, R. D. "Overcoming Teacher Resistance to Behavior Modification." *The Guidance Clinic,* 1976, April, 12-14.

Parsons, R. D., Stone, S. S., and Feuerstein, P. "Teacher In-Service Training: A Tool for Maximizing Counselor Effectiveness." *Guidance Clinic,* 1977, *15,* 545-552.

Phillips, B. N., Martin, R., and Meyers, J. "Interventions in Relation to Anxiety in School." In C. D. Spielberger (Ed.), *Anxiety: Current Trends in Theory and Research.* Vol. 2. New York: Academic Press, 1972.

Piper, T. *Classroom Management and Behavioral Objectives.* Belmont, Calif.: Fearon, 1974.

Rachman, S. "The Role of Muscular Relaxation in Desensitization Therapy." *Behavior Research and Therapy,* 1968, *6,* 233.

Raven, B. H. "Social Influence on Power." In I. D. Steiner and M. Fishbein (Eds.), *Current Studies in Social Psychology.* New York: Holt, Rinehart and Winston, 1965.

Reece, M., and Whitman, R. N. "Expressive Movements, Warmth, and Verbal Reinforcement." *Journal of Abnormal and Social Psychology,* 1962, *64,* 234-236.

Reschly, D. J. "Psychological Testing in Educational Classification and Placement." *American Psychologist,* 1981, *36,* 1094-1102.

Rogers, L. E., and Farace, R. V. "Analysis of Relational Communication in Dyads: New Measurement Procedures." *Human Communication Research,* 1975, *1,* 222-239.

Sarason, S. B., and others. *Psychology in Community Settings.* New York: Wiley, 1966.

Scarr, S. "Testing for Children: Assessment and the Many Determinants of Intellectual Competence." *American Psychologist,* 1981, *36,* 1159-1166.

Schein, E. H. *Process Consultation.* Reading, Mass.: Addison-Wesley, 1969.

Schmuck, R. A., and Miles, M. B. (Eds.). *Organization Development in the Schools.* Palo Alto, Calif.: National Press Books, 1971.

Schmuck, R. A., and Schmuck, P. A. *A Humanistic Psychology of Education.* Palo Alto, Calif.: National Press Books, 1974.

Schmuck, R. A., and others. *Handbook of Organization Development in Schools.* Palo Alto, Calif.: National Press Books, 1972.

Schowengerdt, R. V., Fine, M. J., and Poggio, J. P. "An Examination of Some Bases of Teacher Satisfaction with School Psychological Services." *Psychology in the Schools,* 1976, *13,* 269-275.

Schutz, W. *The Interpersonal Underworld.* New York: Science and Behavior Books, 1967.

Scriven, M. "The Methodology of Evaluation." In R. W. Tyler, R. M. Gagné, and M. Scriven (Eds.), *Perspectives of Curricu-*

lum Evaluation. AERA Monograph Series on Curriculum Evaluation. Chicago: Rand McNally, 1967.

Sewell, T. "Shaping the Future of School Psychology: Another Perspective." *School Psychology Review,* 1981, *10,* 232-242.

Simon, S. *I Am Loveable and Capable.* Niles, Ill.: Argus Communications, 1973.

Spivack, G., Platt, J. J., and Shure, M. B. *The Problem-Solving Approach to Adjustment: A Guide to Research and Intervention.* San Francisco: Jossey-Bass, 1976.

Spivack, G., and Shure, M. B. *Social Adjustment of Young Children: A Cognitive Approach to Solving Real-Life Problems.* San Francisco: Jossey-Bass, 1973.

Steinzor, B. "The Spatial Factor in Face to Face Discussion Groups." *Journal of Abnormal and Social Psychology,* 1950, *45,* 552-555.

Stephenson, P. S. "Judging the Effectiveness of a Consultation Program to a Community Agency." *Community Mental Health Journal,* 1973, *9,* 253-259.

Stern, W. *Psychology of Early Childhood: Up to the Sixth Year of Age.* (2nd ed.) New York: Holt, Rinehart and Winston, 1930.

Stroebel, C. F. *Quieting Response Training.* New York: Bio-Monitoring Applications, 1978.

Strong, S. R., and Schmidt, L. D. "Expertness and Influence in Counseling." *Journal of Counseling Psychology,* 1970, *17,* 197-204.

Thibaut, J. W., and Kelley, H. H. *The Social Psychology of Groups.* New York: Wiley, 1959.

Tubbs, S. L., and Moss, S. *Human Communication.* New York: Random House, 1977.

Vygotsky, L. S. *Mind in Society: The Development of Higher Psychological Processes.* Cambridge, Mass.: Harvard University Press, 1978.

Watson, G. "Resistance to Change." In G. Watson (Ed.), *Concepts for Social Change.* Washington, D.C.: National Training Laboratories, 1966.

Webb, E. J., and others. *Unobtrusive Measures: A Survey of Nonreactive Research in the Social Sciences.* Chicago: Rand McNally, 1966.

Wenger, R. D. "Teacher Response to Collaborative Consultation." *Psychology in the Schools,* 1979, *16,* 127–131.

Wilcox, M. R. "Variables Affecting Group Mental Health Consultation for Teachers." Paper presented at 85th annual meeting of the American Psychological Association, San Francisco, 1977.

Wolpe, J. *Psychotherapy by Reciprocal Inhibition.* Stanford, Calif.: Stanford University Press, 1958.

Index